LOCAL GOVERNMENT IN THE COMMUNITY

LOCAL GOVERNMENT IN THE COMMUNITY

COLIN MELLORS
and NIGEL COPPERTHWAITE

ICSA Publishing Limited
Cambridge

Published by ICSA Publishing Limited
Fitzwilliam House, 32 Trumpington Street,
Cambridge CB2 1QY, England
and
27 South Main Street, Wolfeboro,
New Hampshire, 03894–2069, USA

First published 1987
© Colin Mellors and Nigel Copperthwaite 1987

British Library Cataloguing in Publication Data
Mellors, Colin
    Local government in the community.
    1. Local government – Great Britain
    I. Title   II. Copperthwaite, Nigel
    352.041   353111

    ISBN 0-902197-39-8
    ISBN 0-902197-38-X Pbk

Library of Congress Cataloging in Publication Data
Mellors, Colin.
    Local government in the community.

    Bibliography: p.
    Includes index.
    1. Local government – Great Britain. I. Copperthwaite,
    Nigel. II. Title.
JS3111.M38 1987   352.041   87–3310
ISBN 0-902197-39-8
ISBN 0-902197-38-X (pbk.)

Designed by Geoff Green
Typeset by Wyvern Typesetting Ltd, Bristol
Printed in Great Britain by
St Edmundsbury Press, Bury St Edmunds, Suffolk

CONTENTS

PREFACE

This book shares its title with an Institute of Chartered Secretaries and Administrators' (ICSA) course – *Local Government in the Community*. It also shares the objectives of that course, namely 'to provide a framework for the study of local government, emphasising that its concern is with the environment in which people live and the provision of services for them'. In order to understand local government properly, it is important to appreciate the nature of the community and of the environment in which it functions. The book is not intended to provide an exhaustive treatment of local government or its services, nor to be a complete history of British local government. Both of these needs are well served by other texts. Rather, it is designed to link a review of the activities and structure of local government to its social and physical setting. The particular local environment affects not only the resources and policies of local councils, but also their structure and processes. This relationship between the local authority and its functional context is not always recognised. Local authorities work in a complex framework where their actions are influenced by a wide variety of pressures, not least those that result from increasing central intervention and party politicisation.

The text is designed to serve the needs of a variety of readers, especially those who are preparing for professional examinations in local government service, as well as undergraduates who are studying courses in local government, public administration or political geography. It is hoped that, in addition, the book will appeal to the general reader who wishes to know more about the workings of local government and the relationship between the council and the local community.

The authors would like to thank a number of local government officers who helped answer their questions, Pat Copperthwaite and Susan O'Brien who helped with the preparation of the text and Betty Jones who helped with its typing.

Colin Mellors
Nigel Copperthwaite
June 1987

I

WHY LOCAL GOVERNMENT?

Local government is not, in our view, limited to the narrow provision of a series of services to the local community. It has within its purview the overall economic, cultural and physical well-being of that community, and for this reason its decisions impinge with increasing frequency upon the individual lives of its citizens. (Bains Report, 1972)[1]

LOCAL SERVICES AND LOCAL DEMOCRACY

Some form of subnational government exists in most developed societies, although the precise role and power of these systems vary not only between nations but also between one period and another. In some countries, the lower tier may be effectively an administrative agency of central government exercising little or no discretion and hardly deserving the label 'government', while in other places there may be a tradition of strong local power which balances that enjoyed by the central authorities. In some countries, notably those with federal constitutions, there may be several tiers of government. Like all political systems, local government develops and is modified in response to changes in local and national needs and prevailing ideas and beliefs. The UK system of local government serves two particular purposes: the provision of a wide range of services which take account of both specific area needs and certain nationally determined requirements; and, no less important, it gives local control and direction to these services. The first of these purposes is basically administrative; the second is primarily political.

These twin themes – a provider of services and an instrument of self-government – are the essence of our local government system. Although the average citizen might not spend much time thinking about the services that are provided by his or her local authority (except perhaps when the annual rate demand comes through the letter-box or when something goes wrong), we are all consumers of these services. A local authority might own the house in which we live, run the school in which our children are educated, provide the parks in which they play, or send the social worker who gives support to those in need. It operates the police, fire and other protection (including the increasingly important consumer protection) services, art galleries, museums and libraries. In all, there are about three dozen local authority services.[2] Local government may not seem the most exciting aspect of our lives or be a major topic of daily conversation, but its influence is extensive. Local councils spend over 10 per cent of our national income – a quarter of all public spending. About one in ten of those in work are employed by a local council or related body.

No less important than local government's role as a provider of essential services for the local population is its role as an instrument of local democracy. If local government is to be considered democratic, however, it cannot be judged without recognising its interdependence with the other institutions of our political system. Local government is part of a larger national political system, not separate from it. Nevertheless, local government can make distinctive contributions to democratic practice and, for many, these particular political values – greater opportunities for self-government, participation, community action, easy communication between electors and elected – are the primary justification for local government. In 1960, the Herbert Commission on Local Government in London described local government as 'an example of democracy at work'.[3] A century earlier, John Stuart Mill wrote what many regard as the most profound justification for local government when he argued a powerful case for maximum public involvement in the conduct of local affairs.[4] There have been more recent assessments of the value of local government from a political, as distinct from an administrative or technical, perspective,[5] although most written work about local government still adopts an administrative or legal approach rather than a theoretical one. The most recent inquiry into local government, the Widdicombe Report, devotes part of that report to a discussion of the role and purpose of local government in our political system.[6] According to the Committee, the real value of local government derives from three essential attributes:

(a) pluralism, through which it contributes to the national political system;
(b) participation, through which it contributes to local democracy;
(c) responsiveness, through which it contributes to the provision of local needs through the delivery of services.[7]

Moreover, these three attributes of local government – *pluralism, participation* and *responsiveness* – reinforce each other.

Pluralism in this context means that power is dispersed. A justification for having subnational government, as opposed to subnational administration, is that it prevents all the decision-making power in a country residing in one location and, instead, power is spread between socially different decision-making centres. This is a line of argument that was used by some politicians in the nineteenth century, who supported the development and enhancement of local councils as a means of restraining the growth in the powers of central government – which were expanding as a result of the new social legislation being enacted. In other words, local government is a counterbalance to the power of central government.

The participatory value of local government refers to the quality of democracy within the local political system. As noted above, the idea that local government affords the citizen a unique opportunity to participate in the control of local affairs is one that is most frequently associated with the writings of J. S. Mill, who stressed in particular the 'educative' virtues of popular participation in local government. As the Widdicombe Report notes, however, there are two distinct forms of local participation: 'participation in the expression of community views and participation in the actual delivery of services'.[8] The first is achieved primarily through the electoral process whereby local ratepayers can vote or even be elected as councillors to run local authorities, and the latter through a variety of consultative and lobbying processes which help determine what services are provided and how they are delivered.

Local authorities are also called upon to be responsive, that is responsive to the needs and aspirations of the communities they serve. On this point, the Widdicombe Report rightly makes a distinction between the 'efficient' and the 'effective' delivery of services. Efficiency, the report observes, implies merely the nature of the output of services, whereas effectiveness focuses on the meeting of needs. If the local authority is to fulfil its proper function, then 'those delivering local services need to be responsive to the local community'.[9] Indeed, Widdicombe goes further and defines responsiveness in terms of *sensitivity* to local needs; the opportunity to *initiate* and pioneer in response to particular local circumstances and ideas; and, not least, the ability to *co-ordinate* responses to local issues, many of which are multi-faceted. The latter is especially significant, and multi-purpose local authorities are particularly well suited to the task of responding in a coherent way to local needs such as the problems of inner city areas and those who reside in them, social and ethnic minorities and, most

recently, the challenge of local industrial decline. The fact that local
authorities are multi-purpose bodies means that they can respond to
those needs in a variety of ways and do so in a manner that tackles in a
consistent way several aspects of the problem simultaneously. Even
where the authority itself does not have formal powers, it is able to
orchestrate other bodies with which it has links, for example voluntary
agencies, towards the same objective.

   The qualities of pluralism, participation and responsiveness are
therefore the essence of local government and the justification for its
existence and our interest in its health. Without these qualities the
provision of services at the local level would be an administrative activity
rather than a political one – local administration rather than local
government.

A VITAL INSTITUTION

By any test, local government is a vital part of both the administrative
and political life of the nation. First, it is a massive spender – £800
annually for every man, woman and child – and a major employer.
Second, it has an immediate effect upon our lives and our environment.
The services provided by local councils are essential to our expected
standards of living and would be sorely missed if they were withdrawn.
If the schools did not open, if the police and fire services failed to
respond to emergencies or even if the dustbins were left unemptied,
there would be loud cries of public protest. The contribution of local
government, however, extends beyond routine service administration
since these responsibilities, provided the central government allows,
give considerable potential for initiative and experimentation in order to
respond to particular local needs and ideas. Municipal history is rich
with examples of local initiative, one of the most famous being the
radical programme of Joseph Chamberlain in Birmingham in the 1870s
which, among other things, began a project of slum clearance in that
city. Birmingham was not alone in giving scope to enterprising local
leaders and many cities in Victorian and early twentieth-century England benefited from the ideas and energies of these politicians.[10] Local
issues also often acted as the 'focus of party competition' which led to
involvement of political parties in local affairs.[11] There are, of course,
many more recent examples of local councils putting their particular
imprint upon the provision of services, notably those Labour-led
metropolitan county councils which, until abolition in April 1986, were
strongly committed to providing cheap public transport facilities. On
the other side of the political divide, there are the examples of Conserva-

tive-controlled authorities increasing the involvement of private enterprise in the provision of local services. The important point is that the services provided by local government offer extensive political potential. Some early socialist writers even argued that there was more scope for promoting socialism through town halls than through Westminster – a case of 'socialism in one *county*'. Even though local authorities only have those powers granted to them by Parliament (obligatory or permissive powers), and are largely dependent upon central financing, there is still a great deal of scope for partisanship and local ideas and values to enter into the way in which services are provided.

There is a third major claim for the importance of local government, one that is primarily political and stresses the closeness between local government and the community it serves. This is the opportunity it provides for public participation and involvement. A concern with participatory democracy is not recent: it was a prominent theme in the writings of J. S. Mill in the nineteenth century, who stressed not only the need for public involvement but also the 'educating' role in public affairs which such activity engendered. It is significant that the extension of voting rights last century was connected with property ownership: those who had a physical stake in the local community had the right, and perhaps the obligation, to have their say in the conduct of public affairs locally.

Many facets of the local government system provide opportunities for participation, as a comparison with the organisation of central government reveals.[12] The national political system in Britain allows for periodic elections (up to five years at the government's discretion), MPs who need not possess residence qualifications in their constituencies, infrequent opportunities for the average citizen to lobby his MP directly and certainly little scope for seeking election himself. MPs themselves, unless they are fortunate enough to be in office, may well have less influence than senior civil servants, industrialists and leaders of powerful pressure groups. In local government, there are fixed-term elections and, in some areas, annual elections which give more opportunities to change the group in power. There is a closer relationship – geographically and, probably, socially – between the elector, the council and councillors. It is much easier to contact the local authority or the appropriate councillor, the latter having to be a local ratepayer to be eligible for election. Councillors are at least local people. The social composition of local councils is much broader than that of the House of Commons, not least in the proportion of women and working-class representatives who are elected.[13] The average councillor, largely as a result of the committee system which operates in local government, has

more opportunities to question and influence policy than does his back-
bench counterpart at Westminster. Although strong party control of a
local council might diminish the day-to-day significance of the fact,
unlike civil servants in Whitehall who are the servants of the government in power, local government officers are the servants of the full
council and not of any one group or party. Finally, mainly because of
ease of access and communication, there are probably more opportunities for direct involvement in policy-making locally through community
groups, and the supporting role played by the local media in this context
should not be overlooked.

On all three counts – the size of the undertaking, the utility and
political significance of the services provided and the democratic value
of the processes involved – local government forms a vital part of our
political system. Nevertheless, it can also seem to be an undervalued
institution. For its democratic potential to be fully realised, it needs the
active involvement of the electorate. This is not always forthcoming.
The simplest test is, of course, to measure the level of turnout at local
elections. The average figure is low – around 40 per cent, just over half
the figure at general elections – and there is evidence that among those
who do vote, preferences about national parties heavily influence the
way votes are cast in local ballot boxes. Public awareness about local
government is another important question. Here, recent evidence is a
little more encouraging. In 1967, the Maud Committee on the Management of Local Government reported that 'There seems to be a certain
level of general public ignorance concerning local government and the
services provided by the council.'[4] Nineteen years later, the survey
undertaken for the Widdicombe Committee observed more optimisti-
cally: 'Overall, the level of knowledge . . . appears to be quite high.'[5]
The two surveys were not strictly comparable, but the results give some
cause for satisfaction. If local government is to play its full part in the
political system, it requires three things: the involvement and support
of the public, responsiveness by councillors and officials to local needs
and views, and the respect of Westminster and Whitehall from which
the powers and much of the finance of local government are derived, and
which fashion the political and economic climate within which local
councils have to operate.

CENTRALISATION AND DECENTRALISATION

The system of local government which now operates in Britain is the
product of many years of evolution and is only one form of subnational
government. *Decentralised* is the term which is commonly used to

describe the vertical allocation of functions to lower tiers. The word encompasses a variety of forms, all slightly different but sometimes confused because of the loose way in which terminology is used. The three main forms of decentralised government are: deconcentration, devolution (executive or legislative) and federalism. Before discussing these three types of decentralisation, it might be useful to say something about the forces towards and against centralisation.

Perhaps the most basic centralising force is the *need for co-ordination*, in terms of both policy-making and its implementation. Like any large organisation, governments want to ensure that policies are compatible and do not conflict with each other. Virtually every area of government activity will involve more than one department, not least the Treasury since most policies involve expenditure. In order to ensure that policies do fit together effectively, governments will wish to have jurisdiction over all appropriate policy areas. Since 1979, for example, the Conservative Government has been keen to control the level of public expenditure. One of its difficulties in achieving this objective has been the fact that nearly a quarter of public expenditure is incurred by local rather than central government. For this reason, the Conservatives have taken steps to extend their influence over the expenditure and revenue planning of local authorities.

A second reason for centralisation is the desire for *uniform provision* of many services. There are some areas where uniformity is a practical necessity – currency, defence and foreign policy, railway gauges, postal services, etc. There are many more areas where our desire for uniformity is the result of prevailing ideas and values, notably regarding the basic provisions of the welfare state. Since the Second World War, we have come to expect a certain standard provision in education, health care and the social services. This does not imply that needs do not vary between localities or groups of the population, nor that there cannot be local discretion in the way in which services are actually provided, but in these services there is a generally accepted view that all citizens, irrespective of background, location and needs, have the right to expect equality of treatment and the same general minimum level of provision. That being so, there is a need for a central authority to ensure that such a level is provided and that resources are available for this purpose.

Finally, there is an in-built dynamism towards centralisation in modern political systems. This is encouraged by the growing expectations of the electorate, the government's responsibility for managing the economy, and the focus of the broadcasting media on national politics. All tend towards increasing centralisation.

Excessive centralisation, however, brings its own problems. From an

administrative perspective, the machinery of central government
becomes unwieldy and *difficult to co-ordinate*. The 1973 Kilbrandon
Commission on the Constitution repeated a phrase originally used to
describe excessive centralisation in France, 'anaemia in the extremities
and apoplexy at the centre'. The Commission found that the
predominant view of its witnesses was that government in Britain was
too centralised 'to deal properly with the whole range of functions which
are now its responsibility' and that 'it is impossible for them to have a full
grasp of all that is going on'.[16] Alongside the problem of co-ordination
there is that of *remoteness*. Policies can be made in Whitehall, but they
need to be applied in the locality concerned. The fact that nearly all
government departments have regional offices is recognition of this
need. There is also the fact that both *need and resources vary* between
local areas and, even if policies of standardisation and uniformity are
pursued, it will still be necessary to take account of these variations
when formulating national policies. Some recognition of these variations in need is evident in the range of regional policies pursued by
successive governments in Britain since the 1934 and 1937 Special Areas
Acts.[17] The needs of Liverpool and Bournemouth, for example, are
vastly different – differences which are not explained by disparity in
population size, but by marked contrasts in the nature of their populations and economic setting. Liverpool is suffering from considerable
youth unemployment, the decline of one of its major industries, crime
and social deprivation. Bournemouth, on the other hand, is in an
economically prosperous area, but has to respond to the particular needs
of a high proportion of elderly inhabitants. Liverpool and Bournemouth
are extreme contrasts, but the significant point is that *all* areas and local
communities are, in some sense, unique in their needs and their
resources. Although there may be common problems and lessons to be
shared (for example, between areas facing similar problems of declining
industries, or those with high concentrations of immigrants), their
individual circumstances should be recognised. This is why we have
elected local councils to determine and control the provision of most
local services.

The political reasons for decentralisation are equally strong.
Administrative 'apoplexy' and 'anaemia' have their political equivalents.
In a system where all political authority is centralised, parliament finds
it *difficult to control and scrutinise* adequately the actions of governments. The problems are exacerbated by the recent tendency to hive off
important areas, away from direct parliamentary control, to other areas
of the public sector.[18] In the UK system, the decline of parliamentary
scrutiny has been a recurrent theme since the 1930s. Administrative

remoteness also has its political counterpart. Communities which are distant from centres of decision-making are naturally *inclined to feel excluded* from the decision-making process itself. This is unhealthy since political systems, like financial institutions, have a need for public confidence and trust. *Remoteness* between the community and government can be social as well as geographical. A community which is geographically distant can attribute unpopular political decisions to a lack of understanding which results from this geographical separation. The same feelings may be felt by those who define the separation between 'them' and 'us' in social terms. MPs, after all, are not socially typical, being essentially 'male, middle-aged, middle-class, metropolitan and white'. There is much to be said in favour of having a tier of government, like local government, that allows the participation in public affairs on a part-time basis of people who resemble more closely in their social characteristics, and perhaps their attitudes, the electorate as a whole.

The several forms of decentralisation are depicted in Fig. 1.1.

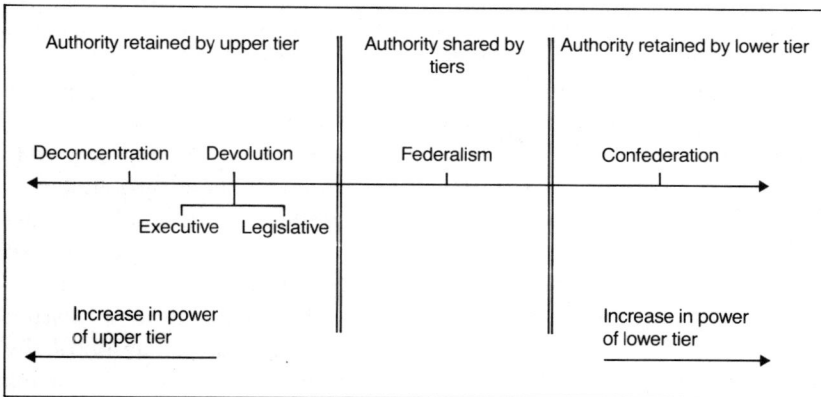

Fig. 1.1 Types of decentralisation

The diagram is necessarily a simplification and the labels used represent no more than points on a continuum rather than absolute and precise forms. Nevertheless, it illustrates the relationship between the various types of decentralisation. The most moderate form is *deconcentration*. This simply means the delegation of administrative authority by central government to public servants who work locally. In strict terms, it involves no transfer of political power and therefore responsibilities for decision-making remain with the central authorities. In essence, it may be likened to decision-making in a military unit where

HQ decisions are passed on to the troops in the field, and an alternative term for the variant is *field administration*. By contrast *devolution* involves some transfer of political responsibilities and therefore gives scope for decision-making to the lower-level body. This lower level of government now has the capacity to act as an institution of general government, is elected and, generally, exercises responsibility over a reasonably large territorial unit. Two specific types of devolution – executive and legislative – may be distinguished. *Executive devolution* is where the central government defines the broad framework of policies and sets national standards, but allows the lower tier to implement these policies and exercise a degree of local discretion in 'fleshing out' skeleton schemes. There will also be a measure of continuing central supervision and, if necessary, intervention. *Legislative devolution* separates the responsibilities of the upper and lower tiers rather than having joint responsibilities: the central authorities retain full responsibility for duties considered to be of national significance while handing over responsibility for other policy areas to the subordinate level. This does not prevent the central government from subsequently changing the allocation of responsibilities or intervening in the actions of the lower tier (especially if it has reserved powers or retains control over the finances of the lower tier), but under legislative devolution an attempt is made to distinguish upper- and lower-tier responsibilities.

Federalism is an even more powerful form of decentralisation. It shares some characteristics of legislative devolution, notably in making a distinction between upper- and lower-tier responsibilities, although the latter tend to be more extensive than under legislative devolution. However, there is a crucial difference. Unlike legislative devolution, the division of powers in a federal system is set out in a written constitution which cannot be amended by the unilateral action of the central government. In legislative devolution, ultimate power remains with the central government so that, for example, it is possible to alter the powers of the lower tier or even abolish it altogether. For instance, the devolved Northern Ireland Assembly at Stormont was abolished in 1971.

To complete the picture, there is *confederation*. In a sense, this is the mirror image of legislative devolution since, while there is a division of responsibilities, formal authority belongs this time to the lower tier which can, at any time, change the powers transferred to the upper tier or withdraw from the arrangement altogether. This was the form of political system advocated by the southern states of America in the 1840s, but it is more usually found as a political form between, rather than within, nations. The lower tier is usually a nation and the upper tier some form of supranational body. The European Community could be described in such terms.

Most subnational government is some form of executive or legislative devolution, but whatever the type, there are a number of common issues. What powers should be devolved? How should the demands for uniformity and standardisation be balanced against the desires for local autonomy and diversity? What is the proper balance between the powers of the upper and lower tiers? Who provides the finance, especially if local resources are insufficient to meet local needs? All of these issues have figured prominently in the development of local government in Britain.

LOCAL GOVERNMENT: THE BRITISH MODEL

The local government system which operates in Britain is a form of executive devolution. Initially, this may seem an exaggerated view of the powers of local government, since the word devolution is usually reserved in Britain for the rather more extensive powers that were being sought in Scotland, Wales and even some English regions in the 1970s. Devolution is sometimes considered synonymous with the concept of regionalism, and the existing local government system falls short of this concept in two ways: the smaller size of units and the limited nature of its powers and financial independence. However, our system of local government does fit the basic framework of executive devolution: it is an institution of general government; it is directly elected; it is granted powers by central government and has discretion, within the limits imposed by statutes and often under the supervision of a department of central government, to exercise these responsibilities in a way deemed appropriate by the local electorate. Even the question of size, which might deter some from classifying our local government system as a form of executive devolution, could be countered since, by comparison with other Western political systems, local authorities in Britain are exceedingly large in terms of both area and the size of population served. English and Welsh local authorities have an average population of approximately 123,000. The average for other Western nations is about 10,000 and even in Sweden, which has the second largest units of local government, the average is only 30,000. The size of council memberships, the size of electoral divisions and the budgets of individual councils are all correspondingly large.

The development of local government, especially during the 50-year period between the 1830s and 1880s, illustrates another important organisational issue that is still topical – the choice between *functional* and *territorial* decentralisation.[19]

Although its antecedents originated in Saxon times and the major units of local government – the county, the borough and the parish – have distant histories, the present system of local government developed mainly in the nineteenth century and the structure that was created during the last two decades of Victorian England largely survived until 1974. In the early years of that century Britain experienced a social transformation which centred on the consequences of industrialisation. The Industrial Revolution led to the creation of new towns, different working and living conditions and the growth of labour organisations which voiced demands for the alleviation of harsh conditions. Concentrations of population in industrialised urban settings created new needs, in particular for housing, water and sewerage services and roads. The radical wing of the Whig party began to promote the cause of the towns, especially as the franchise was extended. The problems of poverty and urban living also led to the creation of reform movements, in which people like Jeremy Bentham, Robert Owen and Titus Salt argued the need for improvement in the conditions of the town. It was not entirely a selfless philosophy since they realised that improving the conditions of the worker meant improving his capacity for work.

In the 1830s two great Acts signposted an important political and administrative principle that dominated the organisation of municipal affairs in the nineteenth century. In 1834 a report was published about the operation of the Poor Law, which dated back to Elizabethan times. The report, largely a result of the energies of Edwin Chadwick, secretary to the Commission, advocated a new and uniform basis for the provision of relief to the poor, and the recommendations were incorporated in the 1834 Poor Law Amendment Act. The Act established the principle of 'less eligibility', i.e. relief was to be set at a level below that enjoyed by the poorest worker. The second principle of the legislation, and for our purposes the more important one, was that the scheme should be administered by locally elected bodies, employing paid officials and operating under strict central control. For the student of modern local government there are two important features of the Act. First, it decreed that the areas of the new boards should be determined on the grounds of administrative convenience (a modern term would be 'administrative efficiency'); and, second, that the bodies should be responsible for this one specific service (the *ad hoc* principle).

The second piece of legislation was passed the following year. The Municipal Corporations Act of 1835 resulted from an investigation into the running of local boroughs, many of which were seats of corruption and privilege. Again, only the major features of the Act are relevant for our present purposes. These were: the identification of the council as the governing body of the borough (three-quarters of the members of which were to be directly elected on the basis of a limited ratepayer franchise); council meetings to be open to the public; their accounts to be audited; and the right to appoint paid officials. Although the 178 boroughs affected by the Act had relatively few powers at the time – they could establish a police force and make certain by-laws – their powers grew piecemeal over the following 50 years and these local, elected, *multi-purpose* bodies laid the foundations of our modern system of city government. By 1882, another 87 boroughs had been added.

The 1834 Poor Law Amendment Act and the 1835 Municipal Corporations Act reveal two distinct and contrasting principles. The first Act established a body to run a single service, under strict central control, using areas defined with regard to the efficient running of that service. It set out a uniform standard of provision. By contrast, the Municipal Corporations Act created multi-purpose bodies, elected by local people, which could operate with a minimum of central supervision. The clash between these two approaches recurred throughout the next half-century, creating an administrative jigsaw of boards operating within different geographical units and levying different rates. Among the many other boards there were, for example, those concerned with schools and with highways.

A step towards rationalisation came with the Royal Sanitary Commission (1868–71). The Report of the Commission argued that:

the administration of sanitary laws should be made uniform, universal and imperative throughout the Kingdom . . . all powers requisite for the health of towns and country should in every place be possessed by one responsible local authority, kept in action and assisted by a superior authority.

The outcome was the Local Government Board – a predecessor of the Ministry of Health – which took over the responsibilities of the Poor Law Board, the public health functions of the Home Office and the related functions of the Registrar-General's Office.

Seventeen years later, local government itself entered a decade of reform which led to the creation of a structure that was to survive until 1974. The 1888 Act created county councils and all-purpose county boroughs which, based on population size, were independent of the county councils. Those boroughs which were of insufficient size to be granted this status remained non-county boroughs – a second-tier authority in the counties. To this structure, urban and rural districts were added by the Local Government Act of 1894 and the system was

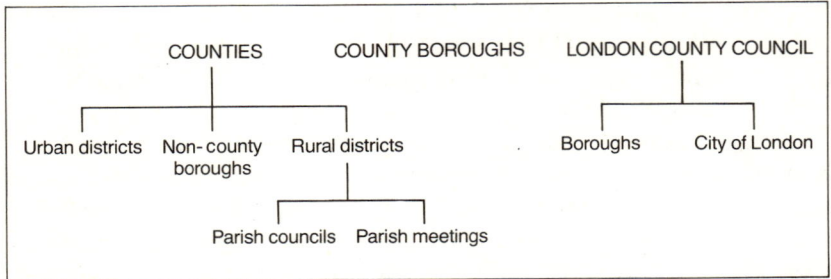

Fig. 1.2 Local government structure 1899–1963

completed in England and Wales when a two-tier structure was devised
for the London area in 1899 (Fig. 1.2).

For the next 50 years, local government enjoyed a gradual expansion
of its role. *Ad hoc* bodies were dismantled and their powers transferred
to local government; local councils involved themselves in the running
of a range of public utilities (gas, water, electricity, etc.), and many
extensions of public provision (especially personal services) were
handed to local authorities. From the 1930s, however, local government
has been in relative decline – losing control of some services to central
government or to *ad hoc* bodies, failing to attract new responsibilities
and becoming increasingly dominated by central government and
dependent upon central funding. Since the mid-1960s it has undergone
a process of considerable scrutiny and, since 1972, an almost continual
process of reorganisation and change in its operation.

This brief and necessarily superficial sketch is not intended to provide
a concise history of the evolution of local government during the last 150
years, but rather to illustrate the organisational choice which is available
for the public provision of those services not administered by central
government. As suggested earlier, there are basically two options:
functional or *territorial* decentralisation (Fig. 1.3). The former is where
a body is specifically created to administer a particular service: there are
estimated to be 3,000 such bodies or quangos (quasi-autonomous non-
governmental organisations) as they are sometimes known. Some of
these are themselves subsequently organised into territorial subdivisions. This practice has been termed 'multiple decentralisation'.[20]
Territorial decentralisation is a process of geographical delimitation
which creates multi-purpose units. Local government is an example of
the territorial principle.

The evolution of local government in England and Wales, and equally
in Scotland, during the last century and a half reveals changing attitudes

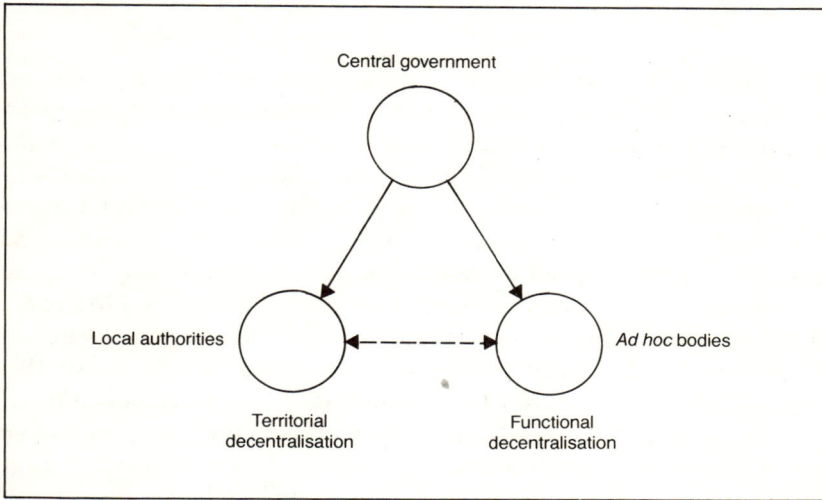

Fig. 1.3 Functional and territorial decentralisation

about the relative virtues of the territorial and functional forms of decentralisation. The functional approach has several advantages – the ability to design optimum-sized units for the service, clear allocation of responsibility, central control, uniform standards of provision – and seemed to prevail between 1830 and 1880. There was a proliferation of *ad hoc* bodies during this period. Over the next 50 years, the advantages of the territorial principle – a single authority for all services, democratic control, relative independence of central government – gained favour and local government was in the ascendancy. During the last 50 years, the functional approach to decentralisation has come back into favour and not only has local government failed to take on new responsibilities, it has lost some of its previous functions. In the earlier part of this period, these were services like gas and electricity; more recently, there have been the losses of responsibility for water and certain aspects of the personal health services following the 1974 reorganisation. Still more recently, there have been the new Urban Development Corporations. As a result, Britain has a tripartite system of administration – central government and a mix of territorially and functionally devolved bodies. In a sense, the evolution of local government can be considered in the context of this choice between the principles of territorial and functional decentralisation. Assessing which of these two principles is in favour at any given time provides an important indicator of the status and health of local government.

A CHANGING ROLE FOR LOCAL GOVERNMENT?

The role that local government plays is determined by the power and financial independence it enjoys and by the perceptions of those who provide and, to a lesser degree, consume services.

Local government derives its powers from Acts of Parliament and can perform only those functions allowed by statute. To go beyond this is to act *ultra vires*. Unlike local authorities in some other countries, local councils in Britain do not possess the power of 'general competence' to do whatever they consider to be in the interests of their area. Most of the functions given to local authorities are obligatory, i.e. requiring councils to perform certain tasks; others are permissive, which means that councils have a certain discretion. In addition, since 1963 local authorities have been able to spend a small proportion of their rate revenue on any scheme considered to benefit their locality. Under section 137 of the 1972 Local Government Act this is now limited to the product of a 2p rate annually.

The range of services provided by local government is extensive; the main ones are shown in Fig 1.4.

CATEGORY	SERVICE
Personal	Education (schools, colleges and careers service) Social services Housing
Environmental	Planning Highways, traffic and transport*, lighting Environmental health Refuse collection and disposal* Cemeteries
Protective	Police* Fire* Consumer protection Licensing
Leisure	Libraries Museums, art galleries, theatres Sports facilities Parks and gardens

*Special arrangements apply in metropolitan areas in respect of these services since the abolition of the GLC and the metropolitan counties in April 1986.

Fig. 1.4 Main local government services

In addition, there is an assortment of trading services which are run on commercial lines. These may include markets, allotments and even, in the case of Hull, its own telephone system.

Local authorities have collected these responsibilities over a long period of time and all of them are subject to frequent modification. Listing them in these broad categories perhaps suggests that they are precise and neat duties set out in single Acts of Parliament. This is far from the case, and every one of them involves numerous pieces of legislation and administrative direction from central government departments.[21] Some, like consumer protection, now even have to accommodate a vast array of EC regulations and directions.

The importance of these services is reflected in financial terms. At the beginning of the twentieth century, local government spent 5 per cent of GNP. Since then, this figure has increased nearly threefold. At the same time there has been a decrease in the financial self-sufficiency of local government; local taxes now provide just one-third of local revenue. Conversely, central grants as a proportion of local revenue have risen from 30 to 50 per cent since the 1950s. These changes have coincided with increasing central control.

For a long time it was customary to view local government as the provider of a range of distinct and separate services. Such a view, which was common until the 1960s, was reinforced by the piecemeal manner in which services had been allocated to local government over time. It was also encouraged by the separatism which typified committee and departmental structures in local government and by the career progressions of those working for local authorities, most of whom saw their career ladders in strict departmental terms. There are, however, alternatives to this *traditional* conception, in particular what have been described elsewhere as *federal* or *corporate* conceptions.[22]

The federal conception derives from a concern for administrative efficiency which was prevalent in the 1960s. It paralleled similar concerns in central government and was characterised by a desire to provide for the most efficient use of resources at local level. Like the traditional model it assumed that services should be separately planned, but recognised that for reasons of efficiency there could be better co-ordination in the provision of these services. The third approach, which was extensively promoted in the 1970s, identified a more interventionist role for local government and stressed the cumulative effect on society and the local environment of the services provided by local authorities. It was also more overtly political.

One of the most widely quoted expressions of the *corporate* approach comes from the Bains Report and appears at the beginning of this chapter. The Scottish equivalent of the Bains Report, the Paterson Report, observed:

The ultimate objective . . . is to achieve a situation where the needs of a community are viewed comprehensively and the activities are planned, directed and controlled in a uniform manner.[23]

A few years earlier, the Royal Commission on Local Government in England defined the role of local government as:

an all-round responsibility for the safety, health and well-being, both material and cultural, of people in different localities, in so far as these objectives can be achieved by local action and local initiative, within a framework of national politics.[24]

The corporate view of local government extends the role of local authorities to one of general responsibility for the well-being of the community. One manifestation of this expanded role can be seen in the employment initiatives undertaken by local authorities in recent times. Although local councils have no statutory duty to engage in job-creation activities, many authorities, especially in employment blackspots, now put considerable effort into promoting economic regeneration. Moreover, there is evidence of public support for such activities. The Widdicombe Report, for example, discovered that 59 per cent of the electorate considered that job creation should become a mandatory function of local government.[25] In essence, therefore, the corporate approach is concerned with the formulation of integrated policies which reflect the changing needs and problems of the local community.

COMMUNITY: A SOCIOLOGICAL AND GEOGRAPHICAL CONCEPT

The word *community* is used frequently, and freely, in newspapers, on television, by politicians, in everyday conversation and, not least, in books about local government. The word often precedes a particular activity – community education, community politics, community health, community policing and, currently fashionable, community architecture. However, the concept itself is left undefined. One popular local government textbook, for example, has no fewer than eight references to specific kinds of community activity or service in its index, but not a line of explanation about the actual concept. It is hardly surprising, therefore, that in spatial terms, 'community' has been used to describe areas from parishes of a few score to regions of several million people.[26] In fact, a community has two distinct aspects – one sociological and the other geographical. It is about people and about places.

Community, in the sociological sense, arises from people sharing common interests, experience and information networks. 'Community news' in a local newspaper, for example, generally refers to items considered to be of interest only to a small section of the paper's readership. There are sometimes 'community newspapers' – broadsheets with limited circulation for readers who wish to share information. Participation, if only passive, in such a network indicates a further sociological aspect of community, namely that it comprises people with a common interest or interests. Such groups of people may or may not form identifiable geographical units: communities which are defined by reference to common social interests or experience are not necessarily limited to people living in close proximity to each other. We may, for example, refer to communities of people having common ethnic or religious backgrounds without suggesting that such groups live adjacent to each other.

In most cases, however, it is assumed that a community of people has a spatial, as well as a social, relationship. Communities exist somewhere and the web of social interaction, of information flow and of common interest has a spatial dimension. In some cases, the notion of community interest focuses upon place, for example in those circumstances where communities unite in order to protect some feature of their location. Communities sometimes only emerge publicly in response to external threats, for example against property development or a particular planning proposal. Many definitions of community include a 'territorial point of reference'.[27] The notion is particularly appropriate where community is defined by birthplace, and it is often asserted that communities develop least successfully in places where newcomers greatly outnumber long-term residents. This is a particular problem in commuter areas outside large towns, and one planning response has been to try to develop a sense of community in these areas by various planning devices. These devices, usually known as neighbourhood planning because 'neighbourhood' is thought to represent the notion of community and associated place, were intended to facilitate a high degree of social interaction and therefore draw individuals into a community network.

There is a crucial dimension to the notion of place and that is scale. Identification of the individual within a given location takes place at a number of levels, from the national 'patriotic' level down to that of personally controlled space, the home or office. Community lies somewhere between these two extremes. We generally understand that a neighbourhood community is smaller than a town but larger than a street, although there are problems in arriving at precise definitions. It may be helpful to consider two extremes of population density – the larger town and the smaller village. The community may be defined by reference to the maximisation of internal interactions (contacts within) and minimisation of external relationships (contacts outside). In the village, the community comprises all residents, whether active in village life or not. Membership is readily delimited by the absence of a population outside the boundaries of the village and, in that sense, the community is isolated. In towns, scale becomes much more important. People and buildings form a continuous surface and interactions are not necessarily bounded. In these circumstances, communities can be defined in different ways and have contrasting territorial components. Geographers and sociologists have attempted to define the limits of communities by examining the spatial patterns of social life (where people travel to work or shop) or by asking people themselves to identify their own community. However, there are considerable methodological difficulties in the latter approach and, as we shall discuss later, attempts to relate the structure of local government units to notions of community have been notably difficult to achieve.

The purpose of this chapter has been to introduce some of the major themes and issues that underlie a discussion of local government and the community it serves. They will reappear in subsequent chapters. It has also served to introduce three key actors that dominate the landscape of local government – people, land and central government. Local government has to respond to the needs and demands of all three, and it is to the first of these that we now turn.

Notes

1. *Study Group on Local Authority Management Structures* (Department of the Environment, 1972), para 2.10.
2. Lord Redcliffe-Maud and B. Wood, *English Local Government Reformed* (OUP, 1973), p. 12.
3. *Report of the Royal Commission on Local Government in Greater London*, Cmnd 1164 (1960).
4. J. S. Mill, *On Representative Government* (1861).
5. Notably, C. H. Wilson, *Essays on Local Government* (Blackwell, 1948); W. J. M. McKenzie, 'Theories of Local Government', *Greater London Papers* (1961); L. J. Sharpe, 'Theories and Value of Local Government', *Political Studies* (1970); D. M. Hill, *Democratic Theory and Local Government* (Allen and Unwin, 1974); G. Jones and J. Stewart, *The Case for Local Government* (Allen and Unwin, 1985).
6. *Report of the Committee of Inquiry into the Conduct of Local Authority Business*, Cmnd 9797 (1986), ch. 3.
7. *Ibid*. para 3.11.
8. *Ibid*. para 3.20.
9. *Ibid*. para 3.26.
10. There are many studies which trace the development of municipal affairs. See, for example, Asa Briggs, *Victorian Cities* (1968); G. W. Jones, *Borough Politics* (1969); D. Fraser, *Power and Authority in the Victorian City*; E. P. Hennock, *Fit and Proper Persons:*

Ideal and Reality in Nineteenth Century Urban Government (1973); W. Hampton, *Democracy and Community* (1970); J. M. Lee, *Social Leaders and Public Persons* (1963). On the development of local government more generally, see J. Redlich and F. W. Hirst, *The History of Local Government in England*, ed. B. Keith-Lucas (1958) and B. Keith-Lucas and P. G. Richards, *A History of Local Government in the Twentieth Century* (1978).

11. K. Young, 'Party Politics in Local Government: An Historical Perspective' in Research Vol. 4, *Committee of Inquiry into Local Authority Business (Widdicombe Committee)*, Cmnd 9801 (June 1986).

12. See D. M. Hill, *Participating in Local Affairs* (Penguin, 1970).

13. The Widdicombe Report, for example, found that 19 per cent of councillors were female. Although this is much less than the 51 per cent of the population who are female, it is significantly higher than the figure of 4 per cent of MPs who are women. The educational and occupational backgrounds of councillors are similarly broader than those found at Westminster. For a general review of the characteristics of both groups see Research Vol. 2, *The Local Councillor*, Cmnd 9799 (June 1986) and C. Mellors, *The British MP* (Gower, 1978).

14. *Committee on the Management of Local Government*, Vol. 3, *The Local Government Elector*, p. 5.

15. *The Local Government Elector*, Cmnd 9800 (1986), p. 28.

16. *Royal Commission on the Constitution*, Cmnd 5460, Vol. 1, paras. 272 and 270.

17. G. McCrone, *Regional Policy in Britain* (Allen and Unwin, 1969). On the question of regionalism more generally, see, besides the Kilbrandon Report above, W. Thornhill, *The Case for Regional Reform* (Nelson, 1970) and A. H. Birch, *Political Integration and Disintegration in the British Isles* (Allen and Unwin, 1977).

18. See W. Thornhill, *Public Administration* (ICSA, 1985), Ch. 1.

19. See Redlich and Hirst, *op. cit.* and Keith-Lucas and Richards, *op. cit.*

20. J. Stanyer and B. Smith, *Administering Britain* (Fontana, 1976), p. 89.

21. See P. M. Lloyd, *Services Administration by Local Authorities* (ICSA, 1985).

22. R. Greenwood and J. D. Stewart, 'Towards a Typology of English Local Authorities', *Political Studies* (March 1973).

23. *The New Scottish Local Authorities: Organisation and Management Structures* (Paterson Report) (HMSO, 1973), para. 5.3.

24. *Report of the Royal Commission on Local Government in England*, Cmnd 4040 (HMSO, 1969), p. 10.

25. Cmnd 9800, Table 5.1.

26. W. Hampton, 'Local Government and Community', *Political Quarterly* (1969).

27. D. J. Herbert and C. J. Thomas, *Urban Geography* (Wiley, 1982).

2

COLLECTION AND USE OF POPULATION
DATA: THE SOCIAL CONTEXT OF LOCAL
GOVERNMENT

THE HISTORICAL BACKGROUND

The purpose of this chapter is to introduce the functioning of local government in its two principal contexts – the social and the physical – and to describe the social context in greater detail. In the twentieth century, local government has come to play an important and direct role in the life of every individual both through historical precedent and because of the intervention of successive central administrations. It has also played an increasingly important part in determining the nature of the physical environment in which the population lives. We can further characterise these two areas of local government operation by suggesting that land and people may be seen as follows:

1. Resources from which local government derives some benefit.
2. Responsibilities for which it must meet some need.

Initially, before the establishment of simple forms of devolved governmental power, the emphasis was upon the land and people as resources for government's use; latterly that emphasis has shifted and it is important to understand the historical context in which these changes have taken place.

The Domesday Survey of 1086 is the first important example in England of a comprehensive attempt by a central government to assess the national resources available to it, and it illustrates a major initial point: that no government is possible at any level without adequate information about the resources at its disposal.

Many surveys and censuses have succeeded that of Domesday, counting and assessing both the ecclesiastical and the lay populations, and their lands and goods. Some were undertaken by central government for the purpose of assessing national taxable resources and raising revenue, others by early local government authorities, such as parishes and dioceses. Gradually the system of national government changed from monarchy towards a liberal democracy, which extended the base of political power. At the same time the economic and social life of the nation became more complex, with interest and pressure groups concerned to impress their needs on those in power. As a result, the exercise of government became increasingly directed towards the needs of the people. This process, supported and justified by the works of great political philosophers such as Mill, was brought more sharply into focus because the character of the population changed from one of a largely homogeneous agrarian society with common basic interests to one of sharp differentiation in class, income and status – and, most importantly, function.

The pace of the evolution of government was slow but more or less in step with changes in the structure of society and of economic life. There were few watersheds of change, but by the nineteenth century it is clear that, at the national level at least, if government was to be responsive to even a limited range of its people's needs, as distinct from meeting the needs of the State itself, then much more information about the population was required. As the nineteenth century progressed there were fundamental changes in the structure of society. At the beginning of the century most people still lived in an agrarian social structure. Their workplaces were the fields surrounding the villages, hamlets and isolated farmsteads in which they lived. Daily life was encompassed in a small area, and social relationships would be conducted within a small group comprising both workplace colleagues and employers. By the end of the century the situation had changed. The majority of the population now lived in large cities which, because of the major problems of public health and housing, required a much greater degree of regulation than the smaller units which had preceded them. Masses of people were drawn together to meet the labour needs of an inflexible factory system. They were increasingly divorced in social terms from their neighbours and from those for whom they worked. The emerging social system was seen by many as the human equivalent of the machines of the new factory age, each individual playing his or her part in the functioning of some much greater system.

It was clear both at local and national level that, aside from any moral or ethical consideration, the large-scale emergent slums of the cities were uneconomic and thus a hindrance to the advancement of trade, industry and commerce. A series of measures were adopted, using enabling Acts of Parliament[1] and local by-laws, to arrest this decline and to institute developments in such areas as public health and sanitation, and working and housing conditions. The principal agency through which such improvements were to be made was that of local government, and, especially in the towns, this promoted the power of local councils and hastened the extension of the franchise.[2]

In the pre-industrial age the needs of each social group were readily identified because communities were small and individuals known to each other. Poor Relief, for example, although eventually organised nationally, was essentially local relief for people who were probably known to their benefactors. In the nineteenth century that close relationship disappeared as the old system broke down and the new emerged. The history of the nineteenth century shows that those needs had increasingly to be met in a more indirect and less personal way through the agency of local government. Local government development can be seen as a response to the need to institutionalise the provision for needs generated within the new social order.

The Local Government Acts of 1888 and 1894 established in England and Wales an administrative structure by which much of the surface area of the country and all of its people were controlled. They provided a context for the operation of the system in both the social and physical environments, so that local authorities would have responsibilities and rights with respect to both people and land.

While it is clear that people function in a variety of social contexts, they equally function within a physically defined compass. We live, work and play in a limited geographical context, our environment. We take that context for granted to the extent that, except for specific activities, we rarely give it a second thought. However, if prompted we would be able to recognise, for example, the importance of the agricultural land from which we derive our food, and impute to it a value in proportion to its ability to meet our needs for food. The value of land therefore may be said to vary in proportion to its productivity in that respect.

Land in cities can also be seen as meeting some of the needs of the people who live on it. It provides space for shelter, for transportation systems, workplaces and the services which the people use. Like agricultural land, its value is dependent upon its 'productivity', and that generally is determined by the sort of function which it can support.

The productivity of agricultural land can be maintained only if it is protected and safeguarded as a resource. It can be seen as having its own needs in respect of drainage, fertilisation and protection from erosion; similarly, land in cities will only continue to be useful while it too is protected. For urban land, however, the protection takes a different form: that of regulating the demands which the urban population places upon it. Because the demands tend to be more intensive in towns than in the countryside, we apply stricter planning controls.

We can therefore see that land and people represent for local government both a resource and a responsibility. Together they constitute the bases for community, but they also have needs. Throughout the nineteenth century the enormous increase in population and the increasing complexity of social and economic life placed greater burdens upon local government because of their attempts to come to terms with these needs. Although such radical social changes have not taken place in the twentieth century, needs have continued to grow as a result of increased affluence, higher expectations and a growing population.

In order to meet its statutory obligations, perform its proper functions and maintain control of its operations, therefore, government at both central and local levels needs adequate information. Well-founded decision-making is impossible without appropriate information, and the essential base of information about the population is the national census. Clearly, the census along with other sources of information is of great significance for the efficient functioning of central and local government, both in the determination of human resources and in the assessment of need at local level and the allocation and distribution of central resources.

CENSUS AND VITAL REGISTRATION

Evolution of census and measurement of populations

Counts of population have been important historically to both Church and State principally in order to assess taxable assets, or the numbers of men available for military service. However, in the eighteenth century another major issue lent weight to the necessity of population censuses at a national level – the fear that, as a result of war and migration, the population was in overall decline. Such a decline could be disastrous for the economy of the country and the well-being of its people because of its effects on trade and commerce and industry.

Some information about the population dynamic was available from local records, the parish register and bills of mortality being the most significant. However, both had limitations. Parish registers dealt only with a population which belonged to the established church, and may not have fully reported births, marriages and deaths even in that group. Bills of mortality were only a very crude and essentially historic measure of population vitality and were virtually useless alone as a device for measuring total population.

The famous eighteenth-century chronicler Arthur Young was convinced of the need for a population census which included not only total numbers, but also data on houses and families subdivided by county, town and city. He was also interested in the numbers in the business or professional classes, and in numbers of landowners, poor and vagrants. His last point reminds us of an additional problem which exercised Britain and its neighbours – that of poverty and the provision for the poor. In Britain a bill was brought before Parliament in 1753 to enable a population census which was justified in *The Gentlemen's Magazine* on the grounds that it would do the following:

1. Provide information about the total numbers and distribution of population.
2. Offer a basis for deciding whether a general naturalisation was desirable.
3. Make it possible to estimate how large an army could be raised in time of need.
4. Provide evidence of the desirability of emigration to the colonies.
5. Give a firmer basis for local government.
6. Show correctly for the first time the burden of the poor to the kingdom and enable new enquiries about and proper provision for them to be made.[3]

But although there was a clear case here for better information for the needs of both central government (primarily for military service) and local government and the people (for example, Poor Law administration), the bill was defeated.

By 1800, however, the mood had changed; apparently at the instigation of John Rickman, who was to become the first Registrar-General and principal organiser, the first national census was held in March 1801. It was an event of considerable importance because, aside from its direct value in furnishing data, it has become a national decennial event and provides a record of the population of Great Britain, unbroken except for 1941.

It has been suggested that the early censuses of population helped to boost public morale during the war with France. In 1811, *The Times* considered that 'These returns of increased population [shown by the census] must afford high satisfaction to every patriotic mind as shewing that the radical resources of the country have not been affected by the war which has lasted so long.'[4] But *The Times* also reflected other opinions about the value of the exercise. Much of the legislation undertaken by Parliament was related to the needs of particular groups of the population; and whereas in the past this had been undertaken 'in the dark' for want of information about these groups, now 'by learning what, as a people, we have been doing . . . we can learn what remains for us as a people to do.'[5] Asking questions about population was recognised as a way of gaining 'a larger grasp of the future', in which the needs and legislation could be brought closer together.[6]

Historical value of the census

The general value of the census was soon recognised and with it came the realisation of its local and specific value. In the first place, a large number of suggestions were made about additional material to be included as each new census approached. This has continued to be the case. Censuses have included labour market statistics, education, reading and writing, agricultural production, food prices, accommodation and industry. The information became ever more useful to local authorities in the emergent cities, giving a firmer basis for their policies with respect particularly towards public health, hygiene and sanitation. An alternative to a more frequent total population count was, however, to improve the accuracy of the *vital statistics* of birth, marriage and death. In 1833 a Commons Select Committee under Wilks inquired into the state of parochial registration and recommended a non-sectarian civil registration procedure organised nationally.[7] Compulsory registration of the births, marriages and deaths of the population was established in 1837 in England and Wales and in 1855 in Scotland.

Changes in the questions

Throughout the 180 years of the census there have been changes in the questions, usually with the effect of increasing the detailed information which it provided, but a milestone was passed in 1920 when the Census Act laid down a number of classes or categories from which all questions were to be derived. They were as follows:

1. Name, sex, age.
2. Occupation, profession, trade, employment.
3. Nationality, race, birthplace, language.
4. Place of abode, character of dwelling.
5. Condition as to marriage, relation to head of family, issue born in marriage.
6. Any 'other matter with respect to which it is desirable to obtain statistical information with a view to ascertaining the social or civil conditions of the population'.[8]

By 1921 revised occupational and industrial classifications were in use, marital fertility questions for married women were replaced by dependancy questions for the head of the household, and a most important addition made in respect of 'place of work'. Information derived from this question has allowed local authorities to determine the extent of daily commuting and helped subsequently to define local catchment areas, important in the distribution of national grant aid.

The census of 1931 was reduced in scope for reasons of economy, and that of 1941 abandoned altogether due to the exigencies of war. By 1951, therefore, there was a substantial need for new information and the census was extended considerably. It included many more questions about the physical quality of life in the home – the so-called household amenities, piped water, cooking stove and oven, kitchen sink, WC and fixed bath, which reflected the need of local and central government for information upon which to base its post-war reconstruction policies.

The census of 1961 took household questions further to enquire into the mode of tenure: whether privately owned, privately rented/ furnished or unfurnished, rented from a housing association or from the local authority. These questions reflected the fact that post-war housing problems were still not solved and indeed new slums were still being created. The principal addition to this data-set in 1971 was a question about parental birthplace, and date of entry into the United Kingdom if the respondent was born abroad, which together were particularly useful in measuring the number of people belonging to ethnic minority groups in the United Kingdom. There was also a question about the availability of a car in each household, reflecting increased concern about the effects of private car usage.

In one major respect the 1981 census was less complete than its forerunners. Ethnic consciousness in both the immigrant population and its British-born children, and in the indigenous population, had reached new heights and revealed substantial social tensions in various parts of the country. Although it was generally agreed that more information was needed, the government faced a considerable reluctance on the part of the immigrant community to acquiesce to an ethnic origin question. Among other reasons it was feared that it could be used to identify those who had entered the country illegally and could thus constitute evidence for deportations. In view of the likelihood that the integrity of the census might be jeopardised if such a question were to be included, and because it was difficult to devise a question which would not be regarded as offensive, it was dropped. Only the country of birth of the respondent was required.[9] This has left a gap in the proper knowledge of a major national minority group which is likely to have special needs at both local and national levels.

Organisation of the census

Until 1837 responsibility for undertaking the local organisation of the census had rested with the parish overseer, for no better reason than that he was familiar with the locality in which he operated. With the compulsory registration of births, marriages and deaths in 1837 responsibility passed from the overseer to the local registrar. Local registrars reported to the Registrars-General of England and Wales and of Scotland, and they acted through a Board of Census Commissioners. They were often doctors so the job of actually administering the census questionnaires was put out to enumerators. Throughout the nineteenth century there is evidence that the enumerators themselves were in some cases unfitted for the job, and of course their conduct is fundamental since the quality of the data relies heavily upon their skills.

Until 1920 the Registrars-General undertook each census under a separate Act of Parliament which made the process compulsory for all respondents, but with the Census Act of 1920 subsequent censuses have required simply an Order in Council. Although the Registrars-General continue to play a role in the census process, from 1971 in England and Wales it has been under the control of the Office of Population Census and Surveys.

From 1911 the principal areal units for census organisation have been the local authority areas. Until the 1981 census in England and Wales these were the county, county borough, municipal borough, urban district and rural district and in Scotland the county, city, large burgh and small burgh, and district. In addition, census material has been made available for other areas such as economic planning regions and hospital or health boards and, latterly, parliamentary constituencies and 'urban' areas.[10]

For census purposes the country is divided first into its local authority areas; these are currently the administrative counties, metropolitan districts and non-metropolitan districts. The local authority is then further subdivided into local council constituencies – the electoral wards. At the 1981 census in England and Wales there were seven metropolitan counties (six plus the Greater London Council), 47 non-metropolitan or shire counties, 33 London boroughs (including the City of London), 36 metropolitan districts and 334 non-metropolitan districts. Together they comprised a total of 9,285 wards. For the census each ward is further subdivided into blocks to be counted by a single enumerator, known as enumeration districts (e.ds). There were 112,300 enumeration districts in England and Wales at the 1981 census and an average therefore of about 12 e.ds. in each ward.

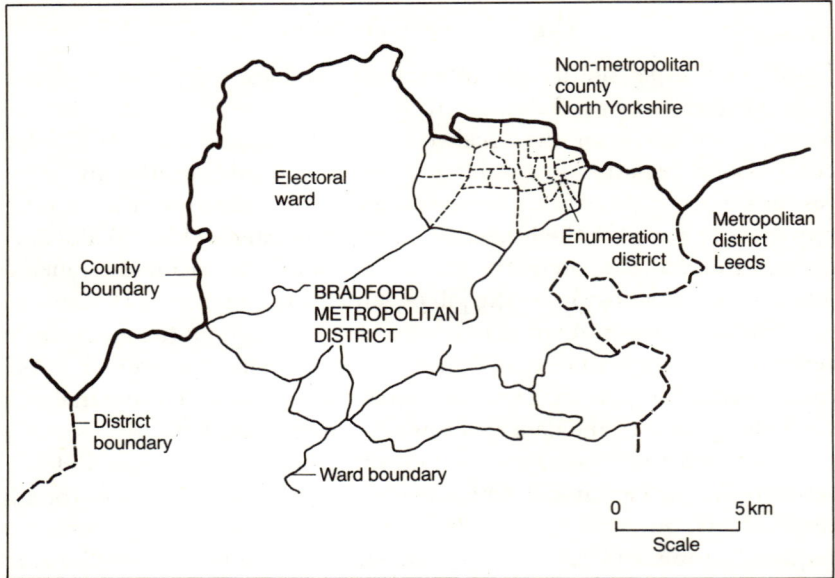

Fig. 2.1 Census 1981 local area structure – a schematic example

An example of this structure may help to clarify the relationships (Fig. 2.1). At the last census the Metropolitan County of West Yorkshire, for example, comprised five metropolitan districts – Leeds, Bradford, Kirklees, Calderdale and Wakefield. In one, Bradford, there were some 30 electoral wards, and in total the district comprised 900 enumeration districts. There was, therefore, an average of 30 e.ds in each ward with rather more in the urban areas and fewer in the rural parts of the district. It can be argued that the enumeration district level is by far the most significant census unit because it is the basis from which all others are aggregated. The e.d. is derived from the area which can be covered in one day by a single enumerator, although in a sparsely populated part of the country the enumerator may be responsible for more than one e.d. An essential requirement of the e.d. is that when aggregated with its neighbours the resulting boundary should be conterminous with that of the ward. The e.d. is equated both in numbers of households and in terrain conditions with the so-called postal walks into which the country is divided for postal delivery services. The planning of e.d. boundaries for the 1981 census also took into account the local authority boundaries which had existed at the 1971 census so that temporal comparisons between areal units could be made more readily. The needs of local authorities for areally based statistics for special purposes such as housing improvement areas, inner city areas and traffic zones were given special attention.[11]

Naturally, the nature of the census and its thoroughness result in the collection of much information which could be considered personal and private. Although the confidentiality of the information is not guaranteed under the 1920 Act, successive governments have provided such guarantees. No information which can be identified by household is revealed; this is achieved statistically by suppressing returns from isolated households where these might be identifiable and by adding random elements to published tables where the numbers of cases are very small, and also by maintaining the secrecy of the raw enumeration data for 100 years after its collection.

The two principal published sources which are readily available to the public are the county reports in which are published the returns aggregated to administrative or metropolitan county level, of which there are 54 volumes, and the Small Area Statistics in which the data are aggregated to ward level. Statistical tables are also produced for other administrative areas in England and Wales, such as the health regions, parliamentary constituencies, urban areas or towns existing before the 1974 local government reorganisation, and new towns. In Scotland published reports include not only planning regions, districts, island areas and postcode sectors, but also less obvious categories such as regional electoral divisions and employment office areas. The Office of Population Censuses and Surveys will also make available statistics for *ad hoc* areas on payment of a fee.

Useful though the published sources may be, it is frequently the case that administrators find direct access to enumeration district level data essential. In addition to the published data available in printed form, e.d. materials are available on electronic media either by direct access through the database of the OPCS computing system, or by the purchase of subsets of that database on magnetic tape for local access. Since the 1971 census considerable strides have been made in improving the availability of data to local authority users through the use of computers. In particular, the local authorities have themselves been responsible for the development of a number of programs to interrogate census data files and to manipulate the results, especially using the suite of programs known as SASPAC (Small Area Statistics Package).[12]

Other sources of information

Although the decennial census is the principal source of information about local and national populations, and is mandatory under existing national law and international agreements, it is not the only source; nor can it provide all of the information needed by either local or central government. In particular, local users find the census unsatisfactory for the following reasons:

1. It is too infrequent.
2. There is too long a time lag between the count and the publication of the results (although this has been falling dramatically in recent years and will continue to do so as electronic methods of collation are refined).
3. They have little control over the contents of the census, which is prepared essentially for national governmental needs on a much larger scale than required by other users (OPCS has increasingly sought the views of other users as to the information they would find most valuable).
4. Special tabulations or forms of output can be very expensive for small authorities.

For both central and local government, some of the gaps can be filled by OPCS, in the first place through the continuous collection of primary demographic data such as the vital statistics (births and deaths) which are published in a variety of forms by OPCS and by the Registrar-General,[13] and second through a range of large-scale surveys for which OPCS is also responsible. There are several categories of information which contribute to the total picture. The most interesting of these is *Social Trends*, a wide-ranging annual publication, but there are a number of other regular surveys such as the *General Household Survey, Family Expenditure Survey* and *Labour Force Survey*. Some material is irregular in its appearance, like the *House Condition Survey*: yet other surveys are conducted to examine specific needs or issues, such as the *National Dwelling-House Survey*.[14]

In addition, valuable strategic information can be obtained as a spin-off from the analysis of returns to other administrative agencies. The National Health Service maintains a central register recording movement of national health service patients from the care of one Family Practitioner Committee to another, which provides a useful though limited surrogate measure of population migration. Local authorities frequently supplement these sources with their own surveys and undertake their own collation of statistical sources for planning purposes in many of their departments.

WHAT THE DATA SHOW

People in the United Kingdom

When addressing the Conference of World Population in 1981, the British representative Lord Glenarthur described the current state of the UK population and the government attitude towards it.

I represent a country which viewed from a global perspective, has attained both low death rates and low birth rates. The expectation of life is already high at 73 years, our aim remains to extend further the span of healthy life and to avoid the waste of human potential through premature death. Desired and attained family size is low. The two child family is by far the most popular size; and through the provision of information and services in the field of family planning we aim to help people plan and space their births to avoid unwanted pregnancies. The overall size of the population has changed little in the decade . . . and the prospect is one of relatively little change in the years ahead – it may rise a little, it may fall a little, but the degree of change is likely to be within fairly narrow limits.

Against this background the Government of the UK is concerned with the well-being of the population rather than with its overall size. An ageing population, one of high geographic density and consequent pressures on the environment means that there are many problems to be surmounted in the field of social and economic policy making. But the search for solutions and deployment of resources will be easier in the virtual absence of population growth than it would be with the added pressure of ever increasing numbers.[15]

Lord Glenarthur's remarks were made in light of the early results of the 1981 census, together with the constant monitoring of population trends through registration of vital statistics. The 1981 population census included questions on the following topics: age, sex and marital status; household composition; country of birth; migration; housing; availability of cars and vans for private transport; economic activity; workplace and transport to work; qualified manpower; and in Wales and Scotland the extent of the Welsh or Scottish Gaelic language.

Not all responses were analysed. Some questions are more easily processed than others and in order to limit expense and save time, those questions requiring some classification procedure, such as occupation and higher educational qualifications, were analysed for only a 10 per cent sample. It is also worth noting at this point that gross figures for the largest population groups may be unclear because their geographical base is confusing. Population figures given for the United Kingdom include England, Wales and Scotland together with Northern Ireland and the Isle of Man. More often figures refer to Great Britain and this is simply England, Wales and Scotland together with the Scottish Islands.

Since Scotland is for many purposes, including the census, administered separately from England and Wales, it is often most convenient to refer to these two principal groupings separately.

Gross population

In 1801 the population of England and Wales numbered 8,892,536. It rose continuously to 49,154,687 in 1981, although the rate of change has tended to slow down throughout the period. Between 1811 and 1821 the increase was 18 per cent, while between 1971 and 1981 it had slipped to less than 1 per cent.[16] This continuous decline to very low levels in the last quarter of the twentieth century has raised fears about a declining population similar to those in the eighteenth century (Fig. 2.2). The fears arise because of the likely economic and social consequences of an ageing population, particularly should the population number begin to decline in real terms. In those circumstances fewer active workers would be available to meet the needs of an increasingly large yet unproductive sector.

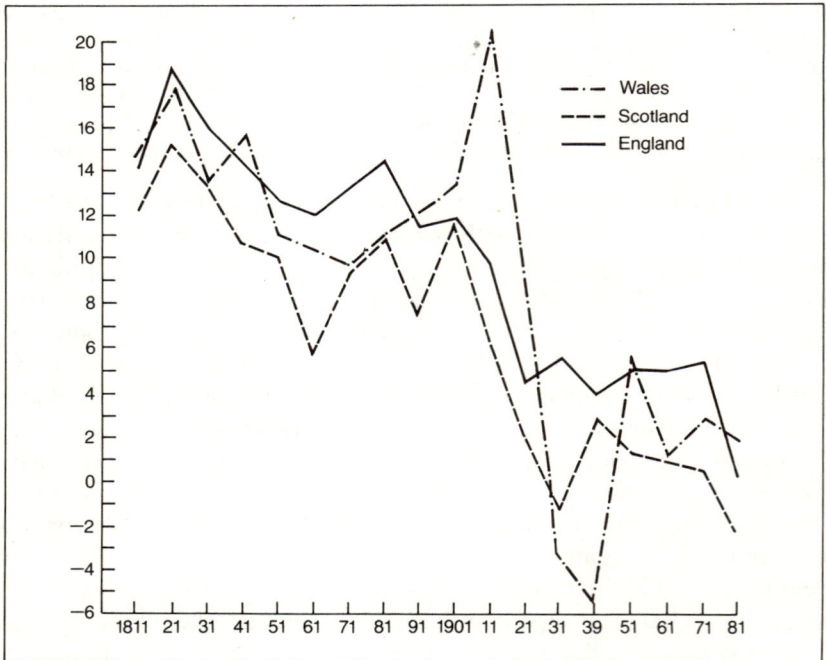

Fig. 2.2 Inter-censal rate of increase and decrease of population (%) 1811–1981
Source: CEN81HT

There are several reasons suggested for the changes in the growth rate in the nineteenth century. Leaving the effect of migration to one side, the principal factor was the decline in mortality rate as a result of better diet, improved hygiene, advances in medical science and, towards the end of the century, the survival rates of infants, which promoted high growth rates. From the 1860s onward deliberate attempts to limit family size became more commonly accepted as the techniques were more widely understood and practised, particularly among the upper and middle classes.[17] The smaller family could enjoy considerable advantages in living standards in a number of ways. In a period before free schooling education was easier in a smaller family, and fewer children meant a reduced demand upon limited family resources. Since the turn of the century birth control has become increasingly effective in limiting family size. In addition, social and economic pressures have reinforced this trend by such mechanisms as increased age at marriage and the entry of more women into the labour market. At the same time there continued to be a net loss to the country as a whole through migration, although the numbers involved varied considerably with time.

During the inter-war period, when the population had reached about 40 million and the rate of increase was about 5 per cent per decade, the fears of a declining population were raised again. The public unease culminated in the appointment of a Royal Commission in 1944.[18] The Commission found that a decline in real terms was possible and did not on the whole believe it to be desirable. A major recommendation was that in order to forestall this decline some attempt should be made to redress the financial disadvantage of large families, and this was one of the factors responsible for the introduction of child allowance and benefits. The importance of migration was also recognised and the Commission recommended that emigration should not be encouraged.

By 1981 the population of Great Britain had risen to 54,285,422 and the annual rate of increase had dropped to only six per ten thousand. It was the smallest inter-censal increase ever recorded. There was a slight increase in mid-1983 due to a shift in migration from a position of predominately net loss to one in which a balance was maintained. However, the rate of increase in England and Wales remained at only four per ten thousand, which masked interesting movements during the decade to 1983. From mid-1973 to mid-1978 the number of births fell and deaths exceeded them. There was a net outflow of migration and therefore there appears to have been a net fall in the size of the population in real terms. From mid-1978 to mid-1983 the death-rate remained steady while migration fluctuated, so that with first an increase in births and then a decrease, the overall rate was slightly increased. These fluctuations in births naturally work through the system producing peaks of demand for services at particular times.

This can be clearly seen in the demand for educational provision. In the period 1966–77, for example, births had fallen lower and lower. Thus 1982 was a year in which the number of 5-year-olds was at a low point, and entry to the school system eased. Falling rolls had continued for a number of years up to that point, but the number of entrants to primary schools has subsequently grown by some 15 per cent over the period 1982–86. In general the size of the school population has remained out of phase with provision because of the fluctuation in birth-rate. In 1984, for example, more children left school (809,000 who were born in 1966–67) than reached school age (564,000 born in 1977–78). It is precisely this sort of information that is required for efficient planning for the needs of the population. However, having the information is only the first step. Effective use has to be made of it. In education provision, for example, the five-year gap between a change in the pattern of births and an adjustment in service provision is barely enough time to evaluate the change and plan for it. Such changes must be considered against the complex effects of population migration, both long- and short-distance, training of teachers and government economic policy. Some embarrassment was caused by governments in the early 1960s, for example, by the lack of preparation for the large cohort of 'war babies' born in the late 1940s. Even though at least ten years had elapsed before some of these children reached secondary school, sixth forms and later colleges and universities were less than adequately prepared, with the result that the nation's human resources were lost or poorly developed.

These fluctuations can be seen to have their effect at other levels of the age structure. We can follow the fate of the cohort of 1917–18 who became pensioners in 1983. They were born in the last year of the First World War, a year in which there was a fall in the number of births. The number in the group was further reduced by the flu epidemic of 1918–19, to which as infants they were particularly susceptible, and by the Second World War, because by then they were in their early 20s, the ideal age for a fighting soldier. In 1983 they were 65 and, because there were so few of them, it resulted in an increase in the relative proportion of pensioners who were more than 75 years old. The middle-age range shows a working population which is still increasing as the post-1945 baby boom makes its way through its working life, while the numbers in the 45+ age range continue to decline due to deaths.

National gross population numbers, however, are only the outcome of a long process of population movement comprising a variety of factors. We can briefly examine each of these factors.

Live births and fertility

In 1983 there were 629,000 live births, about 4 per cent fewer than the recent peak of 656,000 in 1980. There had been a steady fall from the previous peak of 876,000 in 1964, to 569,000 in 1977. These changes are demonstrated by the changes in the number of children a woman might expect to have – the total period fertility rate (TPFR).[19] Up to 1964 it was rising, but by 1977 it had fallen back to 1.66. There was an increase to 1.88 in 1980 and since then it has continued to fall. This most recent decline is due to a fall in the fertility rates for women under 30, who seem likely to have a smaller family. However, there is a continuing rise for those aged over 30, which means that more women are continuing to have children after this age. For the 15–19 age group TPFR is at its lowest since 1955 and for the 20–24 age group the lowest since 1942. These changes can have a substantial impact on the pattern of female employment and on the demand for local authority services because children and families are major consumers of those services.

Age of mother at first birth and social class membership can also be very significant, as Table 2.1 illustrates. The baby booms of both the 1950s and 1960s were due partly to the youthfulness of mothers, and later declines partly due to the increase in the age of the mother at first birth. In 1938 the average age of the mother when she had her first child was 26.4 years; by 1968–70 it was 23.8 but by 1978 it had gone back to 25.0. In 1983 it was 25.6. These changes occurred in all social classes but were more pronounced in the wives of men in non-manual work.[20]

Table 2.1 Age of mother at first birth by grouped social class

Social class	1973	1983
I Professional / II Managerial	26.3	27.9
III Semi-skilled / IV Unskilled	22.7	23.7

These trends in age at first birth are related to social and cultural changes in British society, especially the level of participation by women in economic activity and the development of ideas about female fulfilment in the labour market. Combined with economic depression they result in later marriage, postponement of child-rearing and shortening of the period of active child care.

One result, of course, is that families are getting smaller. The mean size of completed families has fallen from a peak for women born in 1934 of 2.42 children, to 2.1 for those born in 1945. This figure is high enough to ensure replacement of the population, but women of older age groups are slower to have children and there continues to be a danger that there will not be sufficient children to ensure replacement. A factor which is most important locally is the differential in fertility between those born in England and Wales and those whose country of birth is elsewhere.[21]

Infant mortality

Infant mortality is often taken as a useful gauge of overall standard of living and there has been a continuous decline since 1945, when it was about 50 per thousand live births. In 1964 in England and Wales it was 21.4 per thousand, in 1971 17.5 per thousand and in 1983 10.2 per thousand. However, although acceptably low, it is still higher than that of a number of comparable countries in Western Europe[22] and unacceptably high when analysed by social group. In 1979, for example, the infant mortality rate for children born to women in Social Class V exceeded that for women in Social Class I by 90 per cent – almost twice as high. This differential was still 79 per cent in 1980. Again, the problem is exacerbated locally for those areas with large numbers of mothers born in New Commonwealth or Pakistan, where once more the rate is excessively high compared with the average. Much of the reduction in infant mortality is a result of a dramatic fall in neonatal and perinatal rates; the latter, at 10.4 per thousand in 1984, was the lowest ever recorded for England and Wales.

In 1983 there were about 530,000 births within marriage. It was the lowest figure recorded for 100 years, but this is considerably balanced by the addition of some 99,000 illegitimate births, about 18 per cent of all births. In the five years to 1983 births within marriage increased by only 3 per cent while those outside it went up by 79 per cent. The increase was felt in all age groups but most where the mother was aged 20–24. Interestingly there were many more registrations of birth including the father, and where the father's address was given as the same as that of mother and child. This is clear evidence not only of a change in the relative status of marriage and cohabitation, but also of the probability of large numbers of single-parent families for which special help and consideration by the community are required.

One of the principal factors accounting for the decline in the rate of population increase has been the effect of abortion law reform. Although estimates for numbers of abortions before the reform in 1967 are unreliable, it is clear that from 1976 to 1980 they continued to rise, while there was a fall to 128,000 in the year to 1981. It is impossible to calculate how many of these would have resulted in full-term births if legal abortion had not been possible, since some would inevitably have been controlled by other methods. There can be little doubt, however, as to the considerable effect that abortion has had upon the rate of population increase since in the 1970s there was a ratio of live births to abortions of about five to one.

Deaths

The overall crude death-rate has shown a downward trend since 1945 and stood at 11.7 per thousand in 1983. This represented a reduction in absolute terms to 579,600 from 581,900 in 1982. But the lowest number of deaths in recent years was in 1981 – 578,171. The age-adjusted death-rate is known as the standardised mortality ratio; set at 100 in 1968, it had fallen to 84 in 1983. This represents a 16 per cent decrease in the death rate from 1968 if the age-specific death-rates for 1968 had applied in 1983. The smaller number of deaths is partly accounted for by the absence of a flu epidemic in the early part of the year, and by the fact that there was neither very cold nor very hot weather with their accompanying stress for the very young or, particularly, for the aged during the course of the year.

The major causes of death continue to be the circulatory diseases, respiratory diseases and neoplasms (cancer), but there are some detectable changes. Influenza, although still important as a cause of death among the aged and although varying considerably in its effects, appears to be less significant than formerly. For males, the death-rate from bronchitis continued to increase until the 1960s but is now falling. Three factors appear to be important. First, there has been a general decrease in smoking; second, there is the possible effect of the reduction in atmospheric pollution resulting from the Clean Air Act 1956; and last, there is the improvement in medical care. However, bronchitis is a disease associated with a range of social, economic and environmental factors, and declining standards of living for some sectors of society may result in its re-emergence. As a disease closely associated with social and physical conditions it is affected by housing quality. Since local authorities provide housing for up to 30 per cent of households they can clearly have a marked effect on the health of the people through the quality of that accommodation. The largest proportion of fatal neoplasms are lung cancer for men and breast cancer for women, and these continue to increase.

Migration

Internal national

The most ready source of information about internal migration is derived from the reregistration of NHS patients from one Family Practitioner Committee to another as they migrate. In 1983, 3 per cent of the population was affected by such long-distance moves, a relatively low level of internal migration compared with that of the 1960s although slightly higher than that during the 1970s. Probably a further 6 per cent was involved in short-distance unrecorded changes of address. In national terms the movement has been towards England and Wales and away from Scotland and Northern Ireland. The regional position is shown in Table 2.2.

Table 2.2 Losses and gains of population by standard region 1983 ('000s)

North	York & Humb.	E. Midl.	E. Angl.	S. East	S. West	W. Midl.	N. West
−7	−8	+6	+14	+4	+34	−15	−21

Source: *Population Trends* 38, Table K p. 10

International migration

International migration has fluctuated in the recent past. In 1981 there was a net loss of population of 79,000, the highest loss since 1974; 44 per cent of the inflow was from the Commonwealth and 46 per cent of the outflow to the Commonwealth. By 1983 the balance was a positive 17,000, emigration having declined and immigration increased, but the inflow movement was probably largely one of relatives and non-permanent workers on long- and medium-term contracts.[23]

The principal flow of most general concern in the post-war period, however, has been the influx of New Commonwealth and Pakistani immigrants to the United Kingdom starting in the early 1960s. In the decade to 1971 this flow averaged almost 30,000 per year, falling by 1981 to 25,100. In 1982–84 it averaged 25,600 (Fig. 2.3). The figures compare, for example, with an average of about 7,500 a year arriving from New Zealand.[24] It should be remembered that these are gross numbers of entrants and do not necessarily reflect the levels of permanent settlement.

Population movement and government policy

Migration affects the essential distribution of population in Britain, and like density it is an important consideration at the macro level because it affects and influences many of the decisions which central government

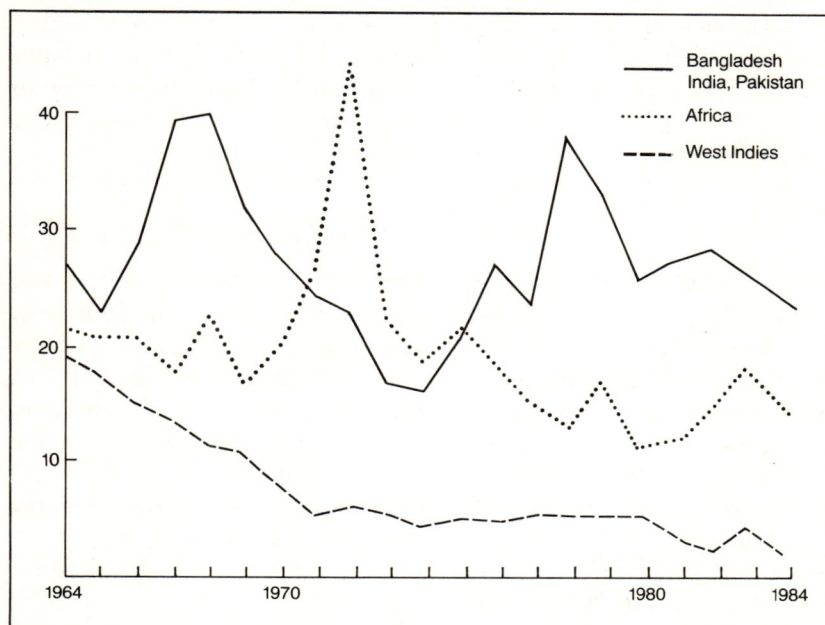

Fig. 2.3 UK–New Commonwealth immigration 1964–84 ('ooos)
Source: OPCS Series MN

must make in order to meet the national need. How government responds to the need, however, may also determine the conditions in which further changes can take place. For example, migration is made easier by better communications. This can be seen by considering briefly the effect of the building of the national motorway network in Britain between 1956 and 1965. The planning of the network was such as to link together the major population centres to and from which goods and people were likely to move. But the detailed routes were themselves of great significance because the alignment was chosen, other things being equal, to optimise the value of the road by making it readily accessible to as many users as possible. The result is a network of some 1,700 miles which, together with 1,500 miles of high-capacity dual carriageway, is within ten miles of every town with a population of 80,000 or more.[25] Not only do motorways meet needs for communication links; they also generate traffic in themselves and, like all transport forms, they have the potential to move goods and people in two directions, opening up previously isolated areas. People become aware that their horizons are now less limited and contemplate moving to work in a district which might otherwise have been considered too far from their families. As a result, it is likely that more daily trips of longer distance will be undertaken, and that there will probably be more long-distance journeys for holiday and recreation. Government response to need on the one hand can be seen to create demand and alter the pattern of national life on the other.

Population distribution and density

We have already noted a number of trends in migration patterns, and changes in migration direction in the period since the Industrial Revolution. The consequence of these movements is the inequality of distribution of the population in the country as a whole and in each of its smaller subdivisions. On the one hand, there is an obvious difference in population density between town and country; 76 per cent of the population in England and Wales lives in urban areas – a much larger proportion than in many West European countries. Densities in some of our cities are well above 100 persons per hectare (116 per ha in Islington), while in rural North Yorkshire or Herefordshire they are about 0.4 or 0.6 persons per hectare.

Some of the regions of Britain are losing population and their urban density is falling. In the ten years to 1981, for example, the urban population of England and Wales fell by 1.9 per cent. Naturally this is a pattern which is most pronounced in the conurbations. In the Greater Manchester area, for example, there was a fall in the population living in towns of 5.1 per cent between 1971 and 1981 (it had remained fairly constant in the preceding decade) but a rise of 23.2 per cent in those living within the county.

Greater London declined in population by 10.1 per cent between 1971 and 1981 and also continued to decline in relative importance. In 1931, at its peak, it accounted for 20.3 per cent of the total population of England and Wales, but by 1981 its share had shrunk to 13.7 per cent. In the same period the outer metropolitan areas of the capital, comprising all of Surrey and Hertfordshire, and parts of Bedfordshire, Buckinghamshire, Essex, Kent, West Sussex, Berkshire and Hampshire, had together increased their share from 6 per cent to 10.9 per cent – a clear indication of the suburbanisation of large parts of southern England.

At the level of administrative county it is not surprising that the highest population densities are to be found in the former metropolitan counties, with London leading at 42.2 people per hectare. West Midlands, Tyne and Wear, Greater Manchester and Merseyside all have densities of around 25 persons per hectare while West Yorkshire and

South Yorkshire have, respectively, 10 and 8.3 persons per hectare. South Yorkshire in fact has a population density lower than one of the shire counties, South Glamorgan, where the density is 9.2 per hectare.

Relatively high rates are also recorded for other non-metropolitan counties which, like South Glamorgan, have highly industrialised areas and large towns. Cleveland has a density of 9.7 persons per hectare. It is a small county in which the built-up area of Middlesbrough accounts for about 80 per cent of the total. The county of Avon is also dominated by a large town, Bristol. Above-average rates are to be found in all of the counties which border Greater London, and in those close to the West Midlands conurbation and to Greater Manchester. The lowest population density is in the Welsh border county of Powys (0.2 pph).

One way of describing current trends in population distribution is to calculate the 'centre of gravity' of the population for a particular region or area and to compare its position over time. For many years there has been a southward drift of the British population, drawn inexorably towards London and the home counties. It is a movement in which England and Wales have benefited at the expense of Scotland and Northern Ireland. That this trend is continuing is shown by the slight southward shift (of about 1 km) in the population-weighted centre of England between 1971 and 1981. The centre of population 'gravity' is to be found close to the point where the boundaries of Northants, Worcestershire and Leicester meet – about 21 km south-east of the physical centre of England.

This national trend is a compound of a number of separate regional and local trends. While the North, Yorkshire and Humberside, the West Midlands and the north-west have lost population, there have been major gains in East Anglia and the south-west. In fact, shifts in the population centres of the regions have been quite small, but in East Anglia the centre moved westward because there the increase in population occurred inland rather than on the coast. In Wales there was a shift to the north because of increases in the north coast towns and in Powys, and decline in the industrial south. The south-west of England also had a large and timely net gain of population, because the immigration helped to offset the surplus of deaths over births in an ageing population. The principal effect of this was in Cornwall, so that the centre for population in the south-west moved in that direction.

At county level the influence of town and conurbations can be clearly identified and there is a two-component movement to be described. Many of the larger urban settlements, including Greater London, continue to lose population from their centres, so that the cores of cities and conurbations are increasingly depopulated and an outward movement can be detected. The zone from which this movement originates is also increasingly large so that urban population densities may continue to fall as cities empty. At the same time, there appears to be a rural migration towards the cities and the smaller towns, a consequent rural depopulation and an inward movement. The two groups of migrants meet in the 'rururban' or suburban fringe, in which the large dormitory suburbs, commuter villages and gentrified settlements are developing, lying within reasonable travelling distance of the workplace and the economic and social activity centres usually to be found at the heart of most towns and cities.[26]

Causes and consequences

The movements outlined above result from two complementary pressures on groups and on individuals. Both elicit government response. First, there are movements created by push factors which initiate mobility but do not determine its direction. Push factors can influence the individual in a number of ways and are usually negative qualities of the current environment. Limited opportunities for satisfying work are often cited as important factors, and government ministers have encouraged work-seeking migration; this is probably the single most significant push factor in longer-distance migration between, for example, the London region and the rest of the country. Poor educational possibilities, the lack or paucity of public and social services, neighbour conflicts or changes in social and family status also play a role in both long- and short-distance moves.

Pull factors may be less significant in initiating moves but do control their direction. Clearly they will tend to be the obverse of the push factors: good work opportunities, better public facilities, etc. A distinction must be drawn, however, between the reality of pull factors and the perceptions which people develop of them; indeed, the migrant's high expectations of a long-distance move can quite easily give way to sour disillusion.

Whatever the factors involved in movement, interregional migration has a significant impact on national governmental policy – both formally, because measures have been taken to control and to accommodate it, and informally in that it is a factor affecting the distribution of national resources and is a resource in itself. Since the inter-war years governments have recognised the need to influence migration. Essentially the measures have been adopted (a) to control the increasing congestion and the development of urban sprawl in the south-east, (b) to reduce the pressure on physical, social and political resources in that region, and (c) to try to restore some balance in national resources because the drift to the south-east is causing a run-down or de-multiplier effect in other areas, and an inefficient use of capital and infrastructural resources such as housing and education provision.

The policy responses have been of two types: those designed to limit the push factors; and those designed to accommodate the migration which does occur. In the first place central government has continued to spend money on the promotion of cultural and recreational activities in the provinces and to support, for example, the establishment of provincially based drama and opera companies. Second, it has encouraged infrastructure expenditure on transport, housing and the like. Most importantly, there has been the development of overall regional policy within which both social and cultural resources could be husbanded and improved, but through which essential economic development could also be facilitated. Accommodation of the changing location of the population has partly been met through development of new town policy, which was initially concerned to solve some of the problems of the south-east but gradually found application in other parts of the country (see page 99).

Social characteristics

Although the range of topics described by the census and by vital statistics is wide, it by no means exhausts the areas for which information might be useful for government departments. Much of that material, the fruits of 11 or 12 major government surveys, is brought together in the annual publication *Social Trends*.[27] Each volume is a mixture of rigorous statistical material, vital statistics and '. . . our best efforts to measure such qualities as altruism (blood donations, time spent in voluntary work)'.[28] Each annual volume is generally arranged so as to correspond to the administrative functions of government.

While a number of topics which are covered in the census are also examined in *Social Trends* (mainly population topics, e.g. the expectation of life for males and females born in 1981 was nearly 70 and 76 years respectively), there is a variety of valuable information on other topics too. This includes households and families, education, employment, income and wealth, resources and expenditure, health and personal social services, housing, transport and communications, leisure, community participation and law enforcement.

National standards of living can be assessed in many ways. *Social Trends* shows, for example, that in 1983 real disposable income per head had risen by about 10 per cent compared with 1973, and that the average weekly wage for employees in manual work was £140, and for non-manual workers £190. By 1984 the figures were £152 and £209 respectively. Wealth was also shown to be still heavily concentrated. The most wealthy 10 per cent of the population owned 54 per cent of the marketable wealth, although this proportion has fallen considerably since 1971. There is good evidence that wealth is more widely spread now than it was then, but only among the most wealthy 50 per cent. The poorer half retains only the 3–4 per cent of the wealth that it has had for the last 25 years.

Ownership of consumer durables has continued to rise and *Social Trends* 16 for 1983 showed that 94 per cent of households had a refrigerator and 83 per cent a colour television. There were computers in 9 per cent of homes. There are some figures which help to assess the overall pattern of food consumption in Britain, although the likely effects on health are very difficult to predict. The country continues to eat fewer fresh vegetables, less butter and milk and more margarine. On the whole life continues to grow safer with a fall in the number of accidental deaths and a particular improvement in the number of road traffic injuries, a likely result of compulsory seat-belt legislation. This is an encouraging trend since *Social Trends* also shows that Britons are travelling more extensively than in the past, especially by private motor car, and total passenger miles have doubled since 1961. But much of the movement must be very short-term since in 1983, 42 per cent of adults did not take a holiday, a figure similar to that for 1971.

The material contained in *Social Trends* is expensive to collect but even with less government intervention in the economy and society, it is still one of the primary functions of the State to provide a wide variety of socio-economic indices so that individuals and institutions can measure the effects of the decisions they take. The very existence of the State implies that society will have some degree of self-knowledge. Equally, it can be argued that a government has a duty to measure and assess the impact of its various positions, and only through careful examination of social, economic and demographic measures such as those in *Social Trends* can those policy outcomes be judged adequately.

There are, however, some major shortcomings in the social statistics collected in *Social Trends*. The first of these is that government statistics contain very little information about the use of land compared with what is known of the people. The second major criticism of the material is that it does not enable regional comparison to be made because generally only national figures are given. However, *Regional Trends*[29] does cover some of the same topics at the level of the standard region and includes a little more information about agriculture. Greater levels of disaggregation are not readily available for this sort of informa-tion, probably since – because it is generally based upon more or less small-scale surveys compared with the universal sample attempted by the census – further breakdown of the data would be statistically unwise.

Census and vital registration material, together with the sort of survey material conveniently collected in *Social Trends*, constitute a consider-able body of information about the people of Britain. The information is of great value to government at both local and national level because it can be used to help determine the national resources available within the population and the policies which should be pursued to maintain their vitality.

Notes

1. For example:
   (a) Poor Law Act 1834.
   (b) Municipal Corporations Act 1835.
   (c) Local Government Act 1888, which created the counties, and county boroughs.
   (d) Public Health Act 1888.
   (e) Local Government Act 1894, which created Urban District Councils from the Urban Sanitary Authorities.
2. K. B. Smellie, *A History of Local Government* (George Allen and Unwin, 1946).
3. D. V. Glass, *Numbering the People* (Saxon House, 1973), p. 19.
4. Quoted in M. Drake, 'The Census 1801–1891' in E. A. Wrigley (ed.), *Nineteenth Century Society* (Cambridge University Press, 1972), p. 8.
5. *Ibid.* p. 9
6. *Ibid.* p. 10
7. *Select Committee to Inquire into the State of Parochial Registration*, Chairman J. Wilkes (1833).
8. J. C. Dewdney, 'Censuses past and present' in D. Rhind (ed.), *A Census Users Handbook* (Methuen, 1983), p. 8.
9. *The Questions and How the Answers are Used*, Census Topics 5 (11/80), OPCS (HMSO, 1980).
10. The areal structure of published census material in 1981 was:

Great Britain	Scotland
England and Wales	Regions
Standard regions	Districts
Counties – metropolitan	Island areas
– non-metropolitan	Postcode sectors
Districts – metropolitan	Localities
– non-metropolitan	Civil parishes
Wards	
Civil parishes	

   Definitions Census 1981, Office of Population Censuses and Surveys (HMSO, 1981).
11. C. Denham and D. Rhind, 'The 1981 Census and its Results' in D. Rhind (ed.), *A Census Users Handbook* (Methuen, 1983), p. 44; B. Bullard and P. Norris, 'User Needs – An Overview' in D. Rhind (ed.), *op. cit.* Ch. 3.
12. SASPAC was written by the Universities of Durham and Edinburgh under contract to the Local Authorities Management Services and Computer Committee.
13. For example, *Local Authority Vital Statistics Series VS*, OPCS (HMSO).
14. K. Francis, 'Large Scale Surveys: Their value to Local Authorities', *Population Trends* 19, OPCS (HMSO, 1984).
15. *Population Trends* 37, OPCS (HMSO), p. 1.

16. *Census 1981, Historical Tables*, Table 1, OPCS (HMSO, 1982), p. 1.
17. R. K. Kelsall, *Population*, 4th edn (Longman, 1979), p. 14.
18. *Royal Commission on Population 1944*, Report (June 1949), Cmnd 7695 (HMSO, 1949).
19. TPFR: Total period fertility rate – the average number of children which would be born per woman if women experienced the age-specific fertility rates for the period in question throughout their childbearing life-span.
20. *Population Trends* 38 (Winter 1984), Table 10, OPCS (HMSO), p. 44; *Birth Statistics 1984*, Series FMI, No. 11, Table 3.11, OPCS (HMSO), p. 32.
21. See, for example, OPCS, Monitor Series FM1 85/4; and OPCS, Monitor Series FM1 85/5.
22. Infant mortality in Western Europe, 1984 rate per thousand live births:

Germany	13
United Kingdom	12
Spain	12
France	10
Denmark	8
Netherlands	8
Norway	8
Switzerland	8
Sweden	7

23. *Population Trends* 38, Editorial Review, OPCS (HMSO, 1984).
24. International Migration 1975 Series MN No. 1, MN No. 2, MN No. 11, Table 2.3, OPCS (HMSO).
25. B. Fullerton, 'Transport' in J. W. House (ed.), *UK Space* (Weidenfeld and Nicolson, 1982), p. 356; and *Britain 1984* (Central Statistical Office, 1985).
26. 'Centres of Population of Local Authorities, Districts, Counties and Regions, 1971 and 1981', *Population Trends* 38 (Winter 1984), p. 31.
27. *Social Trends* 16, Deo Ramprakash (ed.), Central Statistical Office (HMSO, 1985). Sources for *Social Trends*:

    Census
    British Crime Survey
    British National Travel Survey
    British Social Attitudes Survey
    Family Expenditure Survey
    General Household Survey
    International Passenger Survey
    Labour Force Survey
    National Child Development Survey
    National Food Survey
    National Readership Survey
    New Earnings Survey
    Survey of Personal Incomes

28. *The Times*, 11 January 1985.
29. *Regional Trends*, Central Statistical Office (HMSO).

3

PEOPLE AND LOCAL GOVERNMENT:
LOCAL POPULATION, STRUCTURE AND
PROBLEMS

The purpose of this chapter is to consider the social context in which local government operates. The demographic characteristics of the local population are fundamental parameters within which local government works. The chapter begins by examining fundamental aspects of the demographic structure of the population and ways in which changes can be predicted. The population is then examined under a number of more specific headings: social class, employment, educational qualifications. Information about the physical limitations on the operation of local councils such as household amenity and transport are also briefly considered. The chapter continues by examining how local councils use the information and, in particular, how it can help to identify the needs of special groups. Finally, the importance of the role of local authorities is discussed through a consideration of the so-called *distributional effects* of their activities.

As we noted in Chapter 2, the evolution of the present system of local government can be seen in terms of a response to changing population conditions and needs. The decline in the importance of agriculture and the reduction of the agricultural population in the nineteenth century went hand in hand with the development of industry and the growth of an urban population. The twentieth century has seen the extension of the urban culture back into the surrounding countryside and major changes in economic structure. Clearly, local government and local people are inextricably bound together, and local administrations need to be well informed about the nature and characteristics of the local population.

THE LOCAL POPULATION

The information which local government requires about the population derives from its functions, and is of two principal types. First, there is information which is essential in order that it may fulfil its statutory functions and obligations. It is incumbent upon local education authorities, for example, to provide education for all children in the area between the ages of 5 and 16, and for those who wish it within the school system up to the age of 19 years.[1] In order to fulfil these obligations, it is necessary to know at the very least how many children will require the service during a given time period. What constitutes satisfactory provision is decided by the Department of Education, which suggests appropriate standards such as staff–student ratios that local education authorities will apply and which inspects and reports upon schools. In addition to the information required for statutory need, there is information for special purposes defined by the local council through the political process. Such purposes might include the development of strategies for industrial revitalisation or the provision of sheltered accommodation for the mentally handicapped.

Demographic structure

A basic requirement is to know accurately the size of the total population, and the starting-point for assessing total numbers is usually the national census. The figures reveal the broad general directions of movement of the population in local areas. They show, for example, that while in some parts of the country urban populations have continued to increase, there are other areas where the city reached its largest number in the decade to 1910, and although the functional urban unit may now be larger the city itself has not grown. Such statistics about the size of the local area and the changes which have taken place enable general predictions to be made about the directions of change of population and local demand.

Detailed analysis of the population is possible by disaggregating the overall total in two ways: the gross numbers of people may be subdivided into age and sex, and other demographic and social categories; and it is also possible to disaggregate the numbers territorially into ward or enumeration district subtotals.

Age and sex

The most significant subdivisions of the population age structure are those which demonstrate important features of the local population. For

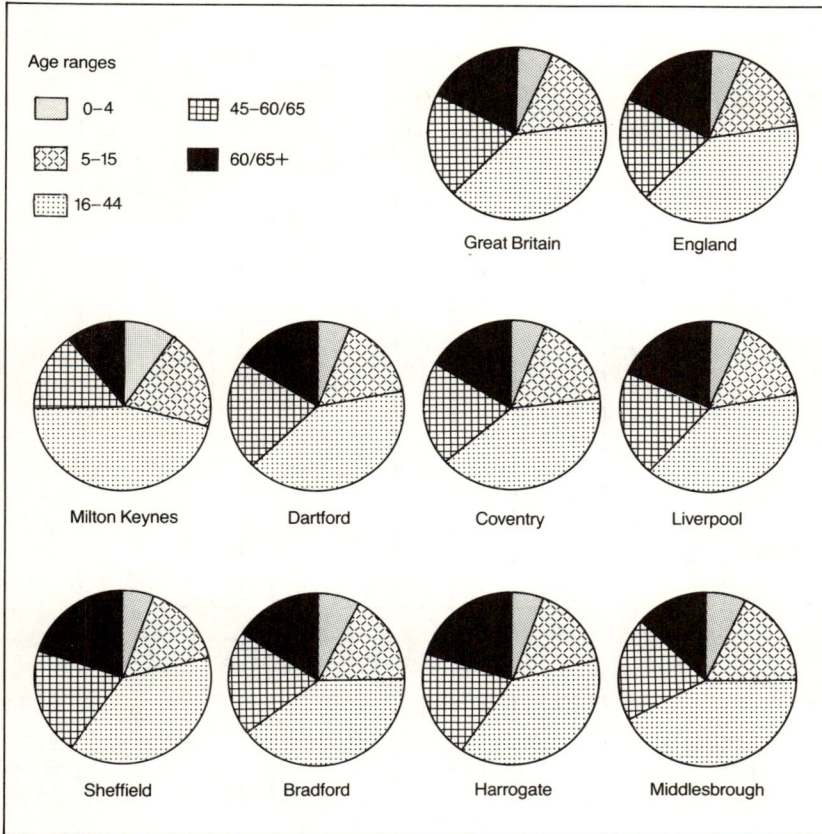

Fig. 3.1 Age structure

instance, local authorities will need to know the number of pre-school children, children at the various school ages, and those economically active and retired. Disaggregation of the total number is therefore usually considered essential to reveal the number of people in the age ranges 0–4, 5–16, 16–65 and 65+. Even at this simple level there are differences between local areas. These are best seen when the numbers are expressed as rates. Figure 3.1 shows the age structure of the population in some English towns; clearly, the pattern of need and of service provision in Milton Keynes is likely to be very different from that in Harrogate.

A popular method of portraying graphically the more detailed age and sex structure of the population is known as the *population pyramid*. It is usual to disaggregate the statistics further and to show the total number

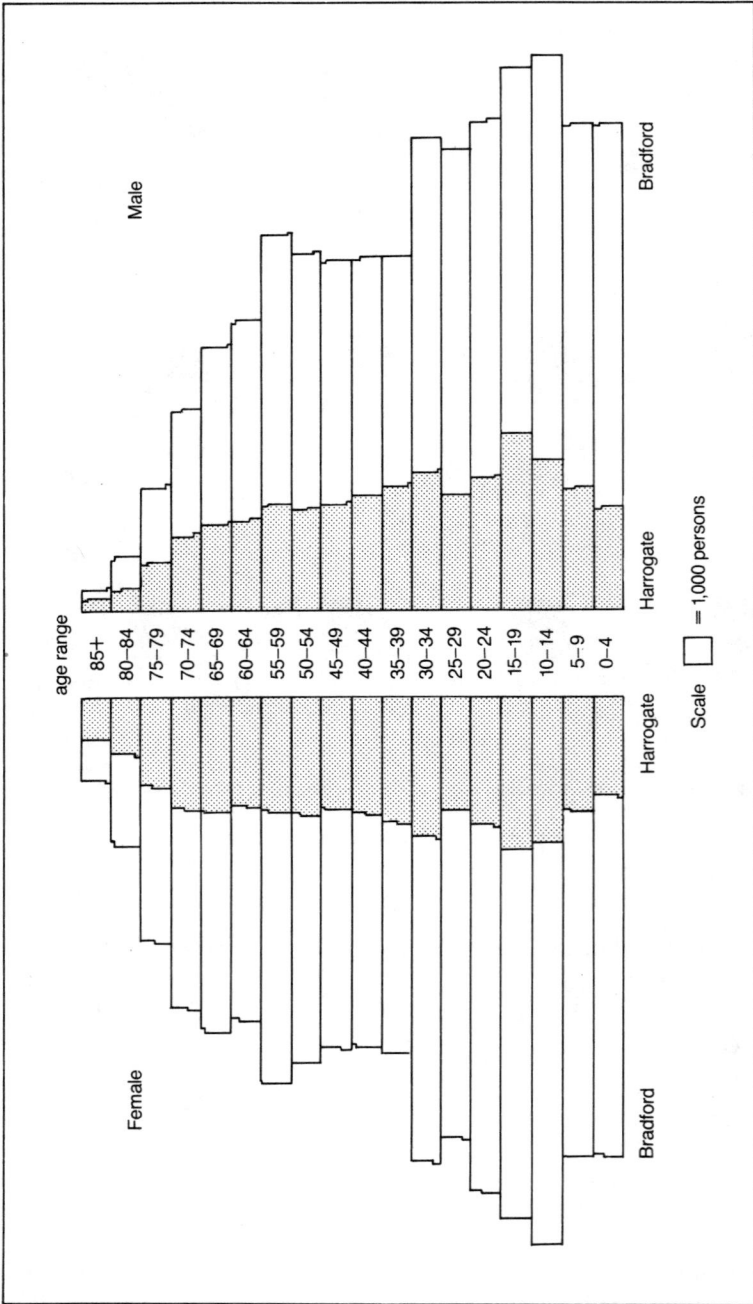

Fig. 3.2 Population pyramid: Bradford and Harrogate
Source: Census 1981

in much smaller, typically five-year, age periods. This facilitates further local comparisons and also helps to elucidate the possible movement of the population during the period between the censuses. Figure 3.2 shows the pyramids for two districts together so that more detailed comparisons can be made.

Predicting changes

As the date for each new census is passed the information collected rapidly decays. Moreover, local authorities must not only assess the present situation; they must also prepare for the future. Many local authorities functions require long planning and gestation periods: some road schemes, for example, may take ten years to plan and build. Techniques for predicting future trends can be both complex and unreliable, but given the need for some sort of basis for future resource allocation or need/demand assessment, such predictions are often attempted. Changes in the numbers in particular age ranges are affected by three factors: the initial size of the group; additions to the group by immigration and by movement up from the group below; and reductions in the number caused by emigration, deaths and losses to the next group above.

Births and deaths can be accurately counted through vital registration as they occur, but prediction is much more problematic. In most cases the techniques involve the application of age-specific birth- and death-rates derived from national figures or from local historical data to the local population, but more sophisticated methods are necessary since local conditions may be quite different from those from which the aggregated national rates are derived. Birth-rates are a function of fertility rates, which in themselves reflect cultural factors such as the age of women at marriage, family size, economic and social status, etc. Demographers will want to introduce the effects of these factors when assessing the likely changes in birth-rates.

Birth assessments are essential where local cultural patterns and demographic structure are diverse. Such diversity may be important, for example, in Belfast or Glasgow between Protestant and Catholic groups, or in many English town between Asian communities and their English counterparts. The complexity of the problem is illustrated by the fact that the crude birth-rate among the Pakistani-born population in Great Britain is almost four times as high as that among the population as a whole. This does not mean that Pakistani families will continue to grow larger than others in the country; rather it is explained by the age structure of that section of the immigrant population, where there are fewer old people and more women in the childbearing stage of their lives than in the total population.

It is equally difficult to identify changes due to migration. Population is not registered by residence in the United Kingdom and it is free to move without restriction. Although at national level it may be possible to identify movement from the changes in location of National Insurance numbers, for example, such information is not generally available. In any case, such figures could give only the crudest estimate of the change since the same statistics might represent either the movement of a single male or female seeking work, or the working member of a household accompanied by several dependants. It is useful to examine the past patterns of movements in the hope of revealing general trends that might be applied to the contemporary situation, although that could do no more than lend weight to an estimate arrived at by another route. There are two other useful, but not in themselves sufficient, techniques. They are derived from secondary sources.

The Family Practitioner Committee of each Area Health Authority maintains a record of the people registered with each GP. Since most people will reregister on changing location, this provides a possible source of information with which to supplement other material. Registration with a doctor is not, of course, obligatory so the record is not complete. The final source of information is the Electoral Register. Each year in October every household is circulated and eligible voters are required to register. The list of registered voters is published each March and is available in Council offices, Post Offices and in many public libraries. Changes in the register may be the result of changes in name, but they usually indicate shifts in residence. There is little doubt that both under- and over-reporting of the numbers of eligible electors takes place, and there is the additional shortcoming that only those over the age of 18 are revealed. However, used judiciously the Electoral Register can provide a further indication of the extent of local changes.

Small Area Statistics

The second level of disaggregation is spatial or territorial. The historical administrative division of the country underlined the difference between town and country. The reorganisation of local government in 1974 resulted in the loss of much of that differentiation because many towns and their functional regions were incorporated into metropolitan districts. There are clear demographic, social and economic differences between the component parts of these districts which can be identified only if the overall local authority data are examined in greater detail.

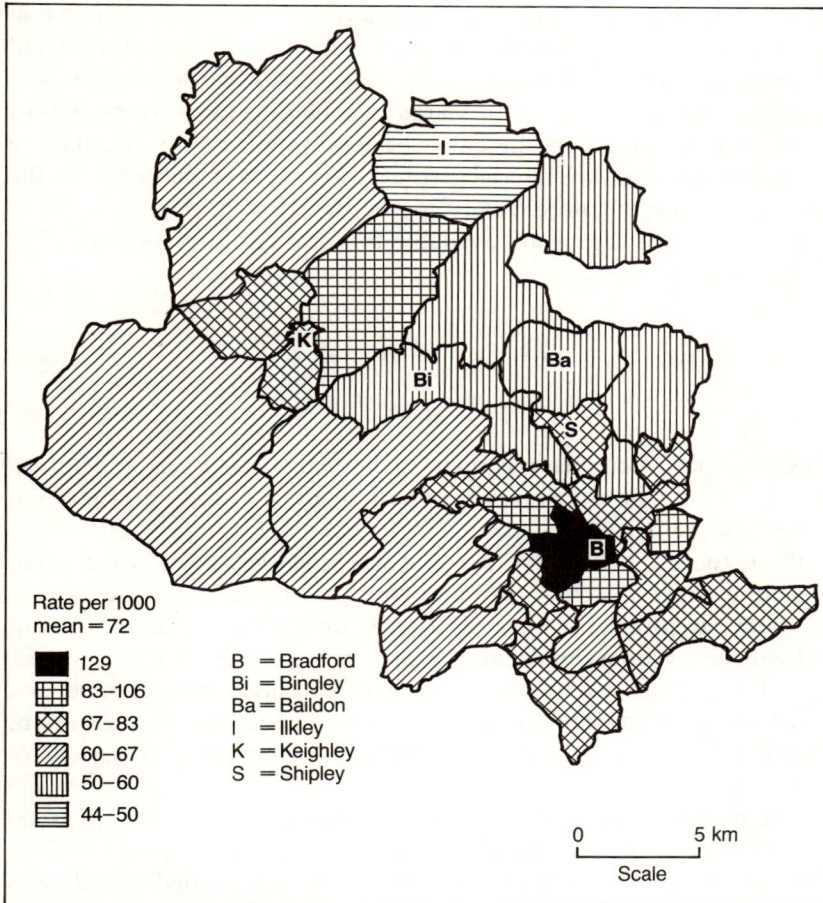

Fig. 3.3 Local variation in age structure (infants aged 0–4 years)
Source: Bradford Metropolitan District Census 1981

Similarly, the extent of demographic differences within urban or rural areas themselves can be staggering. At ward level within Bradford Metropolitan District, for example, the proportion of the population which is in the school-going age range varies between 217 and 148 per thousand population, while the variation in the proportion of infants is between 129 and 44 per thousand (Fig. 3.3). These rates underline the spatial variation in the level of demand for school facilities in the district.[2]

Ward level data, more usually known by the Office of Population Censuses and Surveys as *Small Area Statistics*, are readily available for all parts of the country. They are produced at a level of areal or spatial disaggregation which is a sensible compromise between too much detail and ready comprehension. It is sometimes difficult, however, to understand data-sets at ward level for a large area such as a town of, say, a third of a million people where there may be 30 to 35 wards. It is much more valuable to present the material graphically as maps or charts so that the information may be more readily appreciated (Fig. 3.3).

Small Area Statistics are available for all the information which is gathered in the census.

PEOPLE IN SOCIETY

Social class

The concept of social class is crucial to the analysis of society and human behaviour, and it plays a prominent part in public discussion of political and social events.[3]

While there are generally held and accepted ideas about social class, and simple terms such as 'working class' or 'middle class' are used in everyday language, precise definition is difficult and classification of individuals or households particularly so. Among social scientists, concepts of social class have been developed and terms defined in a variety of ways, depending upon the use intended for the definition. Membership of a class has thus been assessed using a variety of indicators.

The Registrar-General and OPCS have produced and use an operational definition of social class based upon occupation. Such a definition has been in use since 1911 when occupations were classified according to social position. At first there were eight classes; this was reduced to five in 1921, but by the 1981 census seven classes were in use. The current classes are as follows:

(I)   Professional.
(II)   Intermediate.
(III(N)) Skilled Non-Manual.
(III(M)) Skilled Manual.
(IV)   Partly Skilled.
(V)   Unskilled.
(VI)   Armed Forces and those unclassified elsewhere.

The occupational groups included in each of these classes 'have been selected in such a way as to bring together, as far as possible, people with similar levels of occupational skill.'[4] Differences between individuals in the same occupation in terms of, for example, pay or education are not

Table 3.1 Social class composition % variation by location UK 1981

Social class	I	II	III (N)	III (M)	IV	V	Forces
GB	4.5	18.8	9.1	26.2	12.2	4.1	2.4
Inner London	3.8	16.0	11.2	20.6	13.5	5.9	3.7
Kensington & Chelsea	8.1	27.1	12.9	11.3	9.2	3.3	3.8
Newham	1.2	10.1	9.4	26.2	18.0	6.9	4.7
Gateshead	2.6	12.5	8.4	30.5	13.7	5.7	1.2

Source: CEN81KSLA.
N.B. Excludes households where head is economically inactive.

accounted for but those with supervisory functions and higher status as managers or foremen may be allocated to classes different from those to which they would be assigned by occupation alone.

This classification is obviously crude and in some respects lacks objectivity. Occupational skill is not, after all, the only facet of class, and the assignment of a status level to a particular job may be arbitrary. However, the classification has been used in a number of surveys and found to 'correlate well with other measures of the human condition such as housing tenure and amenities, type of education, mortality and morbidity'.[5] To that extent it is a very useful indicator of social condition. The social class composition of the population varies considerably between local authorities (Table 3.1). It also varies within local areas, as Fig. 3.4 shows. Such variation is of considerable important in the planning and everyday operation of local services.

While social class data are obtained from answers to individual census questions, other information is derived from the cross-tabulation of two or more answers. A related statistical classification of local populations obtained in this way is that of the socio-economic group.

Socio-economic group (SEG)
The socio-economic group classification aims to bring together people with jobs of a similar social and economic status and is based upon both employment status and occupation. It is therefore possible to distinguish in SEG 3 those professional workers who are self-employed from those in SEG 4 who are employees. Professional workers are themselves defined as those whose work normally requires a qualification of university degree standard. There are 17 such SEG classes defined by OPCS,[6] and the more detailed allocation of occupation and employment status to social classes and to SEGs is given in the Department of Employment's *Classification of Occupations 1980*, from which OPCS derives its operational definitions.[7]

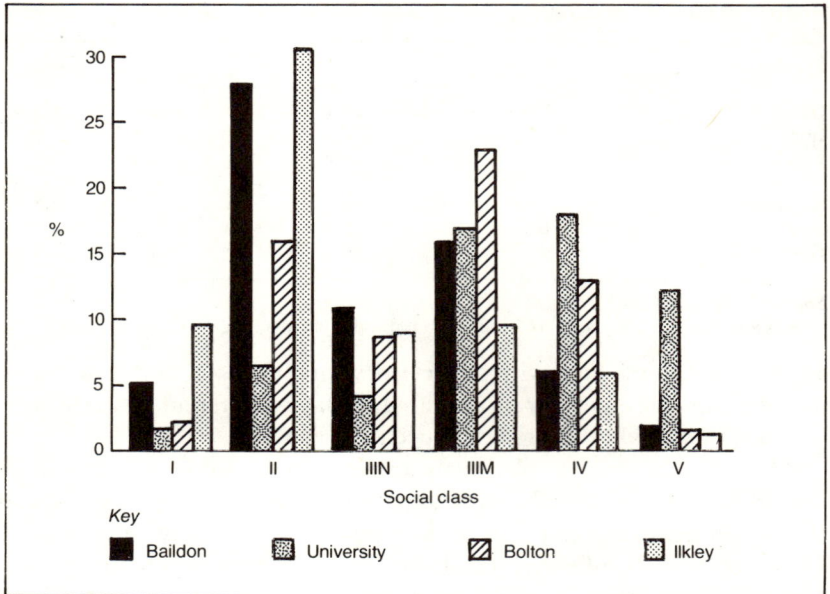

Fig. 3.4 Local variation in social class composition (example wards from Bradford Metropolitan District)
Source: Census 1981 SAS

Economic activity in the community

Economic activity is measured in the community by reference to a variety of local and centrally collected and collated statistics. At national level, short-term trends in employment can be identified through published statistics from the Department of Employment. These data simply indicate the number of people registering as unemployed and claiming State benefits. An analysis of these registrations can show relative levels of employment among men and women, and by industrial sector, and they have a local immediacy. Although not normally published they can be obtained in disaggregated form down to local employment office level.

Their value is limited because it is known that not all of those who are unemployed register. In the past a major group whose unemployment was not recorded in this way was working women who had opted to make limited social security contributions and were thus ineligible for unemployment benefit. In some parts of the country where women constitute a large proportion of the workforce this factor obscured the true extent of unemployment and could result in the inequitable distribution of central government funds. The problem is further exacerbated in that a high proportion of working women, or two-income families, is often associated with areas in which wage-rates are low so that two incomes are necessary to maintain an adequate standard of living. In these circumstances the loss of both income and benefit is damaging not only to the family but also to spending power in the local economy.

However, gauging the extent of unemployment or the growth in employment is impossible without adequate bench-marks; these were provided in the 1981 census, which established the following:

1. The basic economic parameters of the population: whether in full- or part-time employment; awaiting a job-start; seeking work; temporarily sick; or permanently sick or disabled and thus not working; housewife; retired; or still at school or in full-time education. The economically active population are those in employment and those temporarily out of work through sickness or unemployment.

2. Employment status: the number of apprentices, self-employed, employees, etc.

3. Occupation or kind of work performed: the function of the place in which the work is performed has no bearing on this classification of occupation because, for example, all crane drivers will be classified as crane drivers irrespective of the industry in which they work.

4. A classification of economic activity by industry: this is produced from a question in the census about the business or function in which the respondents are employed. The classification has regard 'only to the nature of the service or product to which the labour contributes rather than the nature of the work performed'. Industries are classified according to the Standard Industrial Classification revised in 1980 (HMSO 1979) into ten divisions, 60 classes, 222 groups and 334 activity headings.[8]

The local variation in the structure of employment 1981 is illustrated by comparing figures for the seven major categories of employment shown in Table 3.2 with those for Great Britain as a whole.

From this table it can be seen that the local economies of Barnsley and Walsall are heavily biased towards manufacturing industry and Leominster has a large agricultural sector, while Torbay's dependence on resort functions is clearly evident. This can have important consequences for the local authority. If, for example, there is a nation-wide decline in manufacturing then the effects are clearly likely to be more marked in Walsall than in Torbay; however, Torbay might be affected if many of its visitors are usually from Walsall.

Table 3.2 Variation in the structure of employment. Industry of employment

%	Agric.	Energy % water	Manuf.	Construct.	Distrib. & cater.	Transport	Other services
GB	2.2	3.1	27.0	7.0	19.2	6.5	34.0
Leominster	19.6	0.9	21.7	9.9	18.2	3.6	24.7
Barnsley	0.9	21.8	25.3	6.2	16.6	3.7	24.9
Walsall South	0.2	1.5	45.1	6.1	17.6	5.2	23.6
Pembroke	8.4	9.6	8.2	15.8	26.3	5.1	25.0
Torbay	1.3	1.4	16.2	7.9	33.6	5.2	33.3
York	0.3	1.3	28.3	7.3	20.6	10.2	31.6

Source: CEN81KSLA.

These data, together with material available directly to local authorities such as the number of households claiming rates rebates and other benefits in their localities, form the bases from which an assessment of the social and economic health of the local community can be made.

Household amenity

Demographic characteristics, social class data, and economic and occupational statistics are not direct measures of personal or social well-being, and they are only partly indicative of the overall condition in which people live. The census offers many other measures of the quality of life and standard of living for small groups of people. In 1981 the first question established the nature of household accommodation. This was followed by a series of questions about the number of rooms available to each household. From the responses measures of the density of occupancy and self-containment of accommodation can be deduced, along with the level of provision of basic household amenities and whether they are exclusively available. Table 3.3. shows the variation in the provision of household amenities at regional level.

As can be seen, there are at regional level clear differences in the quality of household provision. To take the two extremes, East Anglia has the lowest room density while Scotland has the highest. Scottish households tend to be more crowded than elsewhere in Great Britain. However, if we examine the provision of WCs Scotland fares better than any other region, while Wales is worst. Similar variations occur at local level. In Rhondda, for example, 17.8 per cent of households lacked an inside WC in 1981. The equivalent figure for Knowsley in Merseyside is only 1.8. Similarly, the proportion of households in Hull without a fixed bath or shower is approximately twice that of Bradford. Clearly such information as this, both in its simple form and when cross-tabulated, is

Table 3.3 Household amenity

	% Households			
	Persons per room	> 1 person per room	Lacking bath or shower	Lacking inside wc
GB	0.55	14.6	1.9	2.7
England & Wales	0.54	12.5	1.9	2.8
England	0.54	12.7	1.8	2.7
S. East	0.54	14.2	1.7	2.0
W. Midlands	0.55	12.8	1.7	3.3
N. West	0.55	12.7	2.1	3.6
Yorks & Humberside	0.55	12.3	1.7	2.7
North	0.56	13.8	1.5	2.7
E. Midlands	0.53	10.5	1.8	3.7
S. West	0.51	9.9	1.8	2.0
E. Anglia	0.51	8.9	2.5	3.4
Wales	0.52	10.0	3.6	5.2
Scotland	0.73	34.7	2.3	1.0

Source: CEN81KSLA.

useful in identifying not only those areas where housing improvements are necessary, but also where General Improvement Area status may be appropriate. It is useful too in pinpointing where there is evidence of overcrowding, together with its likely effects, and in predicting likely housing demand. (See also page 65 and Fig. 3.5.)

Further questions in the census established the nature of tenure for private households (owner-occupiers or freehold or leasehold property, or rental from a variety of public and private sources). Such information reveals national and local trends in owner-occupation and the amount of furnished and unfurnished accommodation rented from private land-lords. It helps in assessing the effects of national legislation and in identifying the directions to be taken in the development of local housing policy, particularly for groups with special housing needs.

Transport

The availability of private transport by car or van is assessed in the census. The growth of private transport has been one of the most striking features of the post-war period. It has been a major factor in altering the pattern of daily life in many households, in changing the overall pattern of settlement, and in expanding recreational and economic horizons. Additionally, it has had implications for the planning of public facilities and services such as shops and health centres. Areas in which there is a low level of car ownership will require better provision

Table 3.4 Availability of private transport

	% Households without a car
GB	39.5
England & Wales	38.5
England	38.6
S. East	35.9
W. Midlands	37.9
N. West	44.5
Yorks & Humberside	45.5
North	31.2
E. Midlands	37.2
S. West	30.9
E. Anglia	30.7
Wales	38.0
Scotland	48.7

Source: CEN81KSLA.

of public transport if their people are to enjoy a level of life opportunities similar to that of the rest. Indeed, it is widely held that lack of private transport is indicative of a poor standard of living and relative deprivation.

The regional rates of private transport availability are shown in Table 3.4. There are more households without transport in Scotland than elsewhere in Britain. If we examine the rates at local level, however, there are many wide variations. In the Inner London borough of Tower Hamlets, for example, 67.4 per cent of households had no personal transport in 1981, while in the Hampshire town of Hart the figure was only 14.6 per cent. Between 1971 and 1981 the number of households with transport available went up by 28 per cent in Britain. Starting from a low level, the rise in the North region was in the order of 50 per cent. Changes like this clearly have a major impact upon public highway and transport provision.

The extent of car ownership is also closely connected to the journey-to-work pattern. The journey-to-work is the most consistent and important of journeys for both the individual and the nation as a whole because of the effect it has on many aspects of the physical environment and local and national services. Questions on the census are designed to establish the normal mode of transport of this daily journey. The information is used in the national context by the Department of Transport in the planning of major road schemes, especially those serving larger urban areas, because the majority of trips are made to and from those areas. It is used by transport operators such as British Rail and bus companies to plan service provision. Local authorities use the data in planning the provision for new jobs and homes and, together with the data on car ownership, related transport services. At the same time, journey-to-work information helps to pinpoint those local areas in which quality of life is adversely affected. Since the journey-to-work is such an important feature of contemporary life and because it defines the principal functional region in which people live, it is also used to define functional regions for other operational purposes. In particular, the current Assisted and Intermediate Areas through which one element of central government regional aid is distributed are defined using journey-to-work catchments.

Manpower and educational qualifications

Questions about educational, professional and vocational qualifications, along with those about economic and social life, are useful in helping to measure the national stock of qualified manpower and to aid in the development of educational policy appropriate to the country's needs. Educational qualification contributes to social class differences within the community. The type of job and its status are closely connected with the extent of the initial educational requirement and thus materially affect social class classification and socio-economic class ascription. In some respects educational attainment also determines the range of people's social contacts, their choice of residential location and, therefore, the journey-to-work patterns. Once again there is considerable local and national variation in the pattern of educational qualification among the population (Table 3.5).

Table 3.5 Higher education participation rates (%)

	Males	Females
GB	13.7	12.2
Inner London	15.1	16.2
Kensington & Chelsea	28.5	22.1
Newham	5.7	8.3
Gateshead	9.2	8.6

Source: CEN81KSLA.

HOW AUTHORITIES USE POPULATION DATA

Most local authorities retain officers who are concerned to a greater or lesser extent with the collection, collation and interpretation of statistical material from the census and from other sources. Indeed, there are few authorities which will not themselves have set in hand surveys and investigations of a nature similar to the census for particular local purposes. Whatever their motives for action – whether obligation imposed by statute or a response to local ideas or pressure – local authorities need information and intelligence to identify problem areas. Combating social problems is a key issue.

Social problems

Social problems can be conceptualised in a variety of ways and under a number of names like 'poverty', 'deprivation', 'disadvantage', 'under-privilege' and 'inequality'. They are words that reflect the way in which we consider these problems. The use of different terms highlights the fact that the problems have arisen in different ways and there may be different explanations and remedies. Those who are disadvantaged in society can be seen to suffer as a result of institutional malfunction – failures of planning, management or administration being responsible for their disadvantage. The underprivileged, however, are under-privileged because resources are inequitably distributed and they fail to get their 'fair' share.[9] Whatever term we use there is no doubt of the existence of some groups and areas which are poor compared with the rest, and these groups or areas are referred to as deprived or relatively deprived.

The most recent comprehensive examination of poverty and depriva-tion at national level was undertaken in 1978.[10] This survey enables yardsticks to be developed by which the problems might be measured and from which, for example, evidence about the value of particular sorts of census questions might be advanced. Many forms of deprivation can be identified: lack of an adequate diet, inappropriate clothing and housing, poor education and physical environment, and so on. Usually these inadequacies are combined and measured in terms of an overall standard of living which falls below a certain prescribed level. Formally recognised standards are objective physical measurements which can be taken or counted in the census or *General Household Survey*,[11] for example, but individual and subjective perceptions clearly influence our general understanding of what constitutes an adequate standard of living. Such perceptions are changed by personal circumstances, class, economic status, background and by stage in the family cycle or life cycle. Those who might fall into the category of deprived will naturally have a particular perception and may feel deprived by comparison, even when objective evidence does not support the view that they are.

Objective deprivation is usually measured by reference to a large number of everyday items and conditions, the lack of which can be shown in practice or according to conventional wisdom to constitute deprivation. These include clothing, consumer durables such as washing machines and dryers, food, and social life – such as the ability to eat out from time to time, to have children's parties, etc. As one might expect, the elderly and young children lack some of these basic items in their lives and there is a 'usually very marked' correlation with occupational class. Compared with households where the head of household worked in a professional or managerial position, far more of those employed in unskilled or partly skilled manual jobs lacked consumer durables in the household, were sometimes short of fuel in winter, did not frequently eat fresh meat, drank little milk and had no summer holiday.

Subjective deprivation is usually a matter of comparison, but that comparison can be difficult to define. Some people make comparisons with national or regional standards, but more frequent are those made with relatives, neighbours or others living in the same locality. Although this is less easy to judge than objective deprivation, some specific groups did appear to feel significantly deprived, especially the elderly, those living alone, and the heads of households with more than four children. Although many recognised that the reasons for their feelings of deprivation were within their own control, the second most important explanatory factor they identified to account for their feelings was 'the government'. It is a point of significance for it underlines the importance attached to the actions of local government and the politicians, who are seen by the deprived as holding the key to improvement.

Housing problems

A principal area of inadequate provision is housing. Housing quality is easy to measure and since the major urbanisation of the country in the nineteenth century it has been a subject of general political interest. The principal measures of housing standard are as follows:
1. Adequacy of the structure.
2. Level of the provision of amenity.
3. Space afforded in relation to the number of users.

The importance of housing to both government and governed is underlined in the succession of committees which have studied the issue. Probably the most significant of post-war reports was that of the Parker Morris Committee (1961).[12] On the whole, these committees have recommended improvement in housing standards in all three of the areas indicated above. In spite of this widespread concern, '. . . emerging and continuing inequalities in housing are minimised . . .'.[13]

The problem is constantly underestimated because there is a failure to recognise deprivation at current levels in the contemporary housing stock, a lack of appreciation of the rate at which deterioration of the stock is taking place, an increase in public expectations of housing quality, and an upgrading of the standards by which housing is measured. As a consequence, in 1978, 22 per cent of households, representing about 13 million people, were living in houses with structural and other defects.

The Housing Act of 1969 laid down a five-point standard against which housing conditions could be judged and housing improvement grants awarded. Houses should have an inside WC, fixed bath or shower, wash-basin, hot and cold water at three points and a sink. The provision of this basic level of amenity together with cooking facilities was examined by the census in 1971, but by 1981 hot water, kitchen sink and cooker were excluded from the assessment. Variation in the results has been shown at national, regional and local levels, but may be acute within the local area (Fig. 3.5).

Limitations of household space may have damaging consequences for personal development and social relationships. Standards have varied widely over the years. In the early nineteenth century it was suggested that a single room was adequate for the needs of the smaller labouring-class family, while later the enlightened Victorian paternalist believed that dignity could not be maintained, nor morality served, unless bedrooms were provided for husband and wife, and children of each sex separately. Sometimes the standards which were applied, while justifiable as measures of density of occupancy, had no relationship to contemporary life-styles. One such was the bedroom standard applied by the Government Social Survey of 1960.[14] What is clear is that lack of space is keenly felt by those who consider themselves deprived and is a real problem for many others who do not (Table 3.3).

It has been found that large families tend to occupy more houses with structural defects than do smaller ones, probably because large families need more rooms and these are to be found more often in older properties which are difficult and expensive to maintain. Single persons are more likely than families to have inadequate housing, and single-parent families more often have insufficient rooms. Not surprisingly, there is a very marked rise in housing deprivation among the lower occupational and social classes. Poor housing is also associated with the nature of tenure. It is much more prevalent in privately rented unfurnished accommodation than in other types of tenure, but while those in council houses have fewer problems with facilities because of the stricter application of housing recommendations, there are struc-

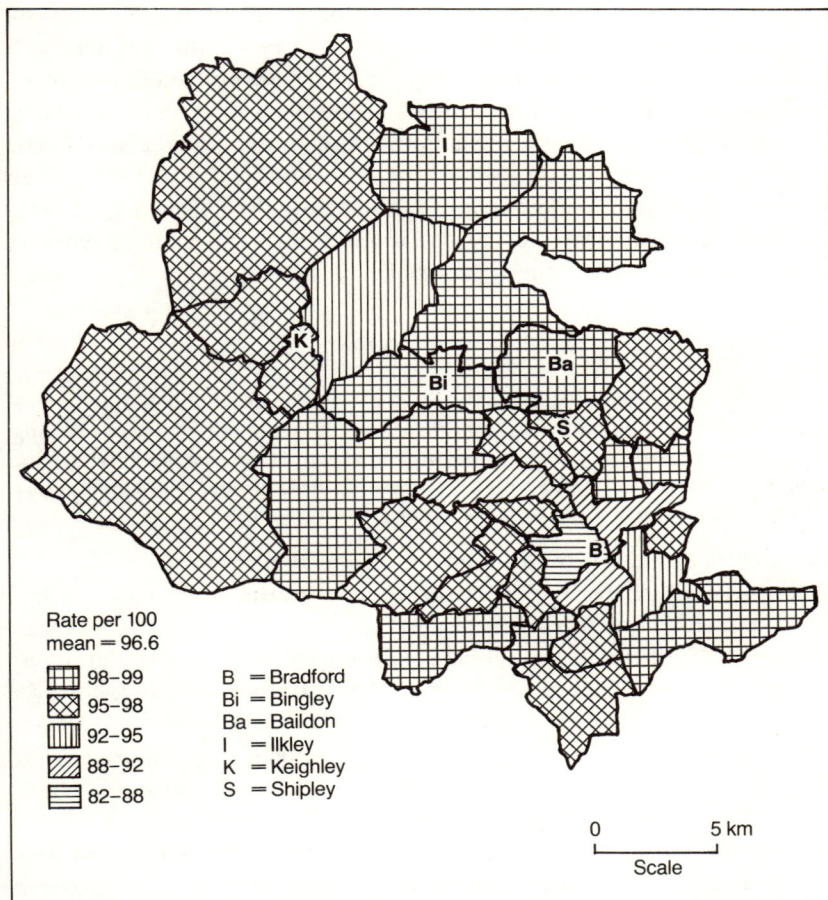

Fig. 3.5 Local variation in household amenity – exclusive use
Source: Bradford Metropolitan District Census 1981

tural and other defects, and social inadequacies such as the lack of play space for children. More people with experience of deprivation were to be found in council houses than in privately rented houses.

Deprivation may also be identified with the external environment in which people live. Objective measurements like size of garden, availability of safe play areas outside and level of air pollution may be made. While they are clearly of direct concern to the individual because of their influence upon personal freedoms, there are other aspects of environmental quality which are less easily quantified but no less important. The general appearance of the landscape, the quality of street maintenance, the presence of non-domestic activities in residential areas, the use of the external space by other residents, and noise are important contributors to the quality of life. These characteristics of an area are often directly related to each other and have been found to correlate well with the three measurable criteria mentioned above. Here regional differences are important, for environmental quality is poorer in the North and in Yorkshire and Humberside than elsewhere. Social differentiations are also important. Air pollution is experienced twice as frequently by the lower social groups as by the higher.[15]

Social minorities

Social minorities are groups of individuals or families which have some characteristic in common which marks them off, or is perceived as marking them off, from 'ordinary' people and which prevents them having access to, or being accorded certain rights which are available to others and who are therefore less likely to receive certain kinds or amounts of resources.[16]

Two distinct types of minority group can be identified:
1. Those who are distinct by reason of race or ethnic origin.
2. Those with a special category or status differentiated from the rest as a result of appearance, physical condition, manner, speech, family or residential situation, or position on the labour market, and who as a result may be treated as inferior citizens.

Clearly the first of these categories is, at first sight, the more readily identifiable, although in Britain for second- or third-generation immigrants it may be simply a question of colour. However, we may all fall into the second group in one way or another, and it thus requires closer description. Some particular groups, such as single-parent families and women living alone with a dependent adult, are often referred to and vocally represented by pressure groups. Others, such as the unemployed, non-white or Irish populations, are popularly identified as minorities, while households with disabled adults can also be included because they probably experience high degrees of poverty. Less easily defined minority groups are households with large families, disabled children or the low-paid.

In many cases these minority groups face compound difficulties, and there are often associated problems of poverty. The head of a single-parent family, for example, may find that caring for the children limits work opportunities, forcing low-paid, part-time or casual work. Low income reduces housing choice, and location is restricted due to the need to limit travel costs or ensure high accessibility to schools, nurseries, shops and work. Such demands can be satisfied only in the inner city, where accommodation is cheap and accessibility high, but where the environment is poor. The alternative is municipal housing, where single-parent families may have priority. A special social geography can therefore be seen to evolve in those circumstances.

Ethnic and cultural minorities

A similar unique social geography is associated with many culturally or ethnically differentiated groups. There is a long history in Great Britain of receiving refugees and immigrants from European countries and from Ireland. During the early nineteenth century Irish immigration was particularly important. They were followed by continental Europeans, refugees from religious and political persecution and economic misfortune, and later large immigrant groups from former colonies like Cyprus, and from southern Europe, such as the Italians.

From the late 1950s there was a trickle and then an increasing flood of immigrants from the countries of the New Commonwealth, especially the West Indian Islands, Pakistan and later Bangladesh, and from India. In all of these examples, with perhaps the exception of the nineteenth-century European immigration, the culmination of the process of migration has been characterised by a high degree of spatial cohesion within the receiving country and in each locality, so that the needs of these groups and the issues raised by their presence have tended to be highly localised and thus not easily recognised in other areas.

For many European societies ethnic and cultural segregation of a part of their population is not new. It was a feature of the treatment of Jewish communities since medieval times. They were often separated from their compatriots in Jewish quarters which became known as ghettos (from the Italian *borghetto*, or from the island of Geto in Venice).

The exclusivity of the ghetto represented a 'community of interest' motivated by the need to preserve a religion and by the strength of the culture based upon it, held together by very strong family ties. Except for very highly localised areas at the level of the enumeration district, few places are entirely dominated in objectively measurable terms by a single group, but so important is the perceived pattern of their dominance that ethnic or immigrant areas were being defined in British cities when it was rare for the ethnic element to exceed 20 per cent of the total population.[17]

Immigrant groups in Britain face particular difficulties of adjustment. While many of these difficulties are individual and personal, and cannot be dealt with through collective action, others certainly can. Assimilation in a non-dominant sense can be promoted by learning the local language, and for many local authorities this was the initial area in which they chose to take substantive action. It was particularly important as the number of children entering the country increased rapidly in the 1960s. These children were required by law to attend full-time education, but could do so only with great difficulty and not much advantage because they could not understand English. Although the operational responses of the local authorities differed, most made direct efforts to provide English instruction at least to the point where children could be transferred to a local school. Language training needs placed a large additional burden upon the resources of the authorities, which were assisted by central government help. Subsequently there were problems of placement in secondary schools. A policy of dispersal which was initially attempted in one district was rejected by the immigrant communities. The cultural and curriculum needs of ethnic minorities must also be carefully considered, since they will have a bearing upon the needs of the whole community.

There is a potential dichotomy between the needs of society and the community at large and those of the minority. It is of fundamental importance whether the minority is ethnic, social, economic or of any other sort because it can only be resolved in the political arena, and the issues therefore become not simply humanitarian or social but inherently political. This point was recognised in the Scarman report on the Brixton riots of 1981.[18] It recommended a fuller and wider involvement of local communities in planning, in the provision of local services, and in the management and financing of local projects. But the report also recognised that a part of the problem was the wider general neglect of a co-ordinated approach to the problems of the inner city. It suggested that there should be a more ready recognition of the problems and needs of ethnic minorities. In particular these needs lay in the areas of housing, where they were discriminated against; in education, where there were a number of complaints; and in employment.

Many of the suggestions and recommendations for assisting local authorities in their treatment of minority groups recognise that the problems are multidimensional, and that identification of groups at risk and areas with problems is a proper function of the local administration. The reason such problems need to be identified is that it makes possible remedial action through a reassessment of the particular pattern of resource allocation in the authority, and indeed the possible allocation of additional resources by central government.

DISTRIBUTIONAL EFFECTS OF LOCAL SPENDING[19]

In 1984 the public sector as a whole provided about 50 per cent of gross domestic product in the United Kingdom. This underlines the importance which national public-sector provisions – such as the National Health Service, social security and unemployment benefit – and local government services, like municipal housing and refuse collection and disposal, have in determining the overall standard of living of the population, particularly those who are less well-off.

The importance of this spending is not simply that it provides services or benefits. It is much more important in its influence because the allocation and distribution of many of these resources often determine to a large extent the life-chances of some social groups. The reason is that those provisions are a means of redistributing wealth depending upon how they are funded and where they are directed, whether they are welfare services or not. It is therefore of crucial importance that services like education are distributed in an equitable manner; otherwise they may create inequality in society. The equity of this distribution can be assessed in two ways. Services should be equally accessible in spatial or physical terms to all members of the community, or all who need them, and they should also be equally accessible or available to all social and economic groups within the community.

These considerations are particularly apposite where there are specific programmes directed at relieving social, cultural or economic deprivation. It has been suggested that inner city initiatives, such as the Urban Programme, sometimes seem to have failed to provide equitable solutions to the problems and in some cases may have exacerbated deprivation simply because those in most need do not or cannot avail themselves of the resources which are being offered.

Naturally, if special policies are to be pursued then it is necessary to try to measure how successful they have been. Sometimes this is done by examining the improvement in service provision (e.g. the number of book-issues in the library) from one time period to another. Local service efficiency or output studies such as that have been used to measure changes taking place as a result of particular allocation decisions. Comparisons between local authorities and within them (e.g. in spending on education) are valuable in determining the effects of particular spending policies (see page 120).

A fundamental question about the allocation of resources is whether it should be measured in terms of the provision made by the authority or the consumption by the client or user. Politicians tend to favour the former, because it can reflect their efforts more readily and it is simpler to understand and present to the public, but on the whole it tells little of the value of the service to the consumer. Similarly, while the distribution of some resources may be directly measured (the frequency of refuse collection or the quality of the road surface, for example), others, such as the quality of education, depend first upon agreement as to what constitutes 'good' education, and may then be dependent upon the characteristics of teaching staff for which only surrogate measures can be used.

It is axiomatic that the consumer must have the opportunity to use the service. Not only is differential accessibility – the location of fixed services such as the careers centre – important, but information about the availability of the service is also essential.[20] Indeed, the dissemination of information to client groups is now a major activity within local government and it has been frequently found that it is the very groups for which a service is intended that have least information about it. Service providers may improve physical accessibility by very simple measures such as the informative signposting of public buildings, and the provision of public transport to locations otherwise difficult for the disadvantaged to reach. If the measurement of service performance reveals a pattern in which there is inequality or inequity, then it is arguable that within the policy constraints in operation the authorities should act to make positive change in favour of those disadvantaged by that pattern.

Social areas

Clearly, many social problems are multidimensional and the delimitation of the scale of the problem depends upon the way in which it is measured, which variables are to be measured and how they are to be combined to identify groups at risk. At national and regional level considerable work has been done to define social problems and the indicators which measure such characteristics as standards of living, social well-being and quality of life. Frequently these indicators seem to have a common spatial or territorial framework, and attention is transferred from the identification of a social group at risk to social areas or territories.

A variety of measurements have been used as territorial indicators and although there is no theory to define what should or should not be included, there is a broad consensus of variables which has been used by the UN, the OECD and the US government to differentiate geographically areas of social concern or to provide criteria of social well-being.[21] Along with some of the variables we have considered so far there are included in most lists indicators of levels of medical well-being; rates of infant mortality; diseases associated with poor housing or diet; and levels of urban crime, particularly vandalism, which is often asserted to be symptomatic of a low standard of living. Frequently these measurements are combined using sophisticated statistical techniques which identify groups of variables that are found most commonly together and which seem to be related statistically to each other. Some procedures involve the reduction of large amounts of data to a smaller number of important factors or components by which relative levels of living can be assessed. Such methods can be in local areas to delimit the spatial extent of deprivation measured by a range of indicators. Usually the methods are applied to urban areas, and they function to identify significant groupings of the elements of the urban social structure. Sometimes this is known as the factorial ecology of an area because it identifies the relationships between factors which characterise the area.

While in general the methods employed are useful for the quantitative description and definition of areas, studies based upon factorial ecological techniques make assumptions which may result in inefficiencies in resource allocation. First, the size of the area to be identified is crucial. Very small areas of perhaps two or three streets, defined by reference to individual census enumeration districts, may be so small as to be impossibly inefficient to assist because while they clearly have needs, they are not sufficiently large as a group to be efficiently serviced. Although larger areas may be more efficient in that respect there are other problems because, of necessity, the techniques assume homogeneity within the area itself. Furthermore, there are some client groups which are not distributed contiguously or confined to small local areas, like the blind or young children. Lastly, there is the ecological fallacy – the translation of the spatially defined need of a group to that of the individual within the group or area. Sharing of common space does not necessarily mean shared need.

However, areal definitions of problems do have some important characteristics to recommend them. First, the areal base is the base upon which much of the data are collected, and thus an areal view seems to be already implied. Often, however, the areal view has too coarse a definition for the sort of analysis suggested so far, and different services are more appropriately defined and examined at different scales. Second, the geography of the area is often also the geography of politics and while distributional allocation decisions are still political, the two match quite well and area-based decisions may be politically sensible. Third, the informational and political areal bases are also the functional bases of many local authority services and there is therefore a clear administrative reason for using the area-based approach.

While the approach is appropriate for analytical purposes and often sensible for service provision, there are many functions of local authorities which do not fall neatly into a single areally defined pattern. It cannot be doubted that one source of consumer confusion lies in knowing to which area he belongs for a particular service. The confusion is compounded by what often appears to be irrationality in the spatial construction of the service and the multitude of different geographical units which are used. This is a dangerous irrationality because it can result in the potential user never becoming an actual user.

Although ecological analysis can be valuable in defining areas which require the attention of the local authority, and a spatial view of service allocation can be usefully defined by mapping techniques, this leads to little concrete understanding of how decisions are made and how they might be changed.

Notes

1. H. C. Dent, *Education in England and Wales*, 2nd edn (Unibooks, Hodder and Stoughton, 1982), p. 85.
2. These figures were obtained from *Small Area Statistics* for Bradford Metropolitan District, Census 1981.
3. P. Townsend, *Poverty in the UK* (Penguin, 1979), Ch. 10.
4. *Census 1981 Definitions*, OPCS (HMSO, 1981), p. 27.
5. P. Townsend, *op. cit.* p. 370.
6. *Census 1981 Definitions, op. cit.* p. 27. Fuller socio-economic group descriptions are as follows:
   1. Employers and managers in central and local government, industry, commerce, etc., large establishments, i.e. >25 employed persons.
   2. Employers and managers in industry, commerce, etc., small establishments.
   3. Professional workers – self-employed.
   4. Professional workers – employees.
   5. Intermediate non-manual workers.
   6. Junior non-manual workers.
   7. Personal service workers.
   8. Foremen and supervisors – manual.
   9. Skilled manual workers.
   10. Semi-skilled manual workers.
   11. Unskilled manual workers.
   12. Own account workers (other than professionals).
   13. Farmers – employers and managers.
   14. Farmers – own account.
   15. Agricultural workers.
   16. Members of the Armed Forces.
   17. Inadequately described and not stated.
7. Detailed allocation of the occupation/employment status groups is given in Appendix B of the *Classification of Occupations 1980*, OPCS (1980). Examples of the allocations of particular occupations is given below:

	SEG	Social class
Judges, barristers and solicitors	3	I
University academic staff	4	I
Teachers	5.1	II
Aircraft flight deck officers	5.1	II

	SEG	Social class
Despatch clerks	6	III(N)
Secretaries	6	III(N)
Petrol pump, forecourt attend.	5.2	III(M)
Chefs, cooks	7	III(M)
Ward orderly	10	IV
Textile workers, dyers, etc.	9	III(M)
Motor mechanics	9	III(M)

8. *Standard Industrial Classification*, revised 1980 (HMSO, 1979).
9. A. Kirby, *The Politics of Location* (Methuen, 1982), Table 2.1, p. 26.
10. P. Townsend, *op. cit.*
11. *General Household Survey*, Social Survey Division Series GHS, OPCS (HMSO).
12. *Homes for Today and Tomorrow*, Report, Chairman Sir Parker Morris, Ministry of Housing and Local Government (HMSO, 1961).
13. P. Townsend, *op. cit.* p. 478.
14. P. G. Gray and P. Russell, *The Housing Situation in 1960*, Social Survey SS319 (Central Statistical Office, 1962); cited in P. Townsend, *op. cit.*
15. P. Townsend, *op. cit.* Ch. 14.
16. P. Townsend, *op. cit.* Ch. 16.
17. D. T. Herbert and C. J. Thomas, *Urban Geography* (John Wiley, 1982), p. 310.
18. *The Brixton Disorders 10–12 April 1981*, Report of an Inquiry by the Rt. Hon. the Lord Scarman, OBE, Cmnd 8427 (HMSO, 1981).
19. B. Webster, 'Distributional Effects of Local Government Services' in S. Leach and J. Stewart (eds.), *Approaches in Public Policy*, for INLOGOV University of Birmingham (Allen and Unwin, 1982).
20. Questions about accessibility and location are fully discussed in relation to health care provision in A. E. Joseph and D. R. Philips, *Accessibility and Utilization* (Harper and Row, 1984). The principles outlined are useful in examining other similar public services.
21. For example, *Measuring Social Well-Being*, The OECD Social Indicator Development Programme 3 (OECD, 1976).

4

LAND AND LOCAL GOVERNMENT: THE PHYSICAL ENVIRONMENT

The purpose of this chapter is to describe the physical parameters in which local government operates. These are essentially the land surface which it controls and for which it is responsible. We shall first consider the bases for the value of land and then examine land use in Britain. This is followed by a closer view of local authorities' responsibilities and duties with respect to the land under their control and an overview of land-use planning, evolution and operation. The chapter ends with an examination of the new towns as examples of the application of land-use planning and the exploitation of land value.

BASES FOR LAND VALUE

As we have seen, the physical environment is important to both local government and the community. It is through the value of land that the locality can raise some of its revenue, and the quality of individual life is materially affected by the nature of the physical environment. Clearly, land has both an intrinsic and an external value. Its intrinsic value lies in the aesthetic appeal of the surface features and its natural fertility, while its external value is imbued through the uses to which it can be put. Initially this value may have been a reflection of the fertility of the soil and its productive capacity. Alternatively, it may have been a consequence of its ability to support wildlife and to act as food reservoir. Wooded land provided fuel and timber for building and manufacturing, and that containing mineral resources, such as coal and oil, could be highly valued.

Land as an economic resource

Commercial land

The factors which most significantly affect the value of land for commercial use are location and accessibility. The relative location of a particular parcel of land affects its accessibility (i.e. the ease with which it can be used and therefore the extent to which its intrinsic value can be exploited). This notion of accessibility is central to an understanding of the relative value of different plots of land, particularly within, or close to, urban areas. This is best explained by a number of examples.

The very large department store is familiar to everyone. It offers a wide range of goods, from food which is perishable and consumed directly to more durable items such as electrical goods or furniture. It may offer personal services such as hairdressing and hire facilities. In order to trade successfully and to offer such a wide range of goods and services, the store must be located so as to make it easy to get to in order to attract the maximum number of customers. In general this has meant a location close to those points with highest levels of accessibility. At its simplest this would be a point at the centre of the area from which the customers were likely to come. Such a central point would minimise their aggregate travelling time and costs. Sometimes this central point is the geometric centre of the customer-zone or urban area, but more often it is defined by reference to the transport network. Where this is at its densest is assumed to be the point of highest accessibility.

Obviously, the central area of a city provides the most attractive location to all those who need to maximise their potential for contact with clients or customers, but the zone of maximum accessibility is limited. There will therefore be intense competition for land and locations in those areas offering high levels of accessibility and land values will tend to be high. The competition for locations will 'bid up' the price of land.

At the other extreme we have the example of the golf club. In general, the use of a golf club is not casual in the way that shopping in a particular store is. The clientele is determined by membership and although it may be useful to have a high degree of accessibility for the convenience of the members, it is much more important that large amounts of relatively cheap land are available. Clearly, the golf club could not afford the high prices of land in the centre, and does not need the accessibility it would gain. The consequence of poor accessibility is a lower level of demand, less competition and thus lower rental prices.

There is therefore a clear distinction in locational requirements that result in the department store locating near the centre of town and golf

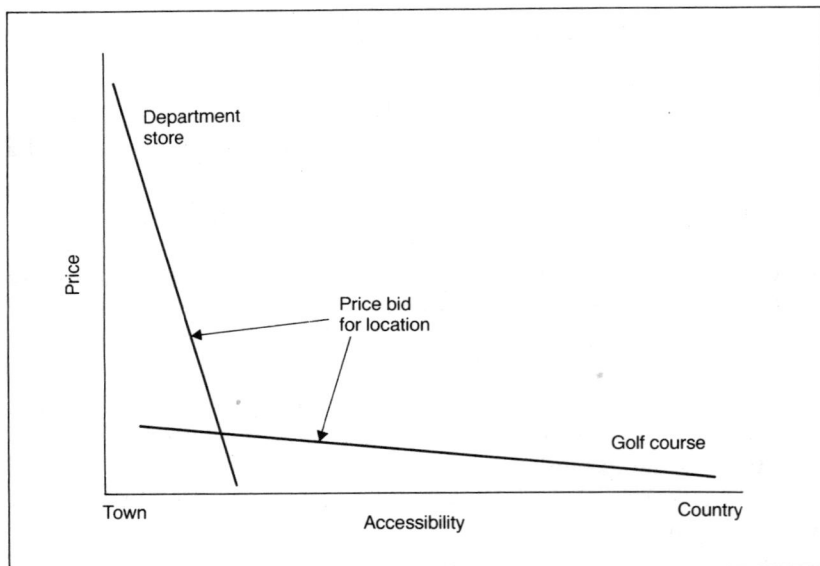

Fig. 4.1 Land value and accessibility

courses on the periphery. Since it is the peripheral areas of towns which are in general least accessible, then it is here also that land values are lowest (Fig. 4.1).

Many land-using activities are located with respect to other factors such as the proximity of similar or associated functions. Industrial users of land, for example, may need to be near railway lines to facilitate the movement of large amounts of raw materials or fuels. They need access to the transport network, but do not need high accessibility for the customer. At the same time they may need large amounts of land for storage purposes, to house plant or to gain economies of large-scale production. They will also need adequate transport facilities to enable the workforce to travel. Their locational requirements are neither so strongly related to general accessibility as the department store nor so poorly related as the golf club. They are prepared to pay the price for land which falls somewhere between the two.

There are many qualifications to the general principle that these examples illustrate. It is a principle which helps to explain the differential value of land between locations and the reasons for the variation in uses to which land may be put. Although the principles of accessibility is important it does not always result in competition for the same sites for specific land users. This is illustrated by the increasing use of out-of-town locations for retailing activities. This is best explained by reference to the change from public to private transport as the principal means of access to large shops. Although urban examples are used here, the principle can also be used, though perhaps less successfully, to explain the variations in the pattern of agricultural land use, both at the level of the individual farm and in a wider regional context.

Residential land use
The differential value of land, because of its varying ability to support human life, contributed to human ideas of territoriality and, therefore, to the attempts of people to control even small parcels of it. This fundamental interest in land is reflected in our social and personal attitudes towards it. There are few who would not welcome the opportunity to own and control some land personally. In Britain we seem to have a clear preference for home ownership rather than for tenancy and for homes and properties with gardens. 'Space' itself has a value. We value gardens not necessarily for what they can produce but because they also give us privacy.

In early settlements and pre-industrial towns, segregation of work-place and home was only minimally possible because people had to be close enough to work to be able to walk there each day. In some ways the overall size of the town was determined by the distance that could comfortably be walked between home and work. Although not necess-arily a limiting factor, the same was true in early industrial towns before the advent of mass transport, and much of the squalor of residential life in the densely packed areas of the early nineteenth-century city can be attributed to that fact. In the absence of transport, homes for the majority had to be built close to work, and indeed were often built at the same time as the factory. As first the horse-omnibus and later the electric tram and motor bus were introduced, the range of possible locations for residential accommodation was extended. In many towns residential development can be seen to have followed the direction and develop-ment of the transport system; and initially, of course, as transport provided improved accessibility, the value of suburban land for residen-tial purposes also increased. All land may be seen therefore to have a residential value provided adequate support is available to link it to workplaces, but commercial or industrial users may be prepared to pay more than residential users for a particular tract of land. This differen-tial value of land for different users in relation to accessibility and distance from some notional centre can be represented graphically.

Figure 4.2 shows how each tract of land successively distant from the city centre is defined in terms of value and use (land being assumed to go to its 'highest and best' use), and the point at which one use changes to

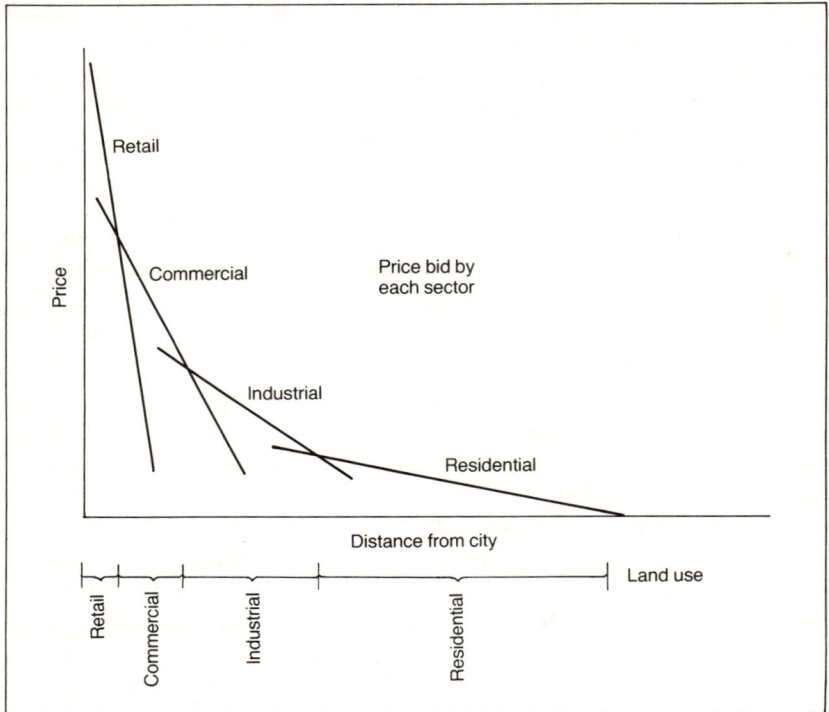

Fig. 4.2 Land use and accessibility

another can be seen. The overall value of land is defined by the maximum value of the bid-price curve.

This change in land value is a basic factor in accounting for differences in the value of rent which might be charged for the use or ownership of that land or space, and thus it is instrumental in determining the value of the land to the local authority which, through the rating system, gains revenue from it. There are, however, many other factors not necessarily connected with accessibility which affect the potential use of space and thus its value:

1. Legal restrictions can limit land use choices. Aside from simple considerations such as ensuring that rights to light and access are maintained, General Development and Use Class Orders under the Town and Country Planning Act 1968 limit changes of land use for some functions or activities. There is, of course, legal protection for buildings and sites of special historical, aesthetic or scientific interest or value. This can include protection for the landscape against damage by change of agricultural practice or land use.

2. Planning principles and aesthetic considerations applied in the planning process can limit the freedom of the individual to build a home or a factory at will. On the whole, residential development is restricted to defined areas so as to limit low density and ribbon-like housing development and to preserve the rural aspect of much of the countryside near to towns.
3. Just as the value of industrial land tends to increase where good transport is readily available, so users may value supporting and infrastructural services such as main drainage or good schools.
4. The quality of the property and land itself, its state of repair and maintenance, provision of services, etc., may also be significant considerations in determining location.

It can be appreciated, therefore, that like the population, land is a resource to be nurtured and developed; but as with people, its parameters must be known if the job is to be done effectively. Local and central governments must be aware of the value of the resource to which they have access so that it may be sensibly and rationally considered and used. Over the last century or so, central and local governments have also had to take powers to control land use and development. Not only do we need population census to assess the needs of, and resources offered by, the people; it is vital that government should also have information about the land on which to base decisions.

UK LAND USE

There are few consistent and extensive sources of land-use data for the United Kingdom, and no government department is responsible for the collation of those sources which are available. Detailed records are gathered and maintained by the Ministry of Agriculture, Fisheries and Food (MAFF), showing the way in which the land is used for agriculture. Some of the information is published using a regional base. Local authorities collect some data about land use in towns on behalf of the DoE, and this has the advantage that it is published on a small scale so that detailed comparisons can be made. Table 4.1 shows a simplified land-use categorisation for the United Kingdom based upon MAFF data.

The figures show the relative importance of arable land, i.e. land lying under crop or fallow, in England compared with the other home countries. The reasons for the distribution are straightforward. In the first place, soils in England are generally more fertile than in other parts of Britain, and the climate is more equable, neither as cold as in Scotland not as wet as in Wales. On the whole, there is a relatively smaller area of

Table 4.1 Land by agricultural and other land uses

	Crop & fallow (%)	Grass & rough grazing (%)	other (%)	Forest & wood (%)	Urban or other (%)	Total (ha)
England	34	40	1	7	17	12,968
Scotland	9	73	0	13	5	7,708
Wales	4	75	1	12	8	2,064
N. Ireland	6	74	2	5	13	1,348
UK	22	56	1	9	12	24,088

Source: Social Trends 16 Table 9.13.
MAFF Agricultural Statistics United Kingdom 1983 HMSO 1984.

elevated land in Engand and thus a wider range of uses for the land is possible. As important, however, is the fact that the larger markets are in England and this higher degree of accessibility makes land which might otherwise be marginal worth while for growing grains such as barley. Agricultural land in England also tends to be more highly capitalised than that in the rest of the United Kingdom and intensive beef production, for example, releases some land which might otherwise be pasture.

The high proportion of grassland and rough grazing in Scotland and Wales, with dairy farming in the valleys and sheep on the uplands, underline their hilly terrain. Northern Ireland is neither particularly elevated nor are the soils especially fertile. Remote from the mainland markets, it nevertheless produces intensively reared beef and pork for them. Like England, Northern Ireland is relatively little wooded, the higher proportions of the economic forestry being in Wales and Scotland. The remainder of the surface is deemed to be mainly urban land, but the figures include a category of great importance – derelict land.

Derelict land is land which cannot be put to gainful use unless it is first treated. Such land amounts to about 0.3 per cent of the land areas of England and is to be found mostly in or near to the main conurbations. It falls into three principal categories. About 28 per cent of the derelict land is spoil heaps resulting from the surface deposit of waste from mining of coal, tin and slate and is therefore a particular problem in the north-east, Yorkshire and Derbyshire, North Wales and Cornwall. Excavations and tips associated particularly with cement and brick-making and pottery industries account for about 18 per cent and are a problem in the Midlands (Table 4.2). About the same amount of land is derelict as a result of abandonment by the railways. It is to be seen in all parts of the country and is an especial eyesore in the major cities. The military are responsible for 6 per cent of derelict land. There are a large

Table 4.2 Derelict land

England	46,000 ha
North	7,500 ha
Yorks & Humberside	5,500 ha
E. Midlands	5,100 ha
E. Anglia	1,000 ha
South-east	4,500 ha

Source: Social Trends 16 HMSO 1986.

number of small parcels of derelict land not accounted for and these include abandoned quarries and land poisoned by the dumping of noxious, usually industrial, waste. These areas pose particular problems for local authorities because they are a possible hazard to public health, for which environmental health officers are responsible. In general, derelict land is of local concern, not just for health reasons but also because it is a waste of local resources. It can be aesthetically unpleasant, though its improvement is assisted by grants from central government.

The UK population of 52 million and land area of 24 million hectares makes it one of the most densely settled countries in the world. High densities of population impose severe conditions on the land surface and its capacity to meet the needs of the people it supports. In the United Kingdom and in much of Europe physical conditions – topography and relief, climate and soils – offer the possibility of supporting high population densities which industrialisation has increased still further. Europeans are among the most highly urbanised people in the world, and the United Kingdom is among the highest of them. Although figures indicate that if the surface were to be equally shared each man, woman and child in the country could expect to occupy an area of 0.44 ha, in practice people tend to congregate in the urban centres and densities can exceed 4,000 per sq. km. In 1971 the most densely population kilometre square in England was in Earls Court, where there were 24,300 people.[1] In the twentieth century, planning restrictions have tended to maintain a large urban population by limiting the building of new houses to areas of existing settlement.

The reasons for these restrictions, although by no means universally accepted, are clear. A widely dispersed population could result in considerable loss of agricultural land and thus a reduction in the ability of the country to feed itself. This would contribute to a continued drain on the country's balance of payments because of the need to import more food and thus make even heavier demands on manufacturing industry and the service sector. Although the problem of Britain's underlying adverse balance of payments position has been largely ignored in the

1980s because of the value of its oil exports, the import of large amounts of food is still felt to be strategically unsatisfactory. For a number of political or economic reasons, it is felt that land with agricultural potential should be preserved. A low density of settlement would place heavy emphasis on transportation, with people in general moving longer distances to work or to shop each day. Not only is this inefficient for them because of the time which is wasted, it is also costly and demands heavy infrastructure expenditure on new roads. This in turn often means the loss of more agricultural land and, because of noise and atmospheric pollution there is a further loss of amenity for those living adjacent to the new highways.

But the countryside is not only a useful and directly productive resource; its value for the majority of people who live in towns is that it provides a different environment from that in which they spend most of their lives. The mere fact that there is a great difference in population density between town and country gives the countryside part of its distinctive value. Allowing it to be developed for industrial or residential use would necesarily reduce that value. Since space is generally at a premium in Britain, and with increasing affluence and car ownership longer journeys from the home for work, shopping and leisure can be contemplated, the countryside has become increasingly at risk through the extension of residential occupancy.

During the latter part of the nineteenth century and in the twentieth century, land-use changes in the United Kingdom have been considerable. The area of built-up land is estimated to have almost doubled between 1850 and 1950. Surveys vary in their definition of what is urban land, but it has been shown that there was an increase of 30 per cent in England and Wales in the period 1935–61. A further increase of 11 per cent occurred between 1961 and 1981, resulting in an overall urban area total of about 12 per cent. The inclusion of the large non-urban area in Scotland reduces the total for Great Britain to 8.5 per cent.[2] Other estimates put the area of settlement at 10.8 per cent in 1963. With a growth rate of about 10 per cent per decade it would total about 13 per cent in 1983.

There are major regional variations in the extent of urbanisation, and also in rates of growth. Although more than ten years out of date, estimates of the urban area as a proportion of the administrative area in each of the economic planning regions put the North-West at the top with more than 25 per cent and the South-East second at 18.7 per cent. Wales, East Anglia and the North had very low proportions by comparison. Since 1971, however, population growth has been highest in East Anglia so we might expect to find that its urbanised area is now higher. On the other hand, it has been shown that in the 1950s even in areas with absolute decreases in population, the urban area has been extended as inner-city redevelopment and increasing personal and domestic space expectations have had their impact.

The effect of urban expansion is considerable but it is not necessarily obvious. It would seem sensible that if a change from agricultural to industrial or residential land use is to take place then it should be on the poorer agricultural sites. It has been demonstrated, however, that while first-class agricultural land amounts to about 7.5 per cent of the total agricultural land area available, it accounts for 9.6 per cent of the land which has recently become urbanised. Even more marked is the loss of land classified as good. It amounts to 37.6 per cent of agricultural land but 43.5 per cent of the new land taken up for building. In simple terms and for clear geological, topographic and geographical reasons, when land is urbanised better land is lost more quickly than poorer land. The underlying geology and relief markedly affect the quality and depth of soils and thus the agricultural potential. Settlements were originally attracted to those locations; towns appeared and expanded on to their agricultural hinterlands, reducing their productive capacity.

In addition, urbanisation has knock-on effects on agricultural management practices, and there is clear evidence that good-quality land is not managed so well, nor is it as productive as it might be, where it is close to large-scale urban settlement. This is partly the result of continuous pressure by the urban population on footpaths, fences and hedges, on livestock-rearing practices and on fertiliser usage. It is a population unsure of the needs of the farmer, and unmindful of the needs of a land surface which appears to it to be both a useful and useable amenity. Equally, the farmer may be insensitive to the effects of his farming methods, the production of noxious smells, pollution of streams and becks, creation of dust and so on. All these factors contribute to making the urban/rural fringe a zone of social and land-use tension.[3]

LOCAL AUTHORITY LAND

While local councils have a wide-ranging responsibility for land and are themselves major landowners, it is difficult to gauge precisely the extent of their holdings. There is no statutory requirement on a local authority to produce a consolidated list of all property and land which it holds or controls, except that which is required under Part 10 of the Local Government Planning and Land Act 1980 to list all unallocated land in the authority. Most officers agree that to produce a comprehensive list of land for which the authority is responsible would be a formidable task. It is estimated that in some districts such land and property could amount to as much as 33 per cent of the surface area. However, this is likely only in those parts of the country where there are large tracts of land which local authorities have inherited from common occupancy, such as open moorland or hill country.

Local authority land and property holdings are of two types. They may be operational, i.e. required in order that the council might expedite its legitimate functions. Schools and their grounds, health centres, nurseries, abattoirs, transport depots and garages, offices and administrative buildings, recreational and leisure facilities, parks and sports centres all fall into this category. Alternatively they may be non-operational, such as farms, plantations or other holdings not essential to the furtherance of council business. In one large metropolitan district, for example, the council is responsible for the maintenance and control of several large areas of upland, and it also has large agricultural estates in the valleys, residential properties and farms, quarries, commercial and industrial premises and sites, and retail and commercial sites in the cities.

Since the individual details for each property are recorded and the complete holdings logged on large-scale ordnance survey plans, though not generally collated, neither the combined value of the capital asset nor the rateable value for those properties that are rated can be calculated. However, an indication of the value to the community of the land and property which is municipally held can be judged from the one example, where property, including housing and land, produces an annual gross rental income equivalent to about 16 per cent of total expenditure and about 28 per cent of the revenue raised locally. It can be appreciated that the financial contribution of this resource is therefore substantial.

How authorities acquired land

Local authorities have acquired these considerable land holdings over a number of years. In some cases land held in common since medieval times has eventually become the responsibility of the authority. At other times, local government has been enabled to purchase land and property in order to satisfy a statutory function and provide a service. Two significant acquisitions of this type in recent years have been for housing development and highways improvement. Compulsory purchase for road-building can result in small parcels of land unneccessary to the scheme itself remaining in the hands of the council. The land may be let or resold to consolidate an existing agricultural holding. It may also be sold for development, in which case the council or purchaser must seek planning permission in the normal way. Much public land was donated to councils by benefactors in the nineteenth century or bought by them for use as public recreation areas, and its function as green space in cities is protected by legislation, such as the Open Spaces Act of 1906.

The provision of public housing became a major local function at the turn of the century and further land was acquired, both for the replacement of poor-quality slum housing and, by the inter-war period, to expand housing provision for the slowly increasing population, particularly the suburban housing estates of the artisan and lower middle classes. Such developments required the purchase of many small tracts of land together with substantial agricultural estates on the edges of cities. At the same time, there was the gradual accretion of land holdings as more and more functions became the responsibility of local government and urban life in particular became more heavily regulated. During the Second World War this house-building slowed, although war damage and emergency rehousing programmes continued to add to the local authorities' stock.

In the post-war period major national changes had a marked effect. In 1948, with the establishment of the National Health Service, responsibility for most of the medical care facilities and services passed from local to central government control, exercised through a series of hospital boards which were in large measure unconnected with the local council. Similar municipal undertakings such as gas and electric power generation and distribution also devolved to public corporations and thus local control was lost. Moreover the site, plant and property became the responsibility of organisations not directly accountable to a local population, and were not owned by the local council. At first, therefore, the stock of council land must have fallen, but in other areas of national life legislation continued to add to that stock.

Many Acts of Parliament, from the Schools Sites Acts of the nineteenth century onwards, had enabled the purchase of land for building new schools. Under the provisions of the 1944 Education Act, which raised the school-leaving age from 14 to 15, there was an increase in the size of the school population; this, combined with the policy of improvement of the existing schools, involved the acquisition of more land for the building of new schools. About half of all local authority schools have been built since 1945 (Table 4.3).

A marked feature of these new schools was the generous provision of outdoor sports facilities and the often extensive playing fields which they included. Many education committees were to find this generosity

Table 4.3 School buildings in England and Wales to 1977

	Total	1919–45	%	Post-1945	%
Primary	23,280	2,360	10.1	10,670	45.8
Secondary	5,030	920	18.3	3,090	61.4
All schools	28,310	3,280	11.6	13,760	48.6

Source: A study of school building p. 90 Table 1 DES and Welsh Office HMSO 1977.

invaluable later when further rapid expansion was called for in a period of more severe financial constraint, since there was often room for new extensions, classrooms and sports halls on the same site.

In the 1950s, as other problems of post-war reconstruction were resolved, housing problems became much more noticeable and new programmes for extensive slum clearance were introduced. The execution of these programmes was dependent upon control of properties first passing to local councils. The mechanism for gaining control was the compulsory purchase order. There is a long history of legislation in this field which was recognised in the Land Clauses Consolidation Act of 1845. Modern legislation dates from the Town and Country Planning Acts of 1947, the New Towns Act of 1965, and a number of planning and local government acts since then.

Privately owned land and property thus passed into public ownership and the amount of locally controlled land increased. At the same time many dispossessed tenants and owner-occupiers were rehoused in property provided for them by the authority, often on large low-density housing estates frequently built on the edges of the cities but owned by the municipality. Some of the cleared sites were reused later and tenants found themselves moved into high-density high-rise accommodation nearer to the city centres, accommodation which was often to prove short-lived because the buildings were subsequently found to have structural defects.

Comprehensive redevelopment

Major redevelopment was also undertaken within the core of many of Britain's larger cities. The concept of comprehensive commercial redevelopment was attractive to many of the groups interested in property development, including local councils, property speculators, retailers and commercial users, as well as the public in general. There was considerable public pride in the new faces of many cities, even if a few voices were raised in questioning the wisdom of a policy which seemed to sweep away the good, pleasant and worthy in the old urban landscape along with the poor and the unpleasant. Large-scale redevelopment of this sort was difficult for the private developer to finance. It demanded total control of the site, and large amounts of capital were tied up in the acquisition of land. Indeed, private developers might be unable to gain complete control of a site since they could not force an unwilling owner to sell. Local authorities did have that power through the compulsory purchase order, and it could be and was used to amass and consolidate plots of land and sites suitable for commercial exploitation in the city centres.

Additionally, local councils had large and powerful financial and capital borrowing resources with which to support these ventures and a strong interest on behalf of the ratepayer in maximising the use and value of the sites and so securing higher income from them in the form of rates and rental payments. Through such activities local authorities began to accumulate the titles to large tracts of prime retail and commercial land and thus to further increase their direct stake or interest in it and the property in their districts. Although the process was one born essentially of the free market, it began to look increasingly like a form of land nationalisation, albeit piecemeal and back-door. Indeed, the Community Land Act of 1975 specifically empowered local councils to purchase land which had been designated for redevelopment and then to sell or lease it to the developer. The Act was intended to facilitate local councils sharing in the value added to land by their own decisions rather than allowing it to accrue solely to private capital. Such land was to be bought at the pre-development market price, and the local authority would thus gain the increased value accruing as a result of its new use.

Changes in attitude to local authority landholding

By the late 1970s, however, the national economic climate, the political outlook, and public attitudes had changed. The 1973 energy crisis had worked through the economic system and ushered in a period of austerity and restraint in public spending. Conservation and preservation became increasingly important influences on local policy-making, especially in the sphere of land use and planning. The problems of comprehensive redevelopment, both in city centres and in housing, became evident.

Local authorities which had begun to utilise the 'belated power' of the Community Land Act 1975 to strengthen the public purse found that the purposes for which it had been created were now restricted; and the Conservative Government took measures to restore a free market in land through the Local Government Planning and Land Act of 1980, which effectively repealed most of the provisions of the Community Land Act (except for Development Land Tax). The Act also required authorities to compile a list of landholdings which were under their control but which were unused, and this register, collated by the Department of the Environment, could be used to compel councils to dispose of such lands by sale. At the same time central government took steps to encourage councils to sell their council houses to tenants on advantageous terms.

The implications of this measure were manifold. First, it released on to the market more land for private development. Second, it can be seen also as a measure aimed at speeding up the process of development in order to minimise planning blight. Third, it has reduced local government financial independence by reducing the level of its capital stock. By encouraging local councils to sell land and liquidate assets it has ameliorated the effects of the reduction in central government funding. In a once-and-for-all sale, control of a vital resource by the community is diminished.[4]

Current situation

Despite these changes local government retains wide powers to acquire land and may do so for a variety of reasons. First, operational needs, such as the building of a highways depot or store, must still be met. Second, statutory and functional obligations continue to require local authorities to purchase unfit housing, to facilitate land use and transport planning, and to build new roads.

Purchases in pursuit of local economic policy objectives are also important. In many local authorities the problem of industrial degeneration and unemployment is acute. There is a limit to the number of people who can be directly employed and a limit to the extent to which an authority can alleviate these problems by direct intervention, especially in a period in which the proportion of public expenditure donated by central funding is being reduced. But there are some measures which can be taken. One is to provide a planning environment in which necessary administrative procedures are expedited and potential employers thereby encouraged to proceed with development schemes. And local authorities can make sites under their control available for development. Site-assembly, the bringing together of small parcels of land to provide appropriately sized units for commercial and industrial development, is thus a major function of local authority estate departments, often pursued under direct council guidelines with the collaboration of planning departments. Such sites are usually let rather than sold off to private companies or individuals. In this way the council retains an interest in the land and in its revenue potential. It is significant that many local councils have set themselves the task of helping to alleviate local unemployment and that the effective use of local land is an important facet of this objective.

LAND-USE PLANNING

Origins and influences

While contemporary land-use planning can be seen substantially in terms of planning for the efficient and effective use of space and the resolution of land-use conflict, its origins are less clear but probably more humanitarian. One may trace the origins of planning almost as far back as the ancient civilisations in Mesopotamia, China, Africa, South America and ancient Greece. The real origins of contemporary West European planning of the city probably lie in sixteenth-century Italy, when builders and architects consciously sought to impose a new order and structure on the townscapes they erected. These architects were aware of the need to provide certain facilities and services within the city without which it could not adequately function and were also aware of the importance of light, open space, and the need to provide an aesthetically satisfying experience both in the structure of the city and in the individual buildings and townscape. The principal elements which they contributed to the modern townscape were the concepts of form, usually geometrical and rectilinear, and aesthetic qualities, with open and enclosed places, piazzas or squares, and parks.

Industrial impact and social change

Other, perhaps more important elements were added in the nineteenth century, inspired by the appalling conditions of the emerging Victorian industrial towns. Here a mixture of philanthropy and economic common sense resulted in the establishment of a number of planned settlements in which work, residential and recreational functions were combined on new sites with vastly improved physical and social environments for those who lived in them.

One such village was Saltaire, built by Titus Salt on the banks of the River Aire some six miles north of Bradford. The village principally housed the workforce for a very large textile mill and the site was probably determined largely on economic grounds. The village included church and chapel, public washroom and laundry, and recreational and self-improvement facilities in the shape of a library and a park. There was accommodation for the elderly and the retired, a hospital but no public house. There is a clear separation of each of the functional zones, with additional shops located at street corners. Although rigidly rectilinear in form and not very sympathetic to the possibilities offered by the sloping valleyside site, it was and remains a clean and neat, if somewhat austere translation of urban homes into a new environment. In many ways the physical plan is a reflection of the Victorian values of hard work, sobriety, self-improvement and religion, but perhaps more importantly it produced a healthy, more reliable workforce and was free of the diseconomies of location of central Bradford; indeed, it was an excellent site from the point of view of economy with turnpike, rail and canal links and a plentiful supply of water.

Such experiments in social engineering were continued throughout the nineteenth century and industrial settlements such as Bourneville, established by Cadbury in 1878, and Port Sunlight by Lord Lever in 1887, are justifiably world famous. Early attempts at this sort of development are perhaps more important because they lay the groundwork for much of the planning for the local authority housing which was soon to follow, and particularly those estates in which there was an attempt to embody elements of a lost rural life and environment. As we shall see, the major influences in this direction in Britain are those of Ebenezer Howard and Patrick Geddes in the building of Welwyn Garden City, and Barry Parker and Raymond Unwin who were responsible for the design of the village of New Earswick near York, built for Joseph Rowntree in the 1890s.

Private attempts to ameliorate the hardships of the urban working classes were soon matched by public action, and a series of building controls, regulation of sewage disposal and other public health measures were passed by Parliament in the second half of the nineteenth century. They can be seen as culminating in 1909 in the Housing and Town Planning Act, which enabled local authorities to tackle the fundamental problem of rehousing those who lived in the worst conditions by preparing town plans and development schemes for housing in new areas under their control. By 1915, 74 local authorities had proposed 108 schemes with new housing extending to some 198,000 acres.[5]

Changing problems in the inter-war years

Further schemes were introduced in the inter-war period, when larger estates were bought and major rehousing projects started on the suburban fringes. Although the extent was not at first known, there was great concern that agricultural land was being swallowed up rapidly in the extension of the towns. The concern was heightened by the publication of the first national land-use survey by Professor L. Dudley Stamp in 1936–37, which revealed the true nature of the problem.

The Town and Country Planning Act of 1932 had sought to provide local planning authorities with the power to control these processes through development schemes, but the procedures required by the Act made it slow, cumbersome and expensive and by 1939 only 2 per cent of the land area of the United Kingdom was covered by such schemes. In spite of its drawbacks, however, the legislation did suggest the direction that land-use planning was to take in order to make the best use of all the urban and rural land in the country. In 1942, the Scott Committee on Land Use in Rural Areas[6] recommended controls on the design of agricultural buildings and the zoning of land to protect it from housing and other development, and the provisions were incorporated into the Town and Country Planning Act of 1947.

Modern planning in Britain

Structure

The post-war political climate was very different from that of the pre-war period. This was evident in the elevated status afforded to government planning. The 1947 Act 'embodied the principle that all development rights belong to the state' and implied a new relationship between government and people on the one hand, and landowners on the other. Planning powers were invested in county councils and county boroughs, which were to formulate proposals for the comprehensive control of land use in the form of development plans. The development plan included a survey and report on the current situation and a statement of policies by which development was to be guided in the future and which would form the basis upon which decisions about land use could be made. Changes in land use could not be undertaken without planning permission and thus control over development and landscape changes could be exercised. If proposed changes were in line with the policy as described in the development plan then permission would normally be granted, although detailed elements of the proposal such as design, materials and access could still result in its being refused. It was in this way that modern development control was established. The Act also required that, where necessary, programme maps should be prepared which showed the stages of implementation of the plan, together with a more detailed town map.

Initially the development process was to be planned for 20 years, with quinquennial reviews and all plans sanctioned by the responsible minister. Ministers could make direct decisions in special cases where a planning application was of national interest or might influence national policy. Additionally, by making general development orders some developments could be exempted, as is the case for some agricultural buildings.[7] Local planning authorities were themselves granted enforcement rights where land-use changes were made without consent, and so the legislation was not only influential in structural land-use terms but it could also be successfully implemented in detail.

Problems

Although the Act was important and far-sighted, its initial operation by local councils posed many problems. Most authorities had no staff directly qualified to oversee the implementation of the Act. Planners were few and far between – the Town and Country Planning Association had been established only in 1935 – and the job therefore fell somewhere between the roles of engineer and architect. Equally, there were few elected representatives with a direct interest in or experience of the field, and novel planning committees had to be established. Similar problems were encountered at central government level to which the local plans were referred; the result was therefore the extremely slow implementation of the Act. This slowed down the process of post-war reconstruction while at the same time laying down a rigid pattern which could be changed only with difficulty.

Policies

The spirit of post-war Britain was one of reconstruction, progress and change, and town and country planning was a part of the new approach. The 1950s seemed to demand large-scale planning and a new vision which the Act was able to provide in tackling the problems and objectives. Many city architects and their colleagues in the emergent planning sections were enabled to initiate major schemes for redevelopment of city centres and the zoning of residential and other functions which had been formulated some years earlier. Although the scale of planning was greater than it had been formerly it was still confined within the county and county borough boundaries and was essentially limited to three areas: housing and reconstruction, including comprehensive demolition of slum and unfit property; city centre redevelopment; and the control of industrial and commercial development. Under this legislation much of the appearance of Britain's major cities was radically altered. It also helped to preserve those which were historically or architecturally valuable and interesting.

Changes of emphasis

Towards the end of the 20-year planning period the operation and value of the Act came to be questioned. Although plans could be prepared and schemes proposed the planners themselves were unable to effect change, merely influencing its direction. The system was criticised as being inflexible, costly, time-consuming and unresponsive to public concerns. In fact, under the Act planning decisions did not have to be publicly justified and there was little consultation over planning proposals. Perhaps more significant was the effect of planning 'blight' on house and property values. 'Blighted' areas are those in which local planning authorities have proposed major changes such as demolition for slum clearance or road-building or the establishment of a change in land use. Such proposals, often necessarily made many years in advance of their implementation, resulted in general uncertainty, the possibility of compulsory purchase and a fall in land values. Legislation introduced in 1959 enabled local authorities to compulsorily purchase properties in this category at current land-use market price, thus both enabling plans to proceed and reducing financial loss. 'Blight', however, is not simply a financial matter and the problems of large-scale redevelopment also extended into the social sphere, where not only was land and property seen to be adversely affected but communities suffered too. The issues involved shifted from the physical landscape and housing to the consequences for people and their locality and neighbourhood. As more and more comprehensive schemes for rehousing were implemented, increasingly loud voices were raised against the destruction, by relocation, of what were asserted to be important communities. This disturbance of the established pattern of life for many thousands of people has been blamed for the emerging social malaise of post-war Britain: higher crime rates, breakdown of family life, vandalism and delinquency. The values of post-war planning came to be questioned. Planners, rather than the elected councillors who actually made the decisions, were increasingly held responsible for the social problems that were considered to be the result of the planning policies they pursued. They were blamed for the destruction of buildings and changes in character of the city centres.

Participation and the new era.

In 1968 a new Town and Country Planning Act was passed. It required the preparation of two separate but interrelated types of plan. First, ministerial approval was necessary for a large-scale coarse-grained county- and county borough-based structure plan with a development time-scale of 15–20 years. These were to establish the aims, principles and framework for the local plan and were to be drawn up in light of existing national and regional policies. The format and content for such plans was indicated by the ministry.[8]

At local level, district and action area plans did not require ministerial approval but were designed to fit into the overall structure plan. They were to contain the detailed information upon which individual decisions about development proposals could be made. When local government was reorganised in 1974 it was logical to retain the two-fold structure, with the structure plans being prepared at county level and local plans left to the district councils. However, such a division of function would mean that the smallest area for which a plan was produced was, in the case of metropolitan districts, unacceptably large. Thus for operational purposes the districts were usually subdivided to correspond to recognisable local areas or even neighbourhoods, or defined in terms of a specified planning problem or objective.

This limitation of the size of practical planning units is important in terms of the provisions of the Skeffington Report of 1969.[9] This report, called *People and Planning*, arose out of the general public disquiet with the planning process and its implementation which had been growing throughout the 1960s. Skeffington recommended that one way to overcome the unease was to make the deliberations of planning committees open to the public and to encourage public participation and consultation during the planning process. Increasingly, planners sought to improve public awareness of the issues and alternatives through leaflets, publicity material, fuller media briefings, and by including local interest groups on consultative committees where this was possible. This practice continues and indeed, some of the more innovative local authorities have used the experience to develop broader policies of open government (see Chapter 8).

Preservation and conservation

Planning functions have also needed to adapt to the new public attitudes and to changing financial circumstances. Comprehensive redevelopment seemed to have failed; the cities still had major problems and in any case there was no more money for grandiose schemes. There was general agreement that much of the valuable social and physical fabric of the cities had been lost by over-enthusiastic planning and commercially promoted solutions to housing problems in the 1960s. The large-scale approach had resulted in worse blight than a more moderate, smaller-scale approach might have done.

In other areas of our communal and private lives, conservation became important and provided a watchword for a change in planning attitudes. Why destroy and dislocate a community, its homes and environment when, at lower cost, it might be refurbished and con-solidated, thus maintaining the social fabric and encouraging local pride? At the same time, it was recognised that the problems of society could not be solved by physical planning alone and that if real changes were to be made, planning should be integrated into an overall strategy which involved many of the other functions of local government as well as agencies outside it.

Such an approach argues for a less definitive land-use plan – one in which changes in the community can be recognised and which is capable of adapting to those changes. At the same time, while the plan should be mindful of large-scale needs it has to be relevant at a smaller scale and understandable to the general public. The moves taken by planners in this direction are important for they heralded a new planning era in which the major thrust was towards identifying and tackling local problems in co-operation with other local authority departments. It implied working with local people as well as for them. The managerial response to these ideas was to set up teams of specialists to examine local areas, and the result has often been an integrated area management approach to the problems of planning and of the inner city in particular. It can perhaps be seen as a smaller-scale version of the overall corporate management philosophy which has been adopted in many city and county halls. Land-use planning in an area management structure matches well with the social area approach to social problems discussed in the last chapter.

NEW TOWNS

In the development of new town policy and planning principles, several of the themes we have discussed come together.

The New Towns Act of 1946 is an area of direct government intervention which has been of considerable local and national import-ance and which came about as a result of the combination of three factors which we have discussed: the need to accommodate population move-ment; the possibility that the State might share in the increased value of land as a result of its actions; and the mechanism of State planning and intervention at a local level, but in the framework of a national policy.

Origins and concepts

For many years it had been suggested that the solution to urban problems lay in the development of new planned settlements specifically designed to try to overcome some of the inadequacies of the old. As the problems of growing urbanisation increased in the nineteenth century, various initiatives attempted to deal with them. People such as Ebenezer Howard, with his Garden Cities Association, and the architects Barry Parker and Raymond Unwin, with Letchworth (1902) and Welwyn Garden City (1919), both theoretically and physically laid the foundations of much of modern planning and of the approaches to new town development.

Early twentieth-century ideas of new town form were combined with national needs in the 1930s. The Marley Committee, reporting in 1935,[10] considered the idea of garden cities and new towns to be so important as to be worthy of direct State involvement. The new town was seen as a way of preventing problems of unplanned development and especially as an alternative to the continued expansion of the suburbs. The view was supported by the Royal Commission on the Distribution of the Industrial Population (1940),[11] which also advocated that there should be more government control of the larger cities and towns. More significant perhaps in the development of the new town concept was the Abercrombie Report (1944) on the planning of Greater London.[12] Its major policy suggestions included the restriction of the outward suburban extension of London by the establishment of a green belt and the foundation of ten new towns about 20 miles from the capital city. They were to accommodate the increasingly large population of the capital, many of whom were moved from their homes in order to facilitate urban renewal. A similar plan was proposed for the Clydeside conurbation in Scotland.

The culmination of these physical planning concepts and regional planning suggestions was the New Towns Act 1946, which paved the way for the establishment of development corporations for the towns initially financed by central government loans, but to be privately funded after 25 years. New town development corporations were enabled to purchase agricultural land at the value of its existing use. Any increase in value as a result of 'betterment' or change to residential, commercial or industrial use was to accrue to the Exchequer. The value of betterment is illustrated by one example in Stevenage, where land originally valued at £750,000 and expected to fetch £3 million, in fact realised £13 million when planning permission for retail development was granted.

Development: failure and success

During the initial phase, from 1946 to 1955, eight new towns were built or extended either as satellite or overspill developments designed to ease some of London's problems. These were at Basildon, Bracknell, Crawley, Harlow, Hatfield, Hemel Hempstead, Stevenage and Welwyn Garden City.[13] Corby was designated a new town in 1950 to house an expanding industrial population in the steel industry. Two new towns were built in Scotland at East Kilbride and Cumbernauld, in response to the need to rehouse people from Glasgow. It was not until the 1960s that the phenomenon was extended to the provinces with the designation of Aycliffe and Cwmbran, where there was existing employment, and at Peterlee and Glenrothes, where they were to be the urban nucleus for alternative employment in areas of declining coal-mining activity. In the third stage of growth, new towns were designated at Redditch in the West Midlands, Skelmersdale and Runcorn in south Lancashire, and Washington in the north-east in order to ease problems of increasingly acute urban congestion.[14]

Population growth projections in the 1960s provided the impetus for further new towns at Northampton, Peterborough, Warrington, Milton Keynes and the Central Lancashire New Town. One such urban centre was Telford in Shropshire, which was originally planned for a population of 250,000 but which had reached less than half that figure by 1981 and is now planned to expand to only 150,000. With the exception of Washington in County Durham, few of the modern towns seem likely to reach their projected targets.

There is little doubt that in other respects many have been successful. Milton Keynes, for example, a London overspill site half-way between Oxford and Cambridge, has been successful in generating large numbers of new jobs, rather than simply transferring existing opportunities, and its expansion has been rapid. The reasons for its success are straightforward. First, there is a public body especially established to develop employment opportunities in the town. Second, there is evidence that the labour market is an attractive one for employers because of its stability, which is due largely to the fact that the incoming population is in the young family stage of its development and thus concerned to retain its economic viability. Third, public housing at reasonable prices is readily available, which helps to foster a contented and stable workforce. Finally, location of the site, peripheral to Greater London but with ready access to services and transport, is attractive to industry, commerce and the workforce because it is relatively cheap and free of pollution and congestion.

It is probably the locational advantage of proximity to the London basin which accounts for much of the recent success of Corby, which was designated a development area after the collapse of what was the virtual monopoly employer, British Steel. Promoting the message that 'Corby Works', the Commission was able to reduce the unemployment rate from 25 per cent to 17 per cent with the introduction of 150 new factories with about 150,000 square metres of building and some 5,000 new jobs.[15] The co-operation between the existing local authority and the Commission is evident in the vigorous advertising policy which was successfully pursued. In the north-east, however, Aycliffe, Peterlee and Washington suffer from levels of unemployment reflecting the deep economic crisis which has afflicted that part of the country. The same is true of Irvine in Scotland, where during the 1970s a number of large employers in the chemical and engineering industries closed and the unemployment rate reached 25 per cent. Much interest has been shown by foreign high-technology industries, although many of the jobs offered are for unskilled or semi-skilled workers. However, about 85 per cent of new foreign investment in Scotland is in the new towns and they therefore constitute Scotland's major growth points. East Kilbride, in spite of its problems, is the most successful and continues to show an annual profit for the Commission.[16]

Changes in attitude to the new towns

The new towns were developed in the first instance as a State activity because they were part of a general policy response towards problems of population and industrial location which could be adequately handled only at national level. In the immediate post-war years State-inspired urban development was both politically acceptable and economically appropriate. In addition, a degree of social engineering could be incorporated in the planning philosophy which might help solve some of the social problems. A central government initiative was required because with the exception of London, where the problems of congestion were already acute, most local administrations were more concerned to deal with the problems of reconstruction as a result of the war.

Perhaps it is not surprising that 30 years later there was a noticeable change in attitude. In the first place, there has been a considerable downward revision of the population projections which initially boosted the need for new initiatives in urban development. The concept of the new town is less interesting both to the authorities, who used the idea to help solve urban problems in the past, and to central government, which had used it as a regional planning mechanism. In addition, the climate of political opinion has changed since the interventionist days of the 1940s, and the role of the State is now more severely circumscribed. This is particularly the case with respect to the notion that the State should be able to benefit financially from the developments that it sponsored, as it had done through the new town development corporations.

The end of the new towns?

In 1984 the New Towns and Urban Developments Act provided a mechanism for the winding up of the programme, the sale of the assets of the NTDCs and the end of the Commission for New Towns. The Act marked the end of a programme in which central government investment exceeded £3.7 billion, creating 340,000 new homes, 10.5 million square metres of factory space, 1.3 million square metres of office accommodation, about 6,500 shops, and many miles of roads, drains and other communal facilities for a total of about 850,000 people.

By 1984 the Commission had, as anticipated in 1947, already taken over from their development corporations a number of new towns in south-east England. It had raised about £360 million from the sale of industrial and commercial property, and £21 million in the towns themselves by selling houses to the tenants. Target dates for the sale of the assets of the remaining towns are likely in the late 1980s and 1990s. The Commission is committed to disposing of the assets at a fair market price and in maximising returns to its investors. It is also committed to maintaining the existing social patterns of tenure and to preventing large-scale ownership by private landlords. Clearly the Commission must balance the interests of taxpayers and ratepayers with the welfare of those who live and work in the community.[17] Much of the disposal of the assets of the new town development corporations is expected to be to local authorities. However, difficulties of transfer from appointed to elected bodies will be small in comparison with the problems many authorities fear they will inherit in new towns, where the original housing stock is already in serious need of renovation.

Urban development corporations

While the new town development corporations appear to have served their purposes, and are coming to the end of their projected life-span, the ideas which they represent, particularly those of collaboration between public and private sectors, continue to be investigated but are not dealt with by the Urban Development Corporations, for which the NTDCs have provided the model.

The UDCs were established under the Local Government Planning and Land Act 1980 with wide-ranging powers to tackle the problems generated in the London and Merseyside Dockland areas by the shift in national trading relationships and the changes in mode of transport and in the nature of cargo-handling. These changes had resulted in under-used port-facilities and derelict land and buildings, and in a general decline in environmental quality and social life in those areas. The role of the UDC is to take measures to revitalise these areas by encouraging new uses for the buildings and docks, improving and renovating the physical environment, and providing new housing and social infrastructure. To that end the UDC can acquire, hold, manage, reclaim and dispose of land and other property and can carry out building and other measures. It is expected that these measures will attract new commercial and industrial users to the docklands, providing employment opportunities, and that people will be encouraged to move back to the docklands because both homes and work will be found there.

A number of developments have taken place both in London and in Liverpool. Converted and refurbished warehouses have found new uses as offices, shops and small industrial premises, and there are plans for residential occupation also. New functions in the docklands include recreational and leisure activities and the site for a new airport – with obvious advantages of proximity to the centre of London.

UDCs form a part of the Urban Programme Measures introduced since 1980 (see p. 132) and, while not without their critics, they have been seen as generally successful within a limited local context. In 1987 five additional UDCs were established – Trafford Park, Cardiff Bay, Black Country, Teeside, and Tyne and Wear – and it is possible that more will be created in the future. Although some councils have been concerned that UDCs effectively bypass local government, the Conservative Government sees them as a way of combating the problems of industrial change and urban decay.

Notes

1. *People in Britain: A Census Atlas*, Census Research Department, University of Durham with OPCS and General Register Office Scotland (1980), p. 18.
2. *UK Monograph on the Human Settlements Situation and Related Trends and Policies*, UN Economic Commission for Europe, Committee on Building and Planning (DoE, 1982).
3. Land use is fully discussed in M. L. Parry, 'The Changing Use of Land' in R. J. Johnston and J. C. Doornkamp (eds.), *The Changing Geography of the United Kingdom* (Methuen, 1982), Ch. 2.
4. H. Elcock, *Local Government* (Methuen, 1982), Ch. 9.
5. L. Allison, *Environmental Planning: A Political and Philosophical Analysis* (Allen and Unwin, 1975).

6. *Report of the Committee on Land Utilisation in Rural Areas* (Scott Committee), Cmnd 6378, Ministry of Works and Planning (HMSO, 1942).
7. Planning permission is not required for agricultural buildings which do not exceed 465 sq m in floor area and 12 m in height, and which are more than 25 m from the nearest highway.
8. The form of the plan, information to be included and symbolism to be used in the preparation and illustration of development plans at each scale are laid down in *Development Plans: A Manual on Form and Content*, Ministry of Housing and Local Government and Welsh Office. Interesting information about the way large-scale planning applications are to be considered is contained in *A Manual for the Assessment of Major Development Proposals*, B. D. Clark *et al.*, DoE (HMSO, 1981).
9. *People and Planning*, Report of the Committee on Public Participation in Planning (Chairman A. M. Skeffington MP), Ministry of Housing and Local Government, Scottish Development Department and Welsh Office (HMSO, 1969). The principal recommendations of the Skeffington Report were as follows:
    1. People should be informed throughout the preparation of a structure or local plan for their area, using many methods including the press and broadcasting.
    2. There should be an initial public statement with a calendar.
    3. Continuous consideration should be given to representations, especially over the presentation of choices and in the presentation of proposals.
    4. There should be an opportunity for meetings and the establishment of discussion forum.
    5. Publicity should be disseminated to both people and groups so that they can participate.
    6. Community development officers should be appointed.
    7. The public should be informed of the reasons for decisions.
    8. More information about the nature of the planning process should be available.
10. *Garden Cities and Satellite Towns*, Report of a Departmental Committee (Chairman The Lord Marley), Ministry of Health (HMSO, 1935). The brief of the Marley Committee was to examine the experience already gained in regard to the establishment of garden cities and villages, and satellite towns and to make recommendations as to the following:
    1. The steps, if any, which should be taken by government or local authorities to extend the provision of such cities, villages and satellite towns.
    2. In particular, how the location of industries in them can be stimulated.
    3. The question of finance and local government connected with their establishment.
    4. What further measures, if any, can and should be taken for securing that in the extension of existing towns, industrial, residential and other development are properly correlated.
11. *Distribution of the Industrial Population*, Report of the Royal Commission (Chairman The Rt. Hon. Sir Montague Barlow KBE, LL D), Cmnd 6153 (HMSO, 1940).
12. *Greater London Plan*, Report of the Working Party (Chairman Sir Peter Abercrombie), Ministry of Town and Country Planning (HMSO, 1944).
13. J. H. Nicholson, *New Communities in Britain* (National Council for Social Services, 1961).
14. S. Potter and R. Thomas, *The New Town Experience*, Urban Change and Conflict, State Intervention II (Open University Press, 1982).
15. *The Times*, Special Report on Corby, September 1983.
16. *The Observer*, 30 June 1985, on Irvine New Town.
17. *The Times*, 17, 18, 19, 20 December 1984.

5

NEEDS, RESOURCES AND POLICY

The main purpose of local government is to provide a range of public services to the local area – services which are provided *for* the community as well as *to* the community. It is the aim of this chapter to consider the principal determinants of service levels and the ways they are modified both locally and by the influence of central government. The chapter builds upon the description of the social characteristics and physical environment of the local community and considers how some of these characteristics affect the level of service provision by local government. First, client-group, demand-based and financial determinants of service levels are considered. A discussion of the mechanisms for the allocation of central government financial resources to local areas and the role of indicators is followed by a description of contemporary systems of raising local revenue and possible alternatives to the rating system. The constraints upon local spending, and therefore upon local service provision, are considered with a special emphasis upon the influence of central government policy. This is exemplified in the important fields of housing, transport, planning and regional policy, although the same determinants affect most of the other services and functions of local government.

ASSESSMENT OF NEEDS

In providing for the needs of the community local government has to gauge accurately what is required as well as what resources are available. Need in this context is usually identified with service provision, while resources, though they may be manpower, plant, or land, are seldom divorced from finance. While assessment of the need for a service is important in the first instance, crucial questions are always 'how much will it cost' and 'to what other purpose might the money be spent?'. The local need for a service can be determined in many ways, but the two main bases of assessment are by 'client-group' and 'demand'. They are often identified separately as distinct and exclusive methods but in practice need-assessment is likely to be derived from a number of different sources and using a variety of methods.

Client-group assessment

Client-group assessment of need is based upon an estimate of the number of people (the client-group) for whom a council is obliged to provide a service or who are likely to need a service. By far the most important of services planned in this way is the education service. It is perhaps also the one in which it is easiest to see the operation of client-group-based assessment of need. Since all children must attend school, it is the duty of the local council to provide sufficient places for the children in its area. At the most fundamental level, therefore, the size of the client group should determine the number of school places available. In detail, the client-group will be subdivided in various ways, certainly into different age ranges and probably also in terms of special needs. The overall service level necessary can, however, be defined quite closely and changes identified fairly quickly, though accommodating the changes may be more difficult. Most people who need home-help services are elderly so the number of home-helps required can be determined by counting the number of elderly people in the local population, although the relationship between numbers and need cannot be defined so closely as it can for education. It appears, for example, that local areas might need about 9 home-helps for every 1000 of the population aged 65 or more. Such a widely based, global average can conceal considerable variation in need among different client-groups. Those who cannot supplement their pensions with additional earnings, for example, are likely to have higher levels of need than others, and the chronically sick or disabled clearly need more assistance than the able-bodied. It would also be unusual to find precisely the same requirement in different parts of the country. Some locations have large elderly populations, living independent of their families, while others retain a close-knit and supportive family structure. In Greater Manchester, for example, the annual number of home-help contact hours in each district varies between 21,142 and 12,673 per thousand of the population aged 65 or over, while in Richmond-upon-Thames the figure was 6,723 hours and in Hackney 28,901.

The client group is also a major determinant of need in other areas of local government service provision. The need for a waste-collection, for example, is obvious and the extent of the need can be fairly accurately assessed by a local council simply by reference to the numbers of households to be served and the number of people included. Much greater complexity is introduced, however, when the detailed definition of the service is attempted. Clearly the need will be influenced by the characteristics of the local area and population. City centre refuse is different in nature to that in the residential suburbs, and more frequent collection may be required in some areas than in others. Service efficiency also may be involved in the decision, since client-need may be best served by, say, a weekly collection service whereas operational efficiency might be most readily satisfied by a two-weekly collection cycle. Such differences can easily be identified in the case of the rural areas where distance is an important factor affecting cost, and a less frequent service may, therefore, be most desirable from the council's point of view. Nevertheless, as an approximation, and given the possibility of technical refinement, a client-group definition might be adequate. This approach remains one of the principal methods of need-determination.

Demand-based assessment

The need for a service may also be determined by demand. Demand can be measured a number of ways. It can be determined by reference to the number of legitimate applications for the service or it may be gauged by measuring direct usage of a service or facility. Additionally, it may be indicated where direct lobbying of councillors indicates an unfulfilled need. Demand-based assessment of need is used in a variety of contexts where there is choice as to the level of service to be offered and also where there is difficulty in quantifying the size of a client-group.

Clearly the provision of recreational facilities such as swimming pools or sports centres, is based in part upon what local councils perceive as being 'a good thing'. Such 'good things' reflect local cultural values, political ideals and expediency, but they are also provided as a result of demand identified and sustained in the ways indicated above. While some of the demand for services such as children's playgrounds and recreational areas is difficult to quantify, for others, where revenues are expected to meet costs, demand must be accurately assessed.

There are a number of shortcomings associated with demand-based assessment, particularly when it is used to define levels of service for minority or disadvantaged groups:

1. Demand-based assessment of need assumes appropriate knowledge on the part of the potential clients, not simply knowledge of the existence and nature of the service, but also recognition of their need for it. This is a particular problem in the case of services for client-groups such as the mentally-impaired who may be considered incapable of making their own decisions.
2. It assumes the physical ability to go to the appropriate office and complete the correct forms.
3. There may be problems associated with indirect factors such as: the location of administrative offices in relation to the home of the client; the relationship of the client with the social and medical services which often provide the initial impetus for an application (and perhaps the expertise to carry it through); the income level of the applicant which can sometimes be an important factor because, for example, it will determine mobility.

Clearly, many services levels are decided by a mixture of client-based and demand-based assessment. The Home Office will suggest, for example, a level of police or fire service provision appropriate to the local area which is based essentially on quantifiable characteristics of the population and physical environment – a client-based assessment – although the actual manpower requirement will be modified by the observed levels of crime or fire hazard – a demand criterion. Ultimately, of course, the extent to which any of the services can be provided depends upon the financial resources available to pay for them.

Financial determinants

Neither need defined by provider nor need defined by recipient are in themselves adequate and are often used in conjunction with each other. In practice, however, resources seldom seem to be adequate to meet all of the demands, however they are determined. The level of provision is more often decided, therefore, by the relative strength of a particular service when measured in competition with other services for scarce financial resources. Decisions about these priorities are essentially value-judgements which are made by politicians. They are the substance of debate throughout the year, but especially in the weeks preceding the annual budget, when the most important decisions about the identification of priorities and, therefore, the allocation of funds, are made.

DEFINING FINANCIAL RESOURCES[2]

The annual budget fixes the level of spending for the financial year and thus determines a major part of the resources available to the authority. Local financial resources comprise essentially three elements:

1. That which is provided from central government funds.
2. That which is raised through the rating system, and which is dependent upon the rateable value of property in the district.
3. That which is raised from commercial and service activities.

This last category is the least important financially. It consists of revenues from commercial activities and the provision of services, such as the admission charges for swimming pools or recreation centres. It includes housing and other rents, and school meals charges. Some of the charges are discretionary and the council can decide its own scales, but they are clearly influenced by local political policy, market forces where there may be competition, and by reference to national rates or levels. In some cases a prescribed level may be set by government. The level of income which can be generated by these activities varies considerably and is heavily dependent upon the economic characteristics of the local area.

Local authorities can also raise funds through the sale of assets, and in recent years they have been encouraged to try to sell council houses. They are also empowered to borrow money in the money market from both private and public sources, but this power is heavily circumscribed, permission being required of the responsible minister. The more important sources of finance are central grants and rates incomes; the general budgetary process is illustrated in Fig. 5.1.

Central government contributions

The total amount of grant-aid provided by central government is determined by: national economic policy; policy with regard to local autonomy; political expediency; and by the representations of the local authorities themselves. The level of central government support for local spending is also partly a reflection of the political power of the responsible minister, the Secretary of State for the Environment, since financial support to local government is but one area of central government spending and the DoE must compete with other so-called 'spending departments' for limited national financial resources.

The total amount of local government spending is known as 'Relevant Current Expenditure'; in 1984/85 it totalled about £20,345 million.[3] About 52 per cent of that was provided from central resources. This sum

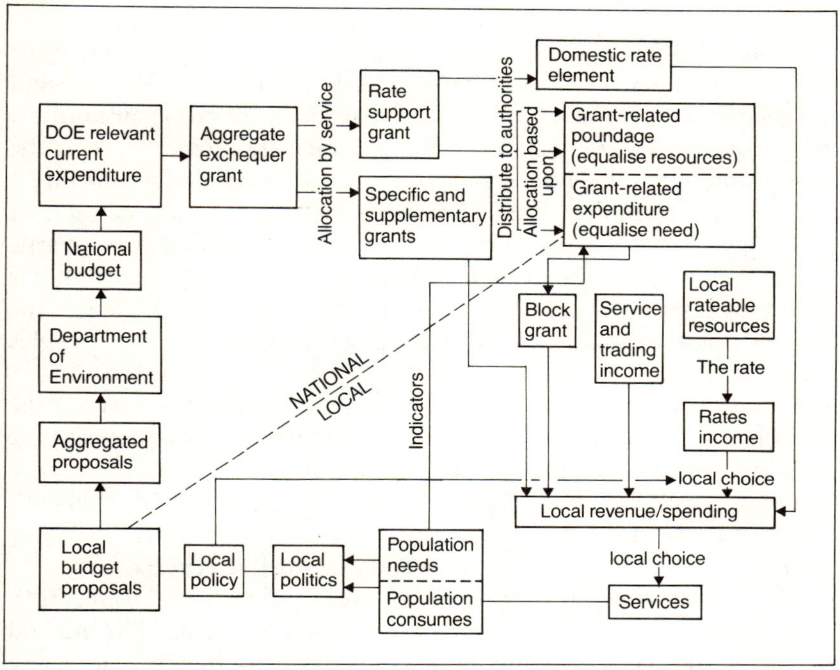

Fig. 5.1 Local government finance schematic flow-chart

is known as the 'Aggregate Exchequer Grant'. When the grant is determined, central government also makes a provisional allocation of expenditure by service, so for 1984/85 the amount allocated to education, for example, was £9,533 million, and for personal social services about £328 million.

The Aggregate Exchequer Grant comprises three parts:

1. Specific grants, which are provided to meet a part of the cost of particular services or projects. The largest of these is in aid of the police service, but it also includes civil defence, the urban programme and derelict land grants.

2. Supplementary grants, which are paid in support of transport and national parks.

3. The Rate Support Grant (RSG) is that which remains from the total exchequer grant after the specific and supplementary grants have been deducted and from which all local authority services can benefit.

Rate support grant

Aggregate RSG (i.e. the total sum before it is distributed to each of the authorities) is made up of two parts – the domestic rate relief grant and the block grant. Domestic rate relief is payable to all rating authorities. It was originally established in 1967 in anticipation of changes in the rating system (which did not occur). Its function is to reduce the direct rating levied upon most domestic properties by a certain fixed rate. In 1984/85 it was 18.5 pence in the pound, as it had been for some years.

Once the basis for the grand total by service has been determined, it is then necessary to allocate the total to each authority. Although the methodology of the allocation has changed in recent years, its principles remain the same.

Formerly, the grant was made in two separate parts. The first was the so-called 'resources element', the function of which was to equalise the rateable resources available to each authority by bringing them to a 'national rateable value per head'. The second was the 'needs element', which was designed to compensate for variations in local needs as defined by a number of measurable and quantifiable criteria.

The block grant system replaced the needs and resources elements in 1981 with a single grant based upon similar requirements. The method of calculating block grant for each authority should result in its being able to provide standards of service comparable to other authorities assuming it levied a similar rate in the pound. The block grant is not earmarked for spending on particular services and each authority is free to decide, within certain limits, how it will spend its grant on the services it provides. It thus retains the right to determine its own priorities.

Grant-related expenditure (GRE)

The grant is distributed among local authorities by reference to an assessment of the costs to each authority of providing a common level of service after allowing for the wide variation in the characteristics and needs of the different areas. That variation is taken into account by calculating the amount of grant-related expenditure, or spending need required to meet a defined level of service in each authority. It is determined by the cost of providing the service to each of the clients who may be deemed to be in need of it, or for each unit of service which is required. These local parameters are adjusted to take account of secondary factors affecting service provision, especially such considerations as low population density, which can result in a higher cost of transport, and lower productivity or multiple deprivation.

Grant-related poundage (GRP)

Since rateable resources vary among authorities, there is a difference in the burden borne by ratepayers in different localities in order to meet the costs of the standard level of service implied by GRE. For each class of authority a grant-related poundage is calculated which assumes that the same rate in the pound is raised for spending at GRE in each authority. The amount of block grant to be paid is the difference between an authority's total expenditure and the yield of GRP from the authority's rateable value.

Service and population indicators

Direct assessment of projected need is not always possible, so indirect indicators such as the proportion of the elderly in the population have to be substituted in the calculation of the GRE. There are altogether about 58 indicators currently in use, and they fall into five categories:[4]

1. Those which describe the population, including the total number resident in each authority and their structural subdivisions.
2. The physical characteristics of the area are described using 15 indicators which include measures of settlement density, sparseness of school population, allocations related to the length and character-istics of the local road network, and commercial, residential and property development rates.
3. Social and environmental needs are assessed under nine headings, and here the multivariate character of social problems is recognised, since a number of indicators are composites which include physical accommodation quality, socio-economic and ethnic status, and need defined by measurement of supplementary benefit receipts. Other indicators in this group measure total and youth unemployment.
4. In some parts of the country, notably in London, the costs of providing services are particularly high. 'London Weighting' for salaries in education, for example, is an addition to the wages bill, and there are two indicators which are intended to take account of high costs.
5. The final category of indicators recognises the special requirements of particular services. Three of these indicators are related to the cost of police, probation and judicial provision, and are measures of criminal and illegal activity in the community. Fire risks and occurrences are measured, as are the actual expenditures in several areas in which the authority has only agency control and therefore little discretion. This includes such expenditure as that incurred over mandatory student grants, rates rebates and land drainage.

A further series of indicators measures strictly financial needs such as the debt charges generated by capital expenditure in transport or education, and the housing revenue account. Complex indicators are used to estimate needs for personal social services such as those for the elderly, children and young people, with services such as residential care, day centres and fostering.

In many cases, the actual values represented by the indicators and used in the calculation for the rate support grant are modified by multipliers, the effect of which is to increase or decrease the numerical value of that particular measure and thus to alter its value in the overall weighting of the value of GRE and the block grant. They are calculated for each class of authority and have the effect of changing the broad direction of financial outlay from central government.

The indicators are themselves combined in various ways to provide the assessment for the different services. For example, grant-related expenditure for refuse disposal, the responsibility of the county councils and the former GLC, was in 1984/85 assigned on the basis of a composite indicator made up in the following way: 42 per cent of the value was determined from total population, 55 per cent from density of settlement and 3 per cent from higher costs in and around London. By comparison, refuse collection, which is a function of the district councils, was allocated principally by reference to the number of domestic properties. That accounted for 78 per cent of the value of the composite, density of settlement was 18 per cent, area 2 per cent, and the additional 2 per cent for higher-cost areas. The cost of collecting commercial and industrial waste is assumed to be met by charges, so the number of such premises is not included and the relative importance of these factors is calculated by reference to statistical cost patterns in the local authorities.

Importance of the indicators

The indicators used by central government are very important because they are used to determine not only the assessment of expenditure likely in each of the services but also the relative distribution of the block grant to each local authority. The number, nature and weighting of the indicators can materially affect both central government disbursements to a local authority and, through the relationship between GRE and grant-related poundage, the weight or proportion of expenditure which can be borne locally and financed through the rates. In its turn, in a period of overall restraint in public expenditure, and when individual local authorities are being limited in the amount of money they can raise locally (rate-capping), it can doubly influence the level of expenditure which the authority can contemplate. It is therefore important to each authority that the indicators which are crucial in determining its own pattern of need, demand and expenditure should be accurate, so that appropriate weight can be given to that area and a fair share of central financial resources be assured.

Locally raised funds: the rates

The rating system

The rating system is based upon an assessement of the rental value of property called its rateable value. The aggregated rateable values of all rated property in a district form the locally available tax base. It may amount to a sum of, say, £500,000. If local projected spending for the financial year is £2 million, central government grants are expected to total £1 million, and £250,000 will be raised from commercial and trading activities, then the local rate must be set at 150p in the pound in order to raise the £750,000 required to balance the budget.

As a form of local tax it has developed from the Tudor Poor Relief Acts of the seventeenth century. The Poor Law, as it became known, was intended to oblige local parishes to look after their own poor and it provided them with a means to do so by raising a household tax. By the middle of the nineteenth century the notion of local provision of services was well established and the principle of local taxation laid. The 'rates' were developed as a refinement of the Poor Law, and the emphasis was placed upon the occupation and use of property rather than its owner-ship. Indeed, by modern definition occupation for rating purposes has to be 'beneficial' – conferring some sort of advantage, convenience or financial gain on the occupier. The tax is raised upon the value of the property in that context and the underlying principle for the tax is the value of 'the rent at which the premises might reasonably be expected to be let, if the landlord were responsible for repairing and insuring the property, and the tenant for the usual tenants rates and taxes'.[5]

Valuation

The valuation of property is the function of the District Valuation Officer, a civil servant employed by the Inland Revenue whose role is to assess the rental value of the property and to prepare a valuation list. Rental values for property are affected by a large number of factors, including the size, services and facilities of the property itself, together with the use to which it is to be put. The quality of the surrounding environment is particularly important for residential property and increasingly so for industrial and commercial users, as is proximity to valued services and facilities such as shops, schools and recreational facilities. Those factors which affect the rental value will therefore influence the rating valuation.

Since valuation is based upon assumed rent, the persons liable to pay rates are therefore those who occupy property rather than those who own it. By implication there should be no liability for rates on property which remains empty or unoccupied. Such properties still have a potential rental value, however, and in the 1960s and 1970s in particular commercial property increased in capital value while remaining unoccupied and without contributing to the rates. This was considered to be unsatisfactory and therefore the General Rate Act 1967 and Local Government Act 1974 gave rating authorities discretionary powers to levy an empty rate after a property had been unoccupied for a continuous period of three months or, if it was a new dwelling, six months. In this way potential revenue from empty property could be realised and there was a disincentive for owners of property to allow it to remain unoccupied.

A number of categories of land and property use are exempted from liability for rates. These include property owned or rented by the Crown, such as government offices, and land and property of the armed services, courts, royal parks and palaces. However, the Treasury does make a contribution in lieu of rates based upon a rateable value. Agricultural lands and buildings were exempted or derated in the 1929 Local Government Act, and churches and other buildings used exclusively for religious purposes have no liability so long as they remain in sole religious use. Mandatory and discretionary relief may be extended to philanthropic, charitable or religious organisations, or where they are clubs or societies which do not exist to make a profit. Voluntary schools fall into this category and are thus entitled to 50 per cent mandatory relief, while local authority schools must pay in full since local authorities are not charities. Local authorities' parks and open spaces are exempt if public access is free and unrestricted, as are police properties although some police authorities do make payments in lieu. Other exemptions may be made – for example, for property occupied by the disabled.

Methods of valuation

There are a number of recognised methods by which the rateable value of a property can be assessed.[6]

The *rentals method* can be applied to both domestic dwellings and commercial premises such as shops, offices and banks. Rates are calculated by reference to actual rental charges. The *contractors test* is also known as the structural method. It is more complicated than the rentals method, depending upon a calculation of the rental value represented by the interest which the occupiers could have obtained if they were able to invest a sum equivalent to the capital value of the property. It is often used to assess the rateable value of large-site, non-residential properties such as large-scale plant, sewage works and public utilities. The third method is known as the *profits test*. It is used in the assessment of some public utilities, theatres and petrol stations. As the name implies an attempt is made to calculate a notional 'profit' from the accounts of the business. The 'profit' is the residue after normal business expenses and profit have been deducted from the income of the business. Many sites and properties, especially those of the nationalised industries, cannot be satisfactorily rated by any of these methods and so for them a *formula assessment* is applied. This is a political compromise rather than a true attempt to establish a real value, although a basic rateable value is calculated by the DoE and fixed after negotiation. The figure is varied by size of industry and is distributed among the local rating authorities as fairly as possible with respect to authorities with major assets of that industry in their area. Formulae assessments are also made for schools based upon the capital cost of each pupil-place.

Variation in rates

Underlying all the methods of assessment of the value of property is the notion of rent, and rent is intimately linked to site characteristics and location. It follows, therefore, that there will be intrinsic differences in the basic value of land and property available within any given local rating area. Apart from any other consideration, there is the problem that revaluations have not been regularly carried out so that the reassessment of older houses and those with improvements affecting their rateable value have not kept in step with the assessment of the value of newly built property. Areas with a large proportion of newer buildings will therefore have a higher overall rateable value than those with older property, although it might naturally be assumed that such new property would in any case command a higher notional rental.

Not surprisingly, there is some variation in rateable value per capita. In Newcastle upon Tyne, for example, it is about £218, while in Leeds it is £157. There is also a large difference between average domestic rates bills, which is probably more significant. In the Inner London boroughs it is about £520 per hereditament, while in the shire counties it is £270. The average domestic ratepayer pays only £184 in the Welsh district councils. The proportion of total rate income derived from each sector (domestic, commercial, industrial) also varies considerably (Fig. 5.2). In spite of the operation of the block grant system of resource allocation

London Inner Boroughs

19%
33%
3%
45%

London Outer Boroughs

12%
10%
55%
23%

England

Metropolitan areas

15%
13%
50%
22%

Non-metropolitan areas

16%
11%
54%
20%

Local examples

Rother

9%
3%
13%
75%

Tewkesbury

15%
8%
40%
37%

Teesdale

32%
48%
9%
11%

Knowsley

12%
27%
48%
13%

Domestic   Industrial

Commercial   Other

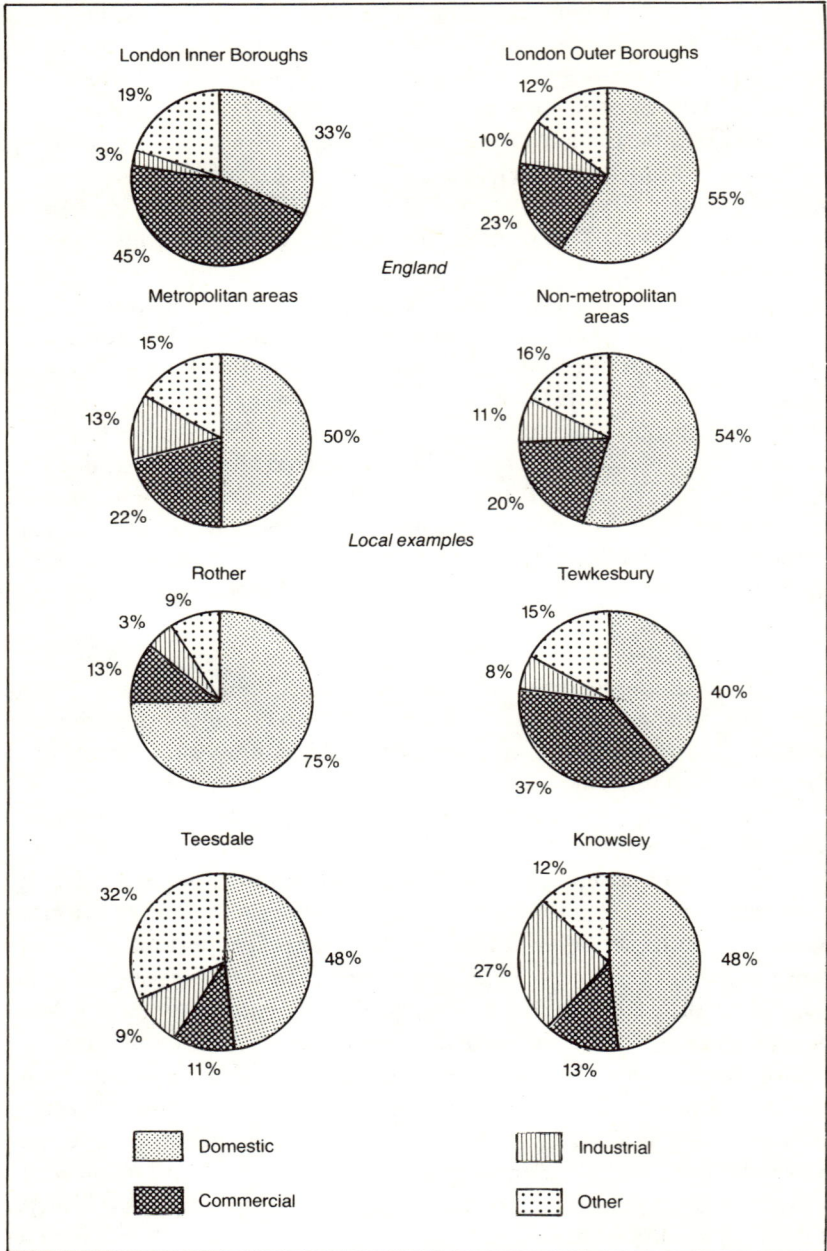

Fig. 5.2 Percentage distribution of rateable value
Source: *Local Government Comparative Statistics 1985* CIPFA

there are anomalies not accounted for simply by the spending patterns of local councils.

Alternatives to rates and changes in local government finance

As we have seen, the system by which local revenue is raised to contribute to the overall budget of councils is a complex one, and for a number of years it has been criticised.[7] The criticisms have been varied according to their source and different suggestions have been made as to changes that ought to be introduced. The criticisms that have been brought to bear can be summarised as follows:

1. It is not clear whether the general public regards rates as a form of taxation or a charge for locally provided services. This leads to misunderstanding of the basic rationale for the payment, which in itself is unsettling for the ratepayer.

2. Rates are a tax upon the occupation of property rather than its ownership and therefore mere possession can result in a capital gain in the value of the property without any contribution to local costs.

3. Rates are a notional or nominal tax, the relationship to any objective measure is difficult to determine.

4. Rateable values vary considerably both between local areas and within them leading to a sense of injustice amongst some sections of the ratepaying electorate.

5. The true rateable value of some property may be concealed as improvements to it take place; this results in inequities in charges.

6. Revaluation is expensive, infrequent and nominal, allowing room for further inequity to creep in.

7. The technical basis of the system is at best only imperfectly understood by those who pay; payment without understanding is undesirable.

8. Valuation relies to an extent upon the judgement of the valuation officer and is thus subjective and may be inappropriate.

9. The tax is one on property but is essentially used to finance personal services, so there is a mismatch between purpose and derivation.

10. As a tax the rates are not related to ability to pay and it can be argued that the burden falls most heavily on those who can least afford it, either because their income is low or because there is but a single income in the household.

11. Equally it can be said that the political responsibility for local government policy is mismatched with those who share the financial responsibility because few pay rates while many are eligible to vote.

12. Changes in patterns of economic life have left an imbalance in the

burden of taxation between domestic ratepayers and non-domestic ratepayers.

13. Inequalities in the burden of rates exist between ratepayers who are single people living alone in a house and the same sort of house in which there may be several wage-earners.

These criticisms have led successive administrations to consider alternatives to the present system. In 1976 the Layfield Committee reported that there was no acceptable alternative to the rates although local income taxes might provide an additional source of revenue. In 1981 the question was again reviewed in a Green Paper *Alternatives to Domestic Rates* (Cmnd 8449) and proposals put forward two years later in a White Paper *Rates* (Cmnd 9008).

In 1986 the Government finally published proposals for changes in the way local finance was raised and in the way central government contributions should be calculated. The 1986 Green Paper *Paying for Local Government* (Cmnd 9714)[8] first differentiated between domestic and non-domestic ratepayers and made a case for the two to be treated separately so as to remove from non-domestic ratepayers the 'distortion of their business competitiveness' that arose simply because of the accident of their location in one authority rather than another. For the domestic ratepayer it set out three criteria which should be met by any new tax:

1. Is it technically adequate?
2. Is it fair?
3. Does it encourage local democratic accountability?

After examining briefly the case for existing domestic rates, and the alternatives of local sales tax and local income tax, the paper came down in favour of a poll tax, or flat-rate charge on all adults, to be called the Community Charge.

The proposed changes

1. *Non-domestic ratepayers*.   The Green Paper suggests that for non-domestic ratepayers a uniform rate in the pound would be set by central government, the proceeds to be pooled and redistributed to all authorities in relation to the size of their adult population. Local councils might also retain the discretion to levy a small non-domestic rate themselves. Since non-domestic rates account for more than 50 per cent of the total rates income, this proposal would clearly operate to the detriment of authorities with larger proportions of young people because of the importance of education in local budgets.

2. *Domestic ratepayers*.   It is proposed that domestic rates be phased out over a ten-year period, to be replaced by a poll tax. The Community

Charge would be the same for all adults in the local area, but would differ between areas. Local expenditure beyond that anticipated by central government would have to be borne by an increased local Community Charge rate.

3. *Central government contributions.* These would comprise a standard grant paid to all authorities as a common amount per adult, together with a needs grant which would compensate for differences in spending between local authorities to meet local needs. The method of assessing needs would be made more simple than it is currently.

While meeting many of the criticisms of the existing rating system for domestic ratepayers, a poll tax or Community Charge is in many ways itself imperfect. Not least of the problems is that the Charge will probably require the creation of a register of adults, which might be difficult to maintain because of population migration. Many people will be able to avoid the Charge altogether by moving, and there are some whose occupations keep them mobile and whose Charge will therefore be difficult to relate to a particular area. Under the existing system, right to a service in a particular locality may be established by a residence qualification; in the future we may have to show that we have registered for Community Charge.

SPENDING AND SERVICES

Irrespective of the way in which funds are to be raised or the sources from which they come, there is a wide variation in the way in which they are spent. The average expenditure pattern for broad categories of local authority services is shown in Fig. 5.3. It can be seen that the largest single item is education, accounting for about a third of total expenditure, with housing and the police service some way behind.

Comparisons between the way each authority allocates its budget are difficult and can be misleading, but variations can be due to the level or quality of service provision, and to efficiency in the use of resources. They may also be due to differences in the social and economic characteristics, to the range of functions which are undertaken by the authority, to the range of manpower and other 'in-house' services available, and to regional variations in costs, e.g. in the price of food for school meals. There are also variations resulting from differences in methods of financing and accounting procedures, and in administrative needs. Some examples will illustrate the extent of variation.

Standards of street lighting are laid down by the DoE, but costs of maintaining street lighting will be different for different locations.

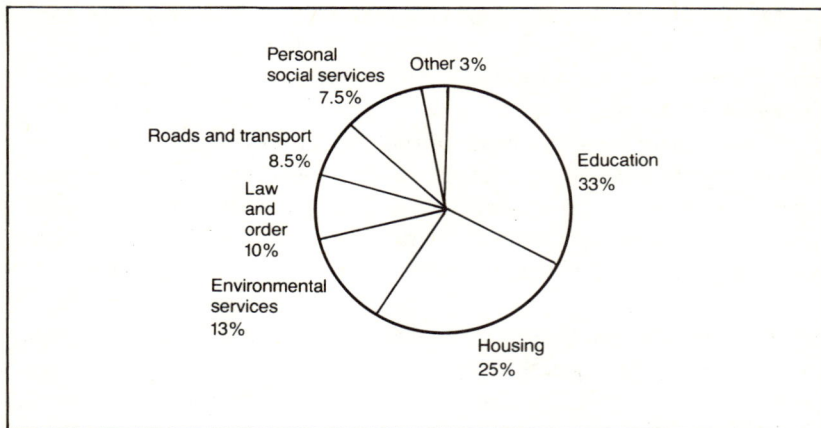

Fig. 5.3 Local authorities gross expenditure 1984/85 by sector
Source: *Paying for Local Government*, Cmnd 9714, HMSO, 1986

Expenditure in the former metropolitan counties varied between £1,122 per km in West Yorkshire and £1,701 per km in Merseyside. In Somerset the comparable figure was £336 and in Leicestershire £1,459.[9] Education is the major item of local spending, and there are numerous ways in which service provision and costs can be compared. In Doncaster more than 65 per cent of children under 5 attended nursery school but in the metropolitan district of Trafford in Greater Manchester it was less than 20 per cent. Not surprisingly, the rate of attendance in metropolitan areas is twice that in the shire counties. As might be expected given the close central government interest in educational spending, the costs of secondary education per pupil are similar in those two classes of authority. Refuse collection and disposal is one of the most important and visible of local authority functions and one which has received considerable attention as a candidate for privatisation. The cost and amount of waste collected are not constant. On average each of us produces about 0.3 tonnes of refuse a year, but within Derbyshire the people of Derby generate only half that amount while those in Bolsover produce about 50 per cent more. Finally, an example from the personal social service sector: it costs about £16,400 per annum to keep a child in a local council residential home in Tower Hamlets in London, but less than £12,700 in Hereford and Worcester, a predominantly rural area.

Constraints on local spending

Irrespective of the value of locally raised revenue, central government can impose considerable constraints on local authority spending. The constraints may be classified in the following ways:

1. The most fundamental is that local authorities exist by virtue of Acts of Parliament, and local authorities can be created or disestablished at the will of Parliament. It was central government, for example, which first created the metropolitan councils in 1972 and then abolished them in 1986.

2. Central government also defines many of the obligations of local councils both to the people and to land through parliamentary legislation.

3. The third group of constraints are financial. Central government is able to restrict local activity by limiting the amount of its financial contribution in a number of ways:

   (a) Although there is consultation with local authority associations, central government fixes the total amount of its contribution and can change it from year to year. In the 1980s there has been a deliberate relative downward trend in support for local spending, whereas in the 1960s and 1970s it increased both absolutely and relatively.

   (b) Central government may limit or change the direction of its funding through its control upon the definitions of the criteria by which the funds are disbursed. This method of control is less obvious than those we have so far discussed because it is hidden in the technicalities of the calculation of the GRE. It is thus apparent only to the specialist and leaves the voter often unaware that there has been a change. In particular, these changes have been used to alter the balance of money flowing towards the urban or rural parts of the country.

   (c) In recent years government has taken steps to limit the total amount of spending by any authority irrespective of the source of the income. This has been achieved by setting overall spending targets and progressively limiting the amount of central contribution to local spending if that spending exceeds the grant-related expenditure target. The 1984 Rates Act also enables the minister to limit the amount of money that an authority can collect from its rates, thus preventing an authority making up from the rates what it was losing from central funds. 'Rate-capping', as it is known, is selective and has been applied to a number of authorities where local expenditure is, in the view of central government, excessively high.

4. The final group of constraints are difficult to quantify and sometimes difficult to identify – but they underpin all the rest. They are constraints deriving from the political priorities of the government of the day. They may be classified under three headings: (a) ideological, (b) policy orientated and (c) electoral, although clearly they are connected with each other:

(a)   Ideologically based constraints are usually stated in very general terms and may even be encapsulated in slogans like 'more freedom – less government' or 'services for people not profit'. They set the climate within which the ruling political party will usually seek to operate, although that may change during the life of a Parliament. To that extent they colour the view which government may have of its relationship with local administrations.

(b)   Policy-orientated priorities are usually easier to identify. The Conservative administration has sought to reduce public expenditure since 1979 as one of the major elements of its economic strategy. This has resulted in a general attempt to reduce government spending at both local and central levels, thus changing the emphasis of the local/central relationship. This policy was initiated, although with different motivation, in 1975 by a Labour administration. One of the Liberal party's principal ideological tenets is that of bringing government closer to the people, a policy supportive of decentralisation. Thus one might expect, under a Liberal government, a shift in the balance of public spending away from Westminster and towards the city and county halls.

(c)   The third political constraint is electoral. Political parties must seek to gain or to retain power, and to do that they must sucessfully influence the electorate. At local level a major dilemma for a political party, and one which is likely to increase rather than decrease if the Community Charge is introduced in England and Wales, is whether maximum electoral benefit can be achieved by increasing service provision or by reducing costs. In part, of course, their views will be determined by whether they see their supporters as primarily consumers of local services or as the financers of them.

CENTRAL GOVERNMENT POLICY

One of the major constraints mentioned above is that the provision of services at local level is sometimes fundamental to central government policy, either because the services are strategically important in a national context, or because they form an issue of major public concern that affects central government. There are several examples of the way that central government's role and influence at local level has been of profound significance, both directly and indirectly, and these include the important areas of housing, transport and regional policy.

Housing

Housing is an issue of constant national interest and direct local involvement. Central government has enacted legislation, commissioned reports, suggested appropriate standards and developed policy affecting both public and private housing provision. It has operated through the local administration in the construction of houses in the public sector, and in the control of private building and planning.

Public housing has served five main functions for central government.[10]

1. Emergency housing was important in the late 1940s to meet what was an acute need for rented accommodation as a result of the war damage to the stock of housing available. The response was to produce what was to be the first age of system or factory-build homes, the 'prefabs'. Though small they were apparently durable, since they are still in use in some parts of the country. Although this type of central government intervention in the housing market was locally significant in the past it is unlikely to be so in the future.

2. General housing initiatives have been an underpinning of many government housing policies at least since the Housing Act of 1919. The relative importance of the idea has shifted, following the complexions of Conservative and Labour governments, from a general requirement to increase and improve housing stock to a determination to reduce the influence of the private landlord. Perhaps the most significant period was that from 1945 to 1967, although the Labour administration of 1964 did accept that owner-occupation would be the preferred mode for the majority of households.

3. The concept of public housing as welfare housing for those most in need or unable to provide for themselves, usually low-income families, has also been significant. It is a view often reinforced in the public mind by the fact that from time to time central government has subsidised public housing and local rents have not necessarily reflected economic costs. Early legislation on housing themes was exclusively directed at the needs of the poorer sections of the community, e.g. the Housing of the Working Classes Act of 1890. This Act and many other pieces of legislation promoted the improvement of living conditions for particular sectors of the community,

and provided local authorities with powers to assess housing standards in their areas, compulsorily purchase and clear unfit stock, and redevelop.

4. A fourth function of public housing lies in the need to facilitate redevelopment in existing urban areas. Such development may be seen as the replacement of housing stock rather than the rehousing of people. Policies essentially controlled by the replanning principle were important in the late 1930s, when large numbers of people were rehoused in low-density 'overspill' estates on the margins of many cities, as well as in high-density estates and sometimes in extensive blocks of flats on clearance sites. Central government financial assistance was severely restricted at the time of their building and clearance site redevelopment attracted the maximum amount of support. Similar restrictions lie behind the second major phase of slum clearance in the years between 1955 and 1962, when financial assistance for slum clearance was more readily available than for general public housing schemes or projects.

5. Finally, public housing may be seen essentially as a part of social service provision. Thus policy is directed towards particular social groups or households for which housing is a part of a wider problem, or to those who could be assisted through rehousing. Such groups include the temporarily homeless; those, such as the disabled, for whom suitably adapted private housing is difficult to find; and the very old, for whom sheltered housing with communal facilities might be necessary.

As noted above, central government policy decisions in this field are principally implemented by local governments because direct housing finance is disbursed to them. Policy is also pursued indirectly through various kinds of assistance to private householders, in which local government is an agency. Central government control of finance also enables it to influence the actions of individual authorities and to determine to a large extent the pattern of local provision of public housing. In addition, the central authority provides special departmental assistance to local housing authorities in the form of advisory groups such as the DoE's Urban Housing Renewal Unit, established to tackle the problem of run-down council estates, and the Housing Estates Priority Unit and Priority Estates Unit, which can offer management advice to local authorities. The aim of these units is to promote schemes for the refurbishment and disposal by sale of empty council properties or the establishment of local management committees for autonomous estates.

It is primarily through the Housing Grant element in the Rate

Support Grant that government policy is implemented; in 1984/85 this amounted to about £2,979 million, a decrease in real terms of about 55 per cent since 1979/80. Such a fall in expenditure has resulted in both a very considerable reduction in house-building in the public sector and a lack of routine maintenance, so that the quality of public housing stock is deteriorating. In England and Wales alone there are an estimated 450,000 unmodernised pre-war local authority dwellings. For many households in cities with large stocks of municipal housing the prospect of modernisation is remote. In Birmingham, where the rate of improvement is about 40 per year, it would take 600 years to clear the task. On the same basis Leeds would take some 40 years and Sheffield 18.

In spite of these problems, the 1981 National House Condition Survey found local authority housing to be in as good or better condition than owner-occupied stock.[11] In this sector government can also be directly influential. The recent imposition of value added tax of 15 per cent to building alterations raised the cost to the consumer and thus cut the amount of work undertaken, while reductions in the funding for improvement grants has also caused valuable work to go undone. Of great importance as well to the demand for housing in the private sector is the mortgage interest rate. It is tied to the Bank Rate and influenced by central government economic policy. Raising the rate will increase costs and limit demand for private houses, thus increasing demand in the public sector.

Public transport[12]

Central government intervention in transport has been multifaceted if one includes such aspects as control of safety and design requirements in transportation vehicles and systems, but there are two principal areas of importance to local authorities in which it is involved: the development of transport networks, especially the road and rail systems; and the control of operations, particularly by bus and air. However, there has never been an integrated transportation policy in which optimal systems or modes of transport were developed within a single framework for the whole of the United Kingdom. Indeed, there appear to be a number of occasions when central government policy for each of the modes of public transport has been in conflict.

In the development of networks, there have been two distinct policy characteristics. First, there is what might be called national network requirements. These are four principal arteries of communication linking the major centres of population and industry which focus mainly in England upon London and include and extend access to industrial areas, ports and airports. These links are principally by road and rail but include air transport and, increasingly, electronic communications. The development of the links is of great significance to both local and central government, and both have played major roles. Second, central government has had a primary role in controlling the use of the network, particularly the road system.

Road transport
The need to develop an integrated road system has been recognised at least since 1936, when about 4,500 miles of major roads were transferred from local to central government control because an efficient trunk road network could be planned effectively only at national level. But even before 1936, the Road Board, which was established in 1910, had been empowered to raise licence fees and excise duty on petrol in order to pay for grants to local highways authorities.[13] In the 1960s and 1970s the trunk road network was supplemented by a motorway system, centrally financed, and designed and built under the auspices of the Department of Transport (later the DoE) and its road construction units. After formal completion of the construction of these motorways, the responsibility for day-to-day operation and longer-term maintenance passed to the county authority in which they are to be found, as did that for the policing and controlling of the roads.

Not only is the network in itself important, but central government also has considerable powers to control the kind of vehicles using it. For 50 years, until 1980, public bus services on all routes were limited, controlled and co-ordinated under the Road Traffic Act 1930, which instituted a route licencing system operated by regional traffic commissioners. The rationale for this system is largely to be found in road safety considerations and the protection of the passenger, but it was also used to ensure services for those areas which due to their location might not be adequately serviced otherwise. Increasingly, bus operation over short-distance routes came to be regarded as a public service and thus the proper province of local government. Both central and local funds were used to subsidise the service. From 1974, passenger transport executives co-ordinated services by public transport bodies within large county and metropolitan areas. There has now been a change of central government policy. The Transport Act 1985, which came into force in 1986, introduced the deregulation of the bus services[14] so as to encourage private enterprise to compete for passengers without restriction and to eliminate the need for heavy subsidisation, which in 1983/84 amounted to a central government contribution of £450 million to transport operations through the Transport Supplementary Grant.

Railways

The privately owned and operated railway system in Britain, which had a network of some 20,000 miles and one of the densest services in the world, was nationalised in 1947 under the Transport Act of that year. By 1963 the system had become very uneconomic and with the publication of a major report *The Reshaping of British Rail*, plans were announced for the reduction of the network.[15] These resulted in a reduction in the route miles open for traffic from about 17,500 in 1962 to 11,300 in 1973.[16]

These reductions in the service were particularly unfortunate in rural areas where trains had often provided an alternative to road transport, and they were a source of some dismay to many local councils which saw parts of their territorial responsibility becoming more and more isolated and marginalised. Rail policy has been increasingly to provide fast, efficient and competitive services between the larger cities for passenger transport and to concentrate on bulk and large-volume traffic for freight. Since central government has continued to influence railway policy and to encourage more efficient operations, it has also had to recognise the need to support local lines on the margins of profitability on a public service basis via the subsidies provided to passenger transport executives through local government. Such direct involvement has resulted in a particularly strong lobby for the maintenance of a number of commuter lines throughout the country.

Air transport

Because of the small size of the country, air transport has never been a major factor in internal transport policy. However, it has become increasingly important to local areas in two ways: first, it can provide a very fast link to the capital and then on to international destinations; and second, provincial airports are seen as valuable local assets generating economic activity in their own right as they service holiday travel needs and provide improved accessibility for the business traveller and for the exporter of manufactured goods. Additionally, they may be seen as symbolic of local pride and aspirations, and an increasingly necessary part of the local and regional economic infrastructure. They are very expensive to maintain but are of such importance that collaborative arrangements between authorities are often necessary.

Central government effectively controls the provision of such services (a) through the control and regulation of the transport medium and its facilities by the Civil Aviation Authority and (b) by exercising strong influence on the siting and development of the airports themselves. Airports are not by their nature welcome neighbours, and planning applications for their development or extension may normally be expected to result in a public inquiry in which national interests will almost certainly be raised and about which there may be conflicts with local interests as represented by the local authority. Sometimes the authority itself might find it difficult to reconcile the twin needs of protecting the people it serves who live close to the airfield and those who need the service offered by the airfield. Airport traffic also generates and calls for additional road and rail facilities which may impose extra burdens at both levels of government.

Private transport and urban planning

In addition to the role of central government in developing and improving a national route network, central government transport policy has been significant in its effects upon local urban planning. Contemporary life has become increasingly dependent upon efficient communications and transport systems, and cities in particular have seen rapid changes dictated by changing patterns of transport. The trend towards suburbanisation and the enormous daily ebb and flow of workers is not without its problems. Not only does it demand a considerable road network, but the increasing numbers of private cars in particular must be accommodated during the day in the city together with those of people journeying into the city to shop or use specific facilities.

Various attempts have been made to try to accommodate these needs, which have become ever greater as successive governments have failed to introduce comprehensive public transport schemes[17] or policies that might have limited private traffic. Early plans such as those implemented in the 1930s at Wythenshawe in Manchester derived from the North American planning experience as attempted at Radburn in New Jersey. There efforts were made to segregate networks according to their function, and to separate pedestrian and cyclists from other road users. In 1963 the Buchanan report *Traffic in Towns* suggested strategies for dealing with the traffic problem which included vertical segregation of pedestrians and motor vehicles.[18] Such ideas as these, generated by central government and advocated by it, have had a major impact on the redevelopment and replanning of many city centres and have resulted in proposals for new urban development by local government.

The importance of the association between improved communications and development can be seen in the recent proposal by a consortium of major house builders for a new town, one of a number planned in green belt land in Essex, close to the M15. Such plans are opposed by bodies like the Council for the Protection of Rural England because of the threat they pose to the green belt, but are welcomed by builders for whom the location is attractive – partly because of its good communications links. The extension of commuter accommodation for London is a significant feature in other villages along the line of the M25 and M40. There are undoubted benefits, however, to a number of villages and small towns which are bypassed by these routes, as a result of the reduction of traffic, noise, pollution and harassment that the motorways bring.

Local transport planning

Beyond this direct involvement in transport, legislation – the Local Government Act 1972 and the Transport Act 1978 – has required the preparation of comprehensive transport policy statements drawn up in light of the needs of the structure plans formulated at county level, so that levels of expenditure can be approved by the DoE and funded through the Rate Support Grant and in the Transport Supplementary Grants. These statements have also offered the possibility of a degree of overall planning of transport provision in local areas.

Regional policy

The final area in which central government policy impinges directly on the actions of local authorities, although not the most costly, is probably the most significant of those we have considered because it is specifically directed to the needs of local areas. The history of the development of centrally directed regional policy in Britain is characterised by the increasing recognition of the inequality and inequity of economic development and opportunity in the provinces and in Scotland, Wales and Northern Ireland as compared with that in London and the south-east. It is a problem which is currently manifest in a number of ways but which has long essentially resulted from differences in physical resources, population characteristics and geographical location.

In the past particular geographical locations and areas have, mainly for economic/locational reasons, had pre-eminence. In the early colonial days, for example, the ports serving the growing merchant and naval fleets and the expanding economies of the colonial trade, such as Bristol, grew rich and powerful. Later, Liverpool and Glasgow rose to the fore as the focus of sea-borne trade shifted. During the industrialisation period rapid growth was experienced and considerable wealth generated in those areas, e.g. Lancashire and the West Riding of Yorkshire, where there were valuable raw materials and most especially coal. At the same time, as the fortunes of the provincial areas waxed and waned, the capital continued to grow. London was always the major port of the country and was the permanent seat of government, both nationally and at the head of a vast world empire, and as it grew in population it continued to offer the largest, richest and most attractive market in the country. Although lacking a physical resource base, it has continued to be a favourite location for many manufacturing activities because of its size and influence.

There is therefore a natural tendency to imbalance in the fortunes of each of the regions in the country which has become increasingly important as the speed of structural economic change and its differential effects have increased. These changes were emphasised during the inter-war economic depression and it is from the Special Areas Act of 1934 that modern regional policy dates. The Act identified South Wales, north-east England, Cumberland and Clydeside as being in special need of economic assistance. Many pieces of legislation have followed, of which the Distribution of Industry Act 1945 and the 1947 Town and Country Planning Act are probably the most significant.

The directions and emphases of regional policy have changed since 1934 but they have usually comprised both administrative and planning measures, along with economic policies. In the 1960s, for example, an attempt was made to tackle the problem of the faltering economic performance in many of the English regions through the mechanism of large-scale regional economic planning.[19] Seven Regional Economic Planning Councils were established in England in 1965, with one in Wales and one in Scotland. The number of regions was increased in 1974, and they now divide Britain into the familiar units: Scotland, Wales, North, Yorkshire and Humberside, North West, West Midlands, East Midlands, East Anglia, South West and South East. It is on the basis of these ten regions that many of the cruder regional comparisons are drawn.

The original brief of each Council was to prepare a regional strategy document which first outlined the social and economic structure of the area, then identified its major economic and economically related problems such as housing, health and social service provision, and finally made recommendations as to the policy which should be developed to combat these problems and issues. The Councils themselves were abolished in 1979 but the Regional Economic Planning Boards, the executive arm of the Councils, continue to function. The policies of the REPBs are to be considered in the formulation of structure plans prepared at county level and thus they become influential on the development of planning and policy at the local level.

The economic policies pursued have usually had both negative and positive aspects. One major thrust, for example, has been to encourage industrial relocation by limiting the areas in which development can take place through the use of a sort of industrial location licence, known as the Industrial Development Certificate, and to make other areas attractive because special financial benefits can be obtained for new industrial development.

Unemployment levels have been a major criterion for defining areas requiring special assistance and much effort in regional policy has been directed at increasing employment opportunities in areas of declining primary and heavy industry such as Tyneside, South Wales and Strathclyde. Incentives have included directed grants and loans for new investment, provision of rent-free buildings for limited periods, reductions or moratoriums on rates, assistance in infrastructural provision, and technical and managerial advice. In addition to industrial-based policy there has been an emphasis on controlling population migration, the principal thrust of which was through the new towns legislation.

The directions and geographical extent of special regional assistance have varied considerably from the simplicity of the four regions identified in the 1934 Act to a complex three-tier system of aid dependent upon rates of unemployment and nature and severity of economic problems. Until 1979 the assisted areas were designated as 'Special Development', 'Development' or 'Intermediate', and thus qualified for differential levels of support. By that time almost 44 per cent of the employed population of the United Kingdom was working in an assisted area. This figure has gradually been reduced by the abolition of one category (only Development and Intermediate areas are now recognised) and by the downgrading of 87 localities so that resources are now concentrated more heavily in areas with the worst problems. The government has also effected a reduction in the level of expenditure in the regional programme, which has been more than halved from £643 million in 1984 to £300 million in 1987/88.

Since the mid-1960s the special problems of Scotland and Wales have also been recognised. Here rural depopulation and the decline of traditional economic activities are more significant problems and the Highlands and Islands Development Board for Scotland and the Development Board for Mid-Wales, together with the Scottish and Welsh Development Agencies, are charged with the task of arresting decline, assisting growth and safeguarding employment. They can provide financial assistance to industry, and are involved in managing industrial estates, building factories and rehabilitating derelict land.[20] Many of these functions are shared with local government and a close working relationship is clearly necessary.

More recently, considerable emphasis has been placed upon the task of urban regeneration and the multifaceted inner-city problem. Often the problems stem from physical decay and degeneration, social distress and disadvantage and economic decline, but they are also partly a natural consequence of changes in public taste and preference, increasing affluence and better transport.

Special assistance for cities with these sorts of problem was initiated through the Urban Programme in 1968. The programme was reformed and developed in 1977 following the publication of a White Paper *Policy for Inner Cities* and a variety of policy programmes were subsequently introduced. Under the Inner Urban Areas Act 1978, Partnership Areas were designated in which local and central government worked together on a wide range of projects for inner-city development and to counter urban deprivation. There were three Partnership areas in London and one each in Birmingham, Liverpool, Manchester/Salford and Newcastle/Gateshead. A further 15 authorities with less severe problems are known as Programme Authorities where the resources are made available for programmes to develop economic opportunities and for environmental improvement. Some 11 areas of economic and physical decay are designated Enterprise Zones. Here simple measures such as the removal of fiscal burdens are thought to be adequate to arrest decline. In these areas, Isle of Dogs, Corby and Liverpool, there are exemptions from rates and Development Land Tax, and 100 per cent tax allowances for capital spending on industrial and commercial buildings together with a simplified and speedier planning procedure.

Urban Programme money is made available through the regional offices of the DoE. Local councils must bid for a share of the resources for particular schemes which may fall within the scope of the programme. The money is available for both private and public use, and may contribute up to 75 per cent of the cost of any individual project. Schemes which have been supported in this way include many which although essentially cosmetic, contribute to the improvement of the environment, such as tree-planting or footpath improvement; and others, such as the rebuilding or improvement of commercial premises, which might themselves create work while at the same time adding to the infrastructural stock of the local area. Directly developmental schemes have included the exploitation of tourist potential through both public service agencies and private enterprise.

EUROPEAN COMMUNITY INVOLVEMENT

An interesting development in the context of the relationship between central and local government lies in the impact of supranational legislation and policy-making from the European Commission. Legislation emanating from Europe may have a direct impact on some areas of local and national policy. Transport policy may be affected, as are trading standards, education and health affairs among others. Central government is responsible, for example, for setting the limits of the axle weight for lorries in the United Kingdom and also for facilitating Community policy which would raise those weights. Here it is in conflict with local councils, which have objected to the proposals on the grounds that such increases would result in damage principally to minor roads and bridges for which they alone were responsible, and on whom the financial burden of repairs would fall.

A major area of local government involvement with the EC is through regional and social policy. Brussels as well as Westminster can be a source of funds for local use. Applying for Community money is not, however, a straightforward business and many authorities have retained advisers to work on their behalf in gaining support for local projects while they rapidly build up expertise among their own staffs.[21] Although this is an additional burden on staff and upon the ratepayer, the potential rewards from the EC Regional and Social Funds are considerable. Projects which have been supported in Britain have included the building of sports and recreational facilities, the renovation of theatres and the reclamation of derelict land for retail development.

In 1984 the United Kingdom was allocated £352.7 million and £379.4 million from the Social and Regional Funds respectively. Ten per cent of the former went to local authority projects.

Notes

1. *Local Government Comparative Statistics 1985*, SIS Ref. No. 44.85 (The Chartered Institute of Public Finance and Accountancy, 1985).
2. N. P. Hepworth, *The Finance of Local Government*, 6th edn (Allen and Unwin, 1980). This book contains a very full discussion of all aspects of local authority finance.
3. *Rate Support Grant (England) 1984/5* (Association of County Councils, for the English Local Authority Associations, 1984).
4. *Rate Support Grant (England) 1985/6* (Association of County Councils, for the English Local Authority Associations, 1985).
5. N. P. Hepworth, *op. cit.* p. 87.
6. N. P. Hepworth, *op. cit.* Ch. II.
7. For example: *Report of the Committee of Inquiry into the Impact of Rates on Households* (Chairman R. G. D. Allan), Cmnd 2582 (HMSO, 1964); and *Local Government Finance, Report of a Committee of Enquiry* (Chairman Frank Layfield QC), Cmnd 6253 (HMSO, 1976).

8. *Paying for Local Government*, Cmnd 9714 (HMSO, 1986). For criticisms of proposed changes see, for example: J. Ross Harper, *Rates Revaluation: The Great Myth*, for The Society of Scottish Conservative Lawyers (1985).

9. *Local Government Comparative Statistics 1985*, SIS Ref. No. 44.85 (The Chartered Institute of Public Finance and Accountancy, 1985).

10. P. Dunleavy, *Public Housing*, Urban Change and Conflict, State Intervention II (Open University Press, 1982), p. 8 and *British Housing Problems and Solutions*, Inquiry into British Housing: Report, National Federation of Housing Associations, 1984.

11. *1981 English House Condition Survey*, Housing Survey Report No. 13, DoE (HMSO, 1981), p. 26.

12. Material for this section has been drawn from S. Potter, *The State and Transport*, Urban Change and Conflict, State Intervention II (Open University Press, 1982); and R. Hambleton, *Policy Planning and Local Government* (Hutchinson, 1978).

13. The Road Board (1910) was established under the provisions of the Development and Road Improvement Funds Act 1909. The Act was to promote the economic development of the United Kingdom and the improvement of the roads therein. The Road Board was to (a) improve facilities for road traffic in the United Kingdom and (b) administer the road improvement grant. It had the power to make advances to highway authorities for the construction of new roads.

14. The Transport Act 1985 also privatised the National Bus Corporation, the Passenger Transport Authorities and municipal bus undertakings.

15. *The Reshaping of British Rail*, Report, Ministry of Transport (HMSO, 1963).

16. J. Simmons (ed.), *Rail 150* (Eyre Methuen, 1975).

17. S. Potter, *op. cit.* p. 64.

18. *Traffic in Towns*: A study of the Long Term Problems of Traffic in Urban Areas, Report of the Working Group (Chairman C. Buchanan) appointed by the Ministry of Transport (HMSO, 1963).

19. H. Elcock, *Local Government: Politicians, Professionals and the Public in Local Authorities* (Methuen, 1982), p. 265.

20. *UK Monograph on the Human Settlements Situation and Related Trends and Policies*, UN Economic Commission for Europe, Committee on Housing and Planning (DoE, 1982).

21. C. Mellors (ed.), *Promoting Local Authorities in the European Community* (International Union of Local Authorities, 1986).

6

THE STRUCTURE AND FUNCTIONS OF
LOCAL GOVERNMENT

The structure of local government and the functions allocated to local authorities are examples of two distinct processes: *horizontal* and *vertical* division. Horizontal division is the separation of a geographical area – in this case a country – into a number of discrete units. This process is also sometimes referred to as *area* delimitation. Vertical division is the allocation of functions between authorities of different status operating within the same territory. Both horizontal and vertical division, and the principles which underlie such processes, are essential to an understanding of the nature of local government. Horizontal division creates the units of local government and determines their size and territorial ranges; vertical division determines which functions are allocated to local councils and which functions are retained by central government and, where there is more than one tier of local government, how responsibilities are divided between these various levels. In the current UK system, this means how powers are divided between central government, county councils, constituent district councils and, sometimes, parish councils. Before considering the principles which influence the processes of horizontal and vertical division, it is appropriate to say something about the political environment in which these constitutional decisions are made.

A PRAGMATIC APPROACH

As a general rule, discussions about the structure of government have tended to assume a pragmatic rather than a theoretical tone in Britain.[1] There are several reasons for this. In part, it results from a lack of opportunity to start building our governmental system from a new beginning since, unlike many other Western nations, we have not suffered major political and constitutional upheavals during the last couple of centuries. It is difficult to achieve radical change in institutions that already exist and, as even a brief glance at the development of institutions would reveal, structures of government have evolved in a piecemeal, even haphazard, manner. Instead of sudden radical changes, we have tended to adapt and adjust institutions in response to either administrative or political need. Thornhill likens these structures to a 'large palatial mansion which has been extended and altered from time to time at the whim of successive occupants [and] for which no complete set of architectural plans exist'.[2] In a very real sense, the structure of government in Britain tends to be 'chronological rather than logical'. Recent books about the British system of government often refer to a variety of reforms – parliamentary reform, civil service reform, health service reform and, of course, local government reform. In reality, many of these reforms would be better understood as reorganisations. *Continuity* and *gradualism* are two key characteristics of a political system that has evolved over a long period of time.

Pragmatism surfaces in another way – the apparent dislike for abstract principle and the preference for institutions and processes that are 'tried and trusted'. Tradition, institutional inertia and even vested interest are powerful forces to overcome. 'Concepts' are quite appropriate matters for consideration in books about political systems, but empirical evidence weighs heavier than theoretical argument when real decisions are taken about the structure and organisation of government.

The pragmatic approach is often reinforced by *political considerations*. After all, the most important decisions about the structure of government are taken by politicians in a party political setting and the ideas and perceptions of politicians are a key ingredient in decisions about government structure. It is important to recognise that structures are designed to promote *objectives* and that objectives in this context are ultimately defined in political terms. Priorities, and therefore objectives, are determined by politicians. Political considerations have certainly played a major part in decisions about local government structure in Britain throughout the nineteenth and twentieth centuries. In the mid-nineteenth century, for example, the country gentry, who were vastly overrepresented in Parliament, succeeded in frustrating a number of attempts to extend the borough system of local government into the counties. Party politics were equally apparent during debates of the late 1960s and early 1970s and when, more recently, the decision was taken to abolish metropolitan county councils. It should not be inferred from this that *principles* are entirely absent from discussions about local government structure; rather that the application of these principles to the structure and functions of local government inevitably takes place within, and is modified by, the political setting.

PRINCIPLES OF HORIZONTAL AND VERTICAL DIVISION

In the first chapter, we discussed the concept of decentralisation and identified the various forms it can take. As we saw then, multi-purpose elected bodies serving particular territorial units represent only one of several options, although in practice local governments organised in this manner tend to be common features of Western political systems. This leads to the more specific issues of horizontal and vertical division – on what basis should we delimit areas of local government and which services should they control? Indeed, there are really four distinct questions to be answered. How many units should there be in total? What size of population should they serve? What geographical area should each unit cover? Should there be a single local authority unit to provide *all* services for a given territorial unit?

National boundaries are rarely discussed or decided in the same way as local boundaries. It is not usual to speculate, for example, about the optimum size of a nation since frontiers between countries are mainly the product of war and geography rather than the application of some kind of size or service principle. In Britain the island location and freedom from invasion for several centuries has meant that, with the notable exception of Northern Ireland, it has not been necessary to give much thought to the siting of national frontiers. In terms of local government, however, the delimitation of areas and allocation of functions are important issues. There are a number of ways in which principles of structure can be applied to these questions.[3]

Some general principles about overall structure are reasonably straightforward and not contentious. It is generally agreed, for example, that the structure should be *complete* and, where possible, *uniform*. In other words, no place should be outside the system and we should try to avoid the kind of confusion which resulted from the separation between county boroughs and administrative counties prior to 1974. There is also general acceptance that, whatever the basis on which they are chosen, local government units should be *distinct* and *discrete*. By this we mean that the units should be easily understood and the boundaries continuous in order to avoid what we might term the 'West Berlin problem' – where part of a political unit is separated from its other parts by being entirely surrounded by foreign territory. As a related principle, some would also argue that units should be as compact as possible in order to achieve maximum internal cohesion.

There is one further principle concerning the overall structure to which brief reference should be made at this point since it has figured prominently in debates about structure during the last two decades. Some people contend that there should be a single local authority unit in each area to administer *all* services allocated to local government. Instead of multi-purpose local councils there would be all-purpose authorities. This was the basis of the unitary structure recommended by the Redcliffe–Maud Commission in 1969. All-purpose county boroughs were previous examples of this approach. The incoming Conservative Government rejected the unitary principle in favour of a two-tier structure.

One of the reasons why the Conservative Government favoured a two-tier structure was its belief that it was impossible to discover one size of local authority that would be operationally suitable for all local authority services. This brings us to the issue of how we might best delineate the units of local government. Two broad approaches can be taken to this issue: the first concentrates on the needs of those who provide services and the second on the needs of those who are consumers of local authority provisions.

One approach to area delimitation is to attempt to specify units by reference to their technical and operational needs. This is the *service principle*, which seeks to identify an optimum area for functional units. Inevitably, this approach gives greater recognition to the needs of the *service provider* than to those of the *service consumer*. Size and scale are often key components of this approach, partly for the reason that both are potentially easy to quantify. On the surface, there is also an initial attractiveness about using population numbers as an indicator of the desirable size of local government units. It seems reasonable to assume that there is a link between the scale of provision and its effectiveness. Sometimes we refer to two types of local services – 'personal' (those requiring small client populations) and 'environmental' (those benefiting from a larger scale of operation). Police and fire services fall into the latter category. Unfortunately, studies have demonstrated that the relationship between the scale of operation and the effectiveness of service provision is rather more complicated than it might appear initially. Apart from any other consideration, size measured by population number may be an unreliable guide to service requirements because of the complexity of population structure. Territories with similar-sized populations may have different needs because of the social composition of the area. When the territorial extent of units, their location, the density of population and physical landscape differences are also considered, there seems little likelihood that simple and generally applicable solutions to the problem of the size of local government units can be achieved. Moreover, even if an ideal population indicator could be found, it is likely that the size would be service-specific, and that it would not be possible to discover one size that would be equally appropriate for all undertakings. Using size or scale as a crude measure to identify territorial areas reveals at most the minimum threshold for the satisfactory provision of services. It does not necessarily indicate an optimum service size. Despite all these shortcomings, we shall see that population number has been the dominant factor in decisions about structure during the last hundred years.

Another way of applying the service principle is to employ geographical analysis rather than statistical analysis. The effectiveness of many services depends upon particular local physical and social characteristics. Appropriate areas for the supply of water services, for example, are dependent upon the location and distribution of water collection and supply facilities – an example of physical geography. Similarly, the spatial requirements of transport-related services are heavily influenced by the distributions of population, travel habits and, therefore, transportation needs – an example of human and social geography. Both indicate the difficulty of taking a single approach to the question of service efficiency and attempting to use it to define territorial units that are universally appropriate. The examination of local government structure using a geographical analysis is not new.[4] Unfortunately, this approach has enjoyed far less attention from politicians than the 'numbers' approach. In fact, some of the main lines of geographical analysis have pointed towards a regional rather than a local structure for subnational government. These ideas will be discussed at a later point in the chapter.

So far, we have concentrated on technical and operational needs. It is equally important to consider those who consume local authority services and we may refer to this approach as the *community principle*. For this group, the desirable unit of local government would be one which (a) is easily recognised, (b) gives ease of access to services, (c) corresponds to the patterns of daily life and (d) inspires some sense of belonging.

One way of identifying a community is to ask people about their own perceptions, and a survey on community attitudes was undertaken for the Royal Commission on Local Government in England (1966–69). The survey confirmed what had been discovered in other studies, namely that communities identified by people themselves are not suitable local government units. As Hampton discovered in his study of Sheffield, 'The areas that constitute the local community for most members of the electorate are much too small to form the basis of local authority areas . . . three-quarters of the respondents described the area in which they felt at home in terms smaller than the size of a city ward'.[5] 'Community' to most people suggests a village or, in a city location, a few streets. It is synonymous in popular usage with the idea of neighbourhood and it is at this level that much informal community involvement occurs through such things as tenants' groups, community action groups and community associations.[6]

A more sophisticated approach to the notion of community is to examine the spatial patterns of people's lives. The area in which people function – the distances they travel to work or to shop or for their recreation – is much more extensive than their perception of community as discussed above. Indeed, as we have seen in a previous chapter, one of the principal physical dynamics of the UK population is the daily journey-to-work which, since the advent of motorised transport and with increased access to private transport, is often quite extensive. This journey links together a number of definable central places – towns and cities – with the suburban and rural areas in which many people now live. Journey-to-work statistics from the census can be used to define these central places and their hinterlands or regions and, with the exception of the London-orientated pattern, these regions are clearly delimited and have strong internal integrity. For large parts of the country, and the majority of the urban population, daily lives operate within the confines of a well-defined territory. This geographical pattern is known as the *city region* and one of its earliest expositions is to be found in R. E. Dickinson's *City, Region and Regionalism*, published in 1947.[7] A related concept, the 'urban hierarchy' was conceived by Smailes (1944) who defined and classified towns by their various functions.

Towns and cities have always had strong relationships with the surrounding countryside; people in urban areas lived on the surplus produced by the land and, in return, provided goods and services needed by the rural community. These links still exist – the village dweller, for instance, may go to town to buy furniture or to the theatre – but better travel facilities and improved communications in general (telephone, etc.) mean that the areal extent of the city's influence has spread. Smailes used the term 'urban field' to denote the 'pull' of the town or city over surrounding rural areas. The analogy is with a magnet and, like a magnetic field, the attraction of an urban area diminishes with distance until a rival urban field takes its place. If, for example, we travel along the Calder Valley from the Leeds/Bradford conurbation towards Manchester, there comes a point where the pull of the former weakens and is replaced by that of the latter. The 'city region' is a large-scale version of the 'urban field'; 'catchment area' may be a similar concept that is popularly used at a more local level. The important point is that town and country are interdependent and that there are techniques available that allow the measuring and representation of these relationships. The concept of city regions resurfaced in Derek Senior's *Memorandum of Dissent* to the Royal Commission (1966–69), in which he proposed a two-tier structure of local government based on regional units and town districts.[8]

There are several ways of assessing territorial integrity. The local transport network, for example, is closely linked to the journey-to-work pattern. Informational links between people are also important, both in the political context and in defining functional areas. These can be identified, for example, by examining the sales areas of local newspapers, which link the centre in which the paper is published with the zone in which it circulates. On a larger scale, the broadcast area of the regional television companies serves a similar purpose. Equally, such functional zones may be defined by shopping and recreational journeys, so that a further facet of everyday life is given a spatial or territorial base. Such methods as these help to identify 'natural' functional units and were used in evidence before the Redcliffe–Maud Commission. Clearly, political and administrative units defined in these ways would have a strong rational justification in terms of the ways-of-life of the people they were intended to represent and serve. They would also mean, incidentally, that there would be a stronger link between the consumption of services (the use of roads, town centres, recreational facilities, etc.) and payment for these facilities since people would be less likely to reside in one locality and work or shop in an adjacent local authority area.

In most cases, the justification for a particular form of territorial subdivision is made by reference to *efficiency*. Efficiency can be measured in a number of ways and an important distinction can be drawn between *operational efficiency*, as defined by reference to those factors required to provide the service or to meet the need and the cost of unit provision, and *consumption efficiency*, defined by reference to the ease with which clients or consumers can avail themselves of the service. The two are seldom compatible. In addition, there is a basic distinction to be drawn between those services which are themselves distributed to the consumer, e.g. refuse collection or fire-fighting, and those where the consumer must travel to obtain the service. The majority of services offered by local government are of the latter type, which leads us to consider the effect of distance on both the provider and consumer of local services.

The field areas which develop can usually be defined in theoretical terms using the concepts of central place theory. In this case, the central place is loosely defined as the location at which the service is to be provided, and the area around that location contains the population which will require the service. The size of the operational area is defined by first the *threshold* of the service (the minimum size of area such that there are sufficient people to make provision of the service worth while) and, second, a *range* (the distance which people are prepared to travel in order to obtain the service). In reality, of course, definitions of range and threshold will vary from household to household and are especially affected by the availability of transport facilities. In some cases, the range concept may not be valid at all, because the consumer is obliged to use the service. All children must go to school and will thus be required to travel as far as is necessary for them to do so. Theoretically, therefore, the range applied to a school is infinite. Facilities where there is an element of choice – e.g. the public swimming pool – require a calculation of an expected range in order to produce an efficient location which optimises use of the facility.

These ideas are valuable in other ways. A threshold population for the library service of a particular size may be, say, 10,000, and as population increases beyond that size further facilities may be thought necessary. However, if the population increase has taken place beyond the range of the service then the additional facilities should be relocated rather than added on to the existing site because the new clients would be unlikely to use the additional facility at the old site. Clearly, for some facilities like primary schools or health centres the range may be limited to a short distance, because of the well-defined and constant need of the consumer. The police and fire service also need to be located relatively closely and within closely defined areas for other operational reasons. Other services, such as refuse disposal, can ignore client convenience and may be best located so as to satisfy administrative and operational efficiency criteria.

In virtually every case, there is a fall in demand or reduction in the perceived level of service with distance from the location of the service – the *distance-decay effect*. In general, those who live further from the swimming pool are less likely to use it than those who live nearby. There are few services which are spatially indifferent in that their location is immaterial to the extent to which they can be used. Optimal levels of service for the consumer are better satisfied when there are a large number of service points, but the administrative and financial interests of the local authority may be better served by large-scale organisation and few outlets. *Agglomeration economies* in the provision of public services are well recognised, and unit costs of services considerably reduced, when large urban areas of dense populations are served compared with small sparse rural populations. Nevertheless, large units generally mean fewer units and increased travel time for either the service provider or service consumer. They can also mean greater physical isolation for certain groups or areas of the population and, because of distance-decay effects, a differential in service level and availability. It is important, therefore, that when fewer and larger service units are contemplated, their location with respect to consumers should be carefully considered.

With these principles in mind, we can now consider how questions of structure and function have actually been tackled in recent years.

REORGANISATION OF STRUCTURE

The structure of local government that was created at the end of the nineteenth century survived for over 70 years, but throughout most of that period it encountered considerable criticism and was the subject of several inquiries by Commissions. As a review of this period reveals, distinctive approaches have been taken towards structure and functions. The key characteristics have been a preoccupation with population size (often to the preclusion of other possible approaches), a reluctance to consider the issues of structure and functions together (or, indeed, to make any attempt to consider in a systematic manner the range of functions that should properly belong to local government), the part played by 'vested interests' in either resisting or modifying proposals for change, and the significance of party political considerations.

In fact, the main issues that have dominated debates about local government structure during the twentieth century were already apparent by the end of the nineteenth century.[9] These were the issues of size and the division between urban and rural patterns of local government. The size problem surfaced during the passage of the 1888 Act. Originally, it had been intended that the population threshold for granting county borough status should be fixed at 150,000. When the Bill was published, pressures had forced this figure down to 100,000 and during its passage through Parliament, the figure was further reduced to 50,000. Even at that time this was a low threshold and the consequence of this reduction was that the proposed number of county boroughs in England rose from an intended figure of ten to an actual figure of 61.

Under the legislation, county boroughs had been intended to be 'exceptional' units of local government; by the time the Act was passed these all-purpose authorities were common units for the major urban centres. By 1922, the number of county boroughs had reached 82. This had consequences for the county areas since it involved the loss of valuable rateable land. As early as 1913, the county councils began to urge the government to prevent the creation of further county boroughs. There was a parallel process taking place which was leading to the creation of more urban districts at the expense of rural districts, and 270 additional UDCs had been established by the mid-1920s.[10] Action was taken to stem this tide of urban expansion in 1926[11] following the report of the Onslow Commission, when the threshold for the creation of new county boroughs was increased to 75,000. (The figure did not apply to existing county boroughs.) In 1956, it was increased again to 100,000 – still a third below the figure proposed 70 years earlier.

Juggling with population thresholds, however, was a response to the symptoms of the problem rather than its cause. Patterns of population continued to shift, still more rapidly with improving transport and communications and especially with increased access to private cars. The effect of these changes on the populations of cities and their suburbs and rural hinterlands continued apace.

By the post-war period, the issue of local government structure was firmly on the political agenda, although there were powerful disincentives to reorganisation. Prominent among these were the array of vested interests articulated through the associations of existing local authorities as well as a lack of any agreement about a substitute structure. Instead, a 'permanent' commission was established to review the actual boundaries of all local authorities. After two years, the Commission concluded that it was impossible to achieve even this modest objective within its terms of reference, and the Commission quoted the minister's own words back at him: 'Everyone who knows about local government feels that it is nonsense to talk about functions and boundaries separately'.[12] Unfortunately, this lesson went unheeded and even 20 years later the Redcliffe–Maud Commission was told that any consideration of *new* responsibilities for local government was outside their terms of reference. In 1948, the 'permanent' Boundary Commission was abolished by the Labour Government, after just three years of existence and without a single boundary redrawn.

In 1958 two Commissions – one for England and one for Wales – were established to look at top-level authorities and the particular needs of conurbations. The piecemeal approach to structural issues continued. At around the same time, a Royal Commission was appointed under the chairmanship of Sir Edwin Herbert to look at local government in the London area. The latter resulted in the extension of the area covered by the old LCC (now to be the Greater London Council) and the creation of 32 second-tier boroughs plus the City of London. The number of boroughs was fewer than recommended by the Herbert Commission and, because of their increased size, they were given responsibility for education services under the overall control of the Inner London Education Authority (ILEA).

The most important period of structural review outside London began in the mid-1960s with the appointment of the Redcliffe–Maud Commission (1966–69) to look at local government in England and Wales and the Wheatley Commission (1966–69) in Scotland. These two Commissions shared broadly similar views about the ills of existing structures, but their conclusions about alternative structures differed. It is worth noting at this point that the Commissions could consider only the 'existing functions' of local government and were not required to consider the tricky issue of finance.

The Redcliffe–Maud Report identified six main failings of the existing local government structure:

1. It was based upon an unrealistic division between town and country which failed to recognise the interplay between urban centres and rural hinterlands. To simply redraw boundaries was not sufficient.
2. The fragmentation between county boroughs and administrative counties made it difficult to plan transportation and land over a sufficiently large area. One consequence of this was that governments created regional policies, and sometimes regional institutions, to deal with these larger-scale needs. This approach bypassed local government.
3. Within the administrative counties, the division between tiers and the allocation of functions was unsatisfactory.
4. Many areas were simply too small. This had two main consequences – the loss of functions to various *ad hoc* bodies over the years and difficulties in raising sufficient revenue to pay for services.
5. Poor communications between councils and their publics.
6. Increasing domination of local government by central government.

The structure of local government in the 1960s seemed to fail both *service* and *consumption* tests of efficiency. In terms of the former, areas were too small, fragmented and paid little regard to the operational needs of service provision. From the latter perspective, local authority areas were unrelated to any sense of community, the division of services was confusing and there seemed little inducement to wide-scale participation in local affairs, even at election time. The Wheatley Commission in Scotland made these concerns even more explicit by stressing four essential principles for reorganisation: ensuring local authorities have the power to play a more substantial role in the running of the country; making local authorities more *effective* in the provision of local services, not least from the consumer's point of view; strengthening *local democracy* and accountability; and maximising *local involvement* in local affairs. 'Community needs' had a central place in the Wheatley Report and were also part of the basis on which the actual units of local government were recommended. The proposed structure in Scotland was based on three main principles: operational viability in service provision; recognition of existing communities; and political viability (i.e. the creation of units that were sufficiently powerful to attract the interest and involvement of the electorate).

The structure recommended by Redcliffe–Maud in England and Wales was essentially based upon the needs of service provision as defined by their scale of operation. Their analysis was as follows:

1. It was possible to distinguish two types of local authority service – environmental (transport, police, etc.) and personal (housing management, welfare, etc.). The integrity of each of these two groups should remain and they should not be further subdivided.
2. Where possible, environmental services and personal services should be under the charge of a single all-purpose authority.
3. Regarding the size of units, it was argued that a quarter of a million population was the minimum threshold for a satisfactory unit of local government. At the other extreme, the maximum which still allowed relatively easy communication across the unit and between electors and the council was regarded as one million. It followed, therefore, that if personal and environmental services were to be linked, all authorities should have a population range of 250,000–1,000,000.

In making these recommendations, the Commission was following a line similar to that of the Seebohm Report on local authority social services, which had likewise argued against the splitting of services between tiers.[13] However, it could be argued that the Commission was concerned more with the ability to provide services than with questions of efficiency. Indeed, selecting a population range between a *minimum* and a *maximum* point does not help indicate an *optimum* point. Even if an optimum point could be established in population terms, there is no reason why it should be the same for all services. One service may be best run with populations significantly below 250,000, while others would be better operated in areas with well over one million. The middle range may be a range where all services operate at their threshold

```
                          Provinces (8)
                               |
         ┌─────────────────────┴──────────────────┐
  Unitary authorities (58)              Metropolitan authorities (3)
         |                                         |
         |                              Metropolitan districts (20)
         |                                         |
    Local councils                          Local councils
```

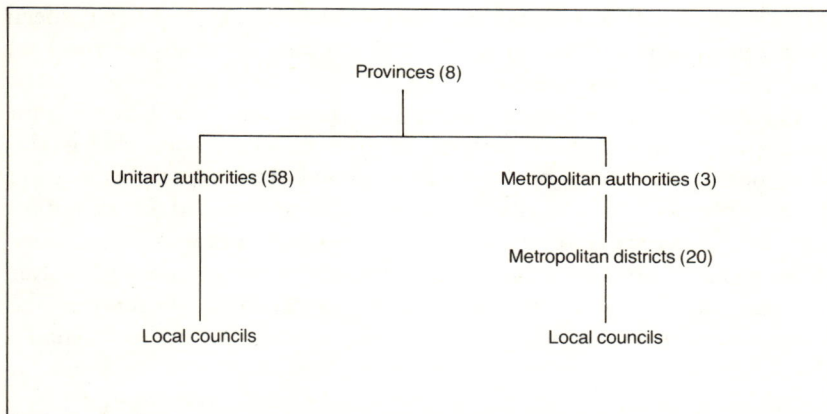

Fig. 6.1 Recommendations of the Royal Commission on Local Government (1969)

of efficiency. In addition, there is the problem of the consumer's ideas of satisfactory areas which, unfortunately, do not necessarily accord with neat numerical packages. For example, the Commission itself had found that, using socio-geographic tests, England could be divided into approximately 140 cohesive town-and-related-country units. Unfortunately, to have created a structure of local government on this basis would have offended against the main analysis about all-purpose units and the size principle outlined above. The compromise was a system based upon unitary authorities, with special arrangements in three major metropolitan areas – Liverpool, Birmingham and Manchester, and the surrounding areas of each. In these three areas an upper tier would be responsible for environmental services and 20 second-tier districts would take control of personal services (Fig. 6.1).

In fact, the phrase 'unitary structure' was something of a misnomer since, even outside these three conurbations, there were to be two additional levels – local councils and indirectly elected provinces to take responsibility for strategic planning. Local councils were intended to voice the opinions and wishes of local communities and, besides taking responsibility for local amenities, could exercise powers delegated by unitary authorities.

The Commission was not unanimous in its recommendations and one of its number, Derek Senior, issued a long *Memorandum of Dissent*. While accepting the Commission's diagnosis of the existing failures, and the recommendations concerning the three metropolitan areas, he argued for a two-tier structure generally, based on city regions (largely defined by travel-to-work data) where environmental and personal services were split between these two levels. He proposed that there should be 35 city regions and 148 second-tier districts. He also proposed five provincial authorities.

The Labour Government broadly accepted the main Commission recommendations, not surprisingly in view of its general belief in the value of the old county boroughs and, some have suggested cynically, the possible electoral benefits of a pattern of local authorities based upon extended urban areas. The Conservative Government which came into office in 1970, however, took a different view and favoured a two-tier structure, with larger counties to exercise responsibility for services like police, fire, refuse disposal, consumer protection, planning and roads. The lower-tier districts were to be given responsibility for housing, public health, local planning and refuse collection. Like the Redcliffe–Maud Commission, the Conservative Government faced a difficulty when dealing with the major conurbations and again it was decided to make special arrangements. As elsewhere, there would be a two-tier structure in six metropolitan areas (Merseyside, Greater Manchester, West Yorkshire, South Yorkshire, West Midlands and Tyne and Wear) but in these areas, the size of the 36 constituent districts was deemed to be sufficient for them to take control of education, social services and libraries. Elsewhere, these services were allocated to the county authorities. As with the Labour proposals two years earlier, it has been suggested that the Conservative Government took some account of electoral advantage in favouring a structure based upon the counties, where their support tended to be strongest.

In Scotland, the recommendations of the Wheatley Commission were broadly acceptable to the Conservative Government. Unlike Redcliffe–Maud's proposals for England and Wales, the Scottish Commission had recommended a two-tier structure based upon seven regional authorities and 37 district authorities. These numbers were subsequently modified by the Local Government (Scotland) Act which came into effect in May 1975, but the two-tier approach taken by the Commission was followed.

The differences between the pre-1974 structure and the unitary and two-tier approaches taken by the Redcliffe–Maud Commission and the 1972 Act respectively are illustrated in Fig. 6.2. This depicts an imaginary county, the external boundaries of which remain unchanged. Prior to reorganisation, the area includes four all-purpose county boroughs which are outside the jurisdiction of the county council. Elsewhere, there is a structure based upon the county level and, beneath that, boroughs, urban and rural districts. Two of the major defects of that system are readily apparent: the confusion of the system and the

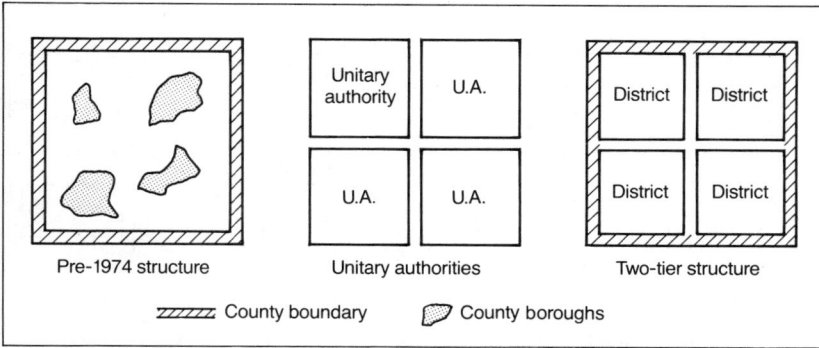

Fig. 6.2 An imaginary county showing pre-1974, unitary and two-tier arrangements

inability to plan services across the area. The county boroughs appear as 'islands', interrupting the spatial flow of services across the territory. Redcliffe–Maud's proposals for all-purpose unitary authorities are depicted in the central illustration. In this instance, the area is divided into four discrete unitary authorities. Finally, the two-tier structure introduced by the 1972 Act is depicted. It shows a county authority embracing the area as a whole, with four component district authorities.

Beneath the main authorities, the 1972 and 1973 Acts established a third tier of local government. In England this meant the retention of existing parish councils (some 7,200) and, where there was a demand, town councils. In Wales, there were similar provisions except that the title 'communities' rather than parishes was used. As in England, these councils are intended to articulate local opinion and, in addition, they have certain consultative rights regarding planning applications. Community councils – there are over 1,300 of them – play a similar role in Scotland.

In the reorganisation, as on other occasions, the question of local authority size was an important consideration, although again in common with other reviews, it had been found impractical to deal in the same way with densely and sparsely populated areas. Hence the distinction between metropolitan and non-metropolitan areas. The Act itself defined the county authorities in shire areas and both county and district units in the six metropolitan areas. However, the task of delineating districts elsewhere was left to Boundary Commissions established by the 1972 Act. These Commissions (an equivalent was established in Scotland) are permanent bodies and are charged with periodic review (i.e. 10–15 years) of local government areas. Their first task was to work out the new district authorities after undertaking local

ENGLAND			WALES	SCOTLAND
Metropolitan areas	Non-metropolitan areas	London		
Counties (6)*	Counties (39)	GLC*	Counties (8)	Regions (9)
				Islands (3)
Districts (36)	Districts (296)	Boroughs (32) plus City of London	Districts (37)	Districts (53)

*Abolished 1 April 1986. The structure shown refers to 'principal' local authorities. In addition, there is a tier of 'local' councils, known as parish, community or town councils depending on their location.

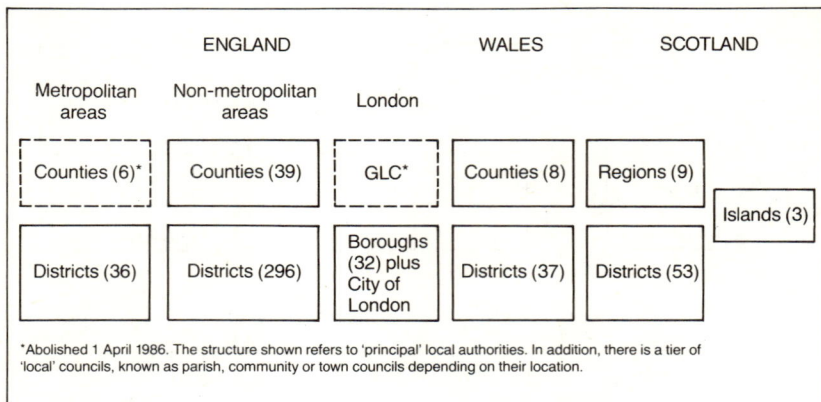

Fig. 6.3 Local government structure, 1975 onward

surveys and public consultation. Their initial plan in England had been to establish 274 non-metropolitan districts, none with a population below 40,000. As a result of local pressures, the number of districts was subsequently increased to 296, of which 14 had fewer than 40,000 inhabitants (see Fig. 6.3). As Keith-Lucas and Richards remark, 'The Commission moved a long way from its original objective which had been a 'preferred population range of 75,000 to 100,000'. No fewer than

---

1. *London Area*

Barking and Dagenham	Hounslow
Barnet	Islington
Bexley	Kensington & Chelsea
Brent	Kingston-upon-Thames
Bromley	Lambeth
Camden	Lewisham
Croydon	Merton
Ealing	Newham
Enfield	Redbridge
Greenwich	Richmond-upon-Thames
Hackney	Southwark
Hammersmith & Fulham	Sutton
Haringey	Tower Hamlets
Harrow	Waltham Forest
Havering	Wandsworth
Hillingdon	Westminster

2. *West Midlands Area*

Birmingham	Solihull
Coventry	Walsall
Dudley	Wolverhampton
Sandwell	

3. *South Yorkshire Area*

Barnsley	Rotherham
Doncaster	Sheffield

4. *West Yorkshire Area*

Bradford	Leeds
Calderdale	Wakefield
Kirklees	

5. *Greater Manchester*

Bolton	Salford
Bury	Stockport
Manchester	Tameside
Oldham	Trafford
Rochdale	Wigan

6. *Merseyside Area*

Knowsley	Sefton
Liverpool	Wirral
St Helens	

7. *Tyne and Wear Area*

Gateshead	South Tyneside
Newcastle	Sunderland
North Tyneside	

Fig. 6.4 Local government areas: counties/regions and metropolitan areas

Western Isles

Shetland

Orkney

■ Island Areas

Highland

Grampian

Tayside

Fife

Central

Lothian

Strathclyde

Borders

Dumfries & Galloway

Northumberland

7

Durham

Cleveland

Cumbria

North Yorkshire

Lancashire

4

Humberside

5

3

6 6

Cheshire

Derbyshire

Nottinghamshire

Lincolnshire

Clwyd

Gwynedd

Staffordshire

Leicestershire

Norfolk

Shropshire

2

Hereford
and Worcester

Warwickshire

Northamptonshire

Cambridgeshire

Suffolk

Powys

Dyfed

Bedfordshire

Hertfordshire

Essex

West
Glamorgan

Mid
Glamorgan

Gwent

Gloucestershire

Oxfordshire

Buckinghamshire

South
Glamorgan

Avon

Wiltshire

Berkshire

1

Surrey

Kent

Somerset

Hampshire

West Sussex

East Sussex

Isles of Scilly

Devon

Dorset

Isle of Wight

Cornwall

111 of the 296 districts fell below the 75,000 preferred minimum'.[14] It seems reminiscent of events back in 1888.

The new system came into effect in April 1974 in England and Wales, and in May 1975 in Scotland (see Fig. 6.4). This time, however, it did not take another 70 years before the structure was reorganised. By the late 1970s, the Labour Government was discussing changing the system, although in the event it was another Conservative administration that actually brought about further change. The abolition of the metropolitan counties and the GLC in April 1986 was a controversial decision even within the Conservative party, and followed a long period of conflict between the Labour-controlled metropolitan counties and the Conservative Government. The decision to abolish the metropolitan counties had been announced three years previously in the White Paper *Streamlining the Cities*. The White Paper gave three main reasons for abolition: simplifying the structure, saving money and removing a source of conflict. The high spending of these authorities, especially on transport services, had been a particular bone of contention, and abolition coincided with other moves to control local authority expenditure. From April 1986 their powers were transferred vertically to their constituent boroughs (planning, highways, waste disposal) or horizontally to new statutory joint authorities or boards (police, fire, public transport, civil defence). Even the duties given over to the boroughs involve some degree of inter-authority liaison and it therefore remains to be seen how far another of the Government's objectives – the avoidance of inter-authority conflict – will actually be achieved by abolition. Reorganisation might not stop at this point. Local government has experienced two decades of fierce debate about structure and there is no sign that the debate has ended. In January 1987, the Labour party published a consultative document on local government reform which proposed, among other things, the re-establishment of the GLC, the abolition of shire counties in England and Wales and, most radically, the establishment of a new regional tier of government. It is clear that the debate about the structure of local government is far from over.

ALLOCATING FUNCTIONS

As the Boundary Commission remarked in 1947, structure and functions need to be considered alongside each other. The purpose of structure is to facilitate the provision of services, ideally to the satisfaction of both provider and consumer. Unfortunately, as we noted at the beginning of this chapter, throughout the last couple of centuries British governments have tended to take an 'evolutionary' rather than 'rational' approach to the allocation of duties to local government. At no time has the simple question been asked: 'What duties properly belong to local government?' At most, official inquiries have reviewed existing activities of local councils and seen how best they might be administered. The sole exception to this was the Commission on the Constitution (1969–73) and even then it was only a minority of the Commission who really tackled this question in a fundamental way.[15] Instead, it has been mainly left to academics, whose interests are often primarily orientated towards regional structures, to give these matters serious thought.

The range of local authority services reveals no consistent plan by central government for the vertical division of power. The current responsibilities of local government are simply the product of responses to separate needs and changing political priorities. In the latter years of the nineteenth century, most of the powers of local councils were the consequence of initiatives by individual authorities, rather than functions handed to them by central government. By the turn of the century, local authorities possessed a mixture of powers derived from several sources, 'some granted by public general Acts; some involved in adoptive and clauses Acts, and some, individual to each corporation, granted by local Acts'.[16] The core undertakings were: sanitary services, police and highways and, in some cases, libraries. In addition, many authorities were involved in public utilities like water, gas and electricity. There were also some particular local powers including, in the case of Leeds, regulatory control over brothels.

Although the range of services operated by local authorities has changed significantly since the turn of the century, the same piecemeal approach has prevailed throughout the intervening period. At no time has any government enunciated a clear basis for the allocation of duties to local government. In failing to do this, they have therefore also failed to identify a precise role for local government. Even on those rare occasions when machinery of government questions have attracted interest at national level – after both World Wars and, to a lesser degree, in the early 1970s – the precise status and role of decentralised government have escaped attention. The issue of vertical division, in so far as it concerns the distribution of powers to local government, has never been planned coherently.

The functions of local councils grew during the first three decades of the twentieth century as existing services were expanded to accommodate new needs. Expanded responsibilities also resulted from developments in social welfare, education and housing. By the Second World War, however, local authorities began to lose services. Hospitals disappeared from local government control following the creation of the

National Health Service in 1946, and remaining personal health functions were lost in 1974. Nationalisation removed gas and electricity and, in 1974, water and sewerage responsibilities were transferred to regional water authorities. Abolition of the metropolitan counties further complicated the allocation of functions by creating new joint boards and in 1986 deregulation of bus services has added to this complexity.

The broad division of responsibilities between counties and districts (or regions and districts in the case of Scotland) is based upon the idea of scale. Counties are responsible for those services where operational needs indicate the desirability of a large unit, while district authorities have control of services where large-scale operation is not seen to be essential (Fig. 6.5). However, the precise division is not quite as simple as this description might suggest: many responsibilities are shared. Indeed, there are several ways in which powers can be shared. For some services, there may be *concurrent* powers which allow both tiers to provide similar services. Amenity services fall into this category and both county and district councils can provide parks and recreation facilities. Then there are *related* powers where the two levels of local government are involved in providing different aspects of a given service. Perhaps the best example of this is the refuse service where, in England, the district authority is responsible for collecting household refuse, but the county authority resumes responsibility for refuse disposal. Similarly, in the planning area there are many instances of related powers. A third kind of sharing results from *agency* arrangements where one local authority can arrange that another authority carries out a particular function on behalf of, and reimbursed by, the former authority. These arrangements usually result in functions being delegated downwards from county to district level. Delegation in local government has a long tradition,[18] although the agency concept that was included in the 1972 Act is more limited. Agency arrangements cannot be made in respect of education, police and social services. A fourth kind of sharing is *joint provision*. This is where a number of local authorities join together (through a joint board or joint committee) to provide a specific service or facility. Municipal airports can be run on such lines and, perhaps more importantly, this has been the device chosen to run fire, police and transport services in the metropolitan areas following the abolition of the metropolitan county councils in 1986.

The allocation of responsibilities is further complicated when we consider the activities of other bodies. These include central government and lower-level units of local government, as well as a variety of *ad hoc* authorities. Central control over local government is discussed later in this chapter and it is sufficient to note here that central government

SCOTLAND

Islands (3)

Consumer protection
Education/Careers
Environmental health[1]
Fire
Housing
Libraries
Planning: structure,
local, planning
applications
Police
Rate collection
Refuse: collection and
disposal
Social services
Transport

Regions (9)

Consumer protection
Education/Careers
Fire
Libraries
Planning: structure
Police
Rate collection
Social services
Transport

Districts (53)

Consumer protection
Environmental health[1]
Housing
Libraries
Markets
Planning: local,
planning applications
Refuse: collection and
disposal

ENGLAND AND WALES

London

Boroughs (32)[4]

Consumer protection
Education[3]
Environmental health[1]
Housing
Markets
Planning: structure[2],
local, planning
applications
Rate collection
Refuse: collection and
disposal[2]
Social services

Fire[2]
Transport[2]

Non-metropolitan areas

Counties (47)

Consumer protection
Education/Careers
Fire
Libraries
Planning: structure
Police
Refuse: disposal
Social services
Transport

Districts (333)

Environmental health[1]
Housing
Markets
Planning: local,
planning applications
Rate collection
Refuse: collection

Metropolitan areas

Districts (36)

Consumer protection
Education/Careers
Environmental health[1]
Housing
Libraries
Markets
Planning: structure,
local, planning applications
Rate collection
Refuse: collection and
disposal[2]
Social services

Fire[2]
Police[2]
Transport[2]

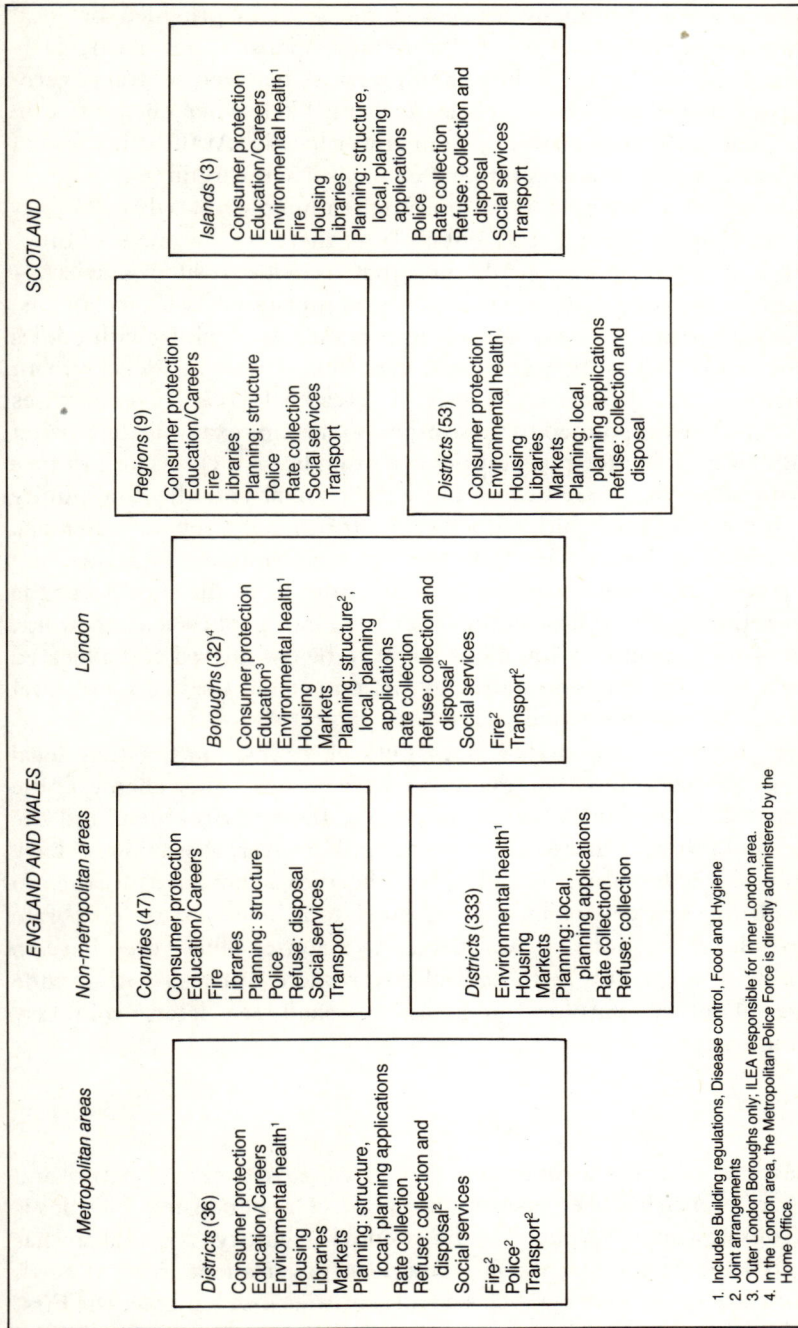

1. Includes Building regulations, Disease control, Food and Hygiene
2. Joint arrangements
3. Outer London Boroughs only; ILEA responsible for Inner London area.
4. In the London area, the Metropolitan Police Force is directly administered by the
   Home Office.

Fig. 6.5 Allocation of main functions to principal local authorities

retains control over many aspects of the services provided by local authorities. This has the effect of blurring responsibilities, particularly where there is a clash of policies and priorities between central government and a local authority. This is especially likely when one party is in power nationally and another one in power locally. At the other end of the scale, parish and community councils have certain rights to be consulted – for example, regarding the planning proposals of higher-level authorities. On the horizontal plane, there are a number of other local and regional *ad hoc* bodies that provide related services – sometimes services that were previously administered by local councils. Local authorities have particularly important relationships with bodies in the fields of health, water, gas, electricity, tourism, development agencies, national parks and the newly created UDCs. In some cases councillors are appointed to these other bodies, for example the district health authorities. Responsibilities can often be very close, for instance the social service activities of the local council and the community health duties of the health authority. Unfortunately, separate financial arrangements, boundaries that are not conterminous and differing priorities and strategies can make it difficult to put the services of the local authorities and those of the other body into a cohesive framework. This is one reason why functions ought to be considered and allocated as part of a comprehensive strategy. At no time in the history of local government has this actually happened.

The foregoing discussion does not, of course, imply that local authorities retain few powers. As we have seen in other chapters, the effect of local authority action on people, their environment and the social and physical landscape is extensive. However, these powers have been achieved haphazardly and local authorities do not have jurisdiction over all the services which are necessary to achieve a truly corporate approach to questions of local need. As a consequence, they have to work closely not only with central government but also with a wide range of other statutory and, as we shall see later, voluntary organisations.

REGIONALISM

At several points in the discussion about local government structure and areas, reference has been made to the notion of 'regionalism'. The idea is far from new and, throughout the twentieth century, regionalism has played some part in discussions about local government areas. Indeed, the lineage of regions goes back several centuries, but it is since the First World War that it has been directly related to the issue of local government structure. In fact, regionalism is not unknown in our contemporary system of government. The Scottish Office has exercised certain departmental responsibilities in respect of that nation since 1885 and the Welsh Office similarly for Wales since 1964. Since the 1930s, governments have recognised regions as units for strategic planning purposes and also now collect and assess data on the basis of the regional unit. Government departments generally have regional offices and, shortly after coming to power in 1964, the Labour Government created a pattern of regional economic planning boards and councils. Two-thirds of all civil servants work in regional and local outposts of central government departments. During the Second World War, Regional Commissioners were designated to assume full control of their areas in the event of invasion. Although they were subsequently disbanded, it is intended that a similar regional network would assume responsibility in the event of nuclear weapons being targeted at Britain. At a more everyday level, regions are features of most organisations ranging through railways, electricity, water, health, tourism and sports authorities in the public domain, to independent television companies, gas boards and most major retail organisations in the private sector. For all these bodies, the region is a meaningful administrative unit.[19] There seems a prima facie case, therefore, for examining its suitability as a unit of subnational government.

As long ago as 1919, C. B. Fawcett used geographical principles to argue the case for the reorganisation of local government on regional lines.[20] This theme was subsequently developed by a succession of geographers who applied a variety of principles to show that the region was a meaningful unit which could be used for the purposes of organising subnational government. As we noted earlier, two particular concepts have been popular: the 'city region'[21] and the 'urban hierarchy'.[22] Both concepts share a common feature: the desire to delimit territorial areas on the basis of *real* spatial patterns of social and economic life. In applying these techniques it is usual to identify between five and nine major regions of England, with additional units in respect of Scotland and Wales.

As we have seen, regions are widely accepted as administrative units in Britain. However, regions have been much less favoured as political units and have been resisted by politicians from both local and central government. In the late 1960s, a Royal Commission on the Constitution (Kilbrandon Commission) was appointed to look at the subject of devolution, separate from the Redcliffe–Maud and Wheatley Commissions on local government structure and areas. The Labour Government saw these as two separate issues. It was a view shared by the

Conservative Government that succeeded Labour, since it went ahead with reorganisation before the Kilbrandon Commission had submitted its report. Like the Redcliffe–Maud Commission, the Commission on the Constitution issued two reports.[23] The second, a *Memorandum of Dissent* written by Lord Crowther-Hunt and Professor Alan Peacock, proposed the creation of five regional assemblies plus two others for Scotland and Wales. Broadly, these assemblies would take over the responsibilities of the regional outposts of central government departments as well as those of most public-sector *ad hoc* regional authorities. The proposals were seen as a means of complementing and strengthening the existing structure of subnational (i.e. local) government in Britain. In the event, nothing came of either the minority or majority recommendations. There was no move to create regional authorities in England and the debate about Scottish and Welsh devolution continued throughout the decade before finally coming to an abrupt end in 1978.[24]

With the demise of the Scottish and Welsh devolution Bills, it might seem as though regionalism retains no interest for the student of local government. This is not the case. As a geographical approach to the problem of territorial units, regions remain relevant. Moreover, as long as many decentralised services are operated by *ad hoc* regional bodies, then it will be important to understand the relationship between these statutory bodies and local government.

CENTRAL SUPERVISION AND CONTROL

The relationship with central government is a crucial aspect of the local government system. The relationship has been variously described as anything ranging from a 'partnership' to an 'agency' arrangement, but in recent years it has become increasingly strained.[25]

In the most basic terms, local government is the creation of Parliament: its powers, structure and boundaries are dependent upon the will of Parliament. National interests are also an important feature of the context in which local authorities operate. We have already seen, for example, how the physical or social needs of the local community have to be set in the context of national patterns of need. The same is true of resources, and one of the most controversial aspects of the relationship has been the financial control of local government by central government. National interests have also become more apparent through the increasing participation in local politics of national political parties.

It is usual to consider central control of local government under three headings – legislative, administrative and judicial. Inevitably, these three kinds of control overlap, but they provide a convenient categorisation. In addition, there is, of course, the issue of financial control that was discussed in the previous chapter. *Legislative or parliamentary control* is the most obvious form of central control since all local authority powers derive from Acts of Parliament. Even local by-laws are subject to government scrutiny. In addition to the main statutory duties imposed by these Acts, individual local authorities can seek to extend their legal competence through Private Bills. However, this is a complex and costly procedure, designed to discourage many local authorities from seeking such powers. One recent case of a Private Bill was the Birmingham City Council Act 1985, which allows the staging of motor racing events in the city streets. A further way of extending the powers of a local council is by application to ministers who, in some matters, may have appropriate powers designated by a piece of parent legislation.

Administrative controls provide the more detailed supervision of local authority work. There is a particularly important characteristic of this form of supervision. In Britain, unlike some other countries, control over local government is not a function of one particular department. Although the Department of the Environment has frequent dealings with local government and comes closest to being the central government department exercising general responsibility for local authorities, the relationship is by no means exclusive. The Department of Education and Science, the Department of Health and Social Security and the Home Office all have considerable connections with the work of local councils. The link with the DES is particularly strong since, although local authorities administer the vast majority of education services in Britain, most of the money comes from central government. It is inevitable that this fact alone will lead to considerable central intervention.

Control by departments can range from regulations which are supported by delegated legislation and which are therefore enforceable, to consultative papers which are not backed by any real sanctions. There is a range of controls between these two extremes, and the provision of most local authority services involves a continuing dialogue with the appropriate central government department. In some matters, local authorities are required to submit development schemes for ministerial approval, for example concerning changes in the organisation of secondary and tertiary education. Planning is another area in which ministerial approval might be necessary, sometimes as a result of an inquiry to arbitrate between the local council and an appellant. Arbitration may also sometimes be necessary as a result of a conflict between local authorities. Finally, ministerial intervention can take the form of default powers, for instance when an authority fails to provide a service to the satisfaction of the relevant minister. In such circumstances, the minister may either assume the power himself or transfer responsibility to another body – another local authority or a specially appointed person or body. The best-known example of the latter was when Clay Cross UDC refused to implement the fair rent clauses of the 1972 Housing Finance Act, with the result that a commissioner was appointed to administer this function. The most systematic form of administrative control is that of inspection. This procedure is an important means of ensuring that satisfactory standards of provision are achieved. It is used in respect of police, fire and education services (via HMIs) and in the social services departments which are subject to review by the DHSS.

The third major category of control is *judicial control*. Britain does not have a system of administrative law; consequently, as with central government, judicial control in respect of local government can take a variety of guises. One aspect is through the principle of *ultra vires*, by which an authority can be prevented from exceeding its powers or incurring unreasonable expenditure. Recourse to law on these grounds is available to an individual citizen or to an external auditor. Legally, all authorities are subject to an annual audit – mainly to ensure that expenditure is incurred legally – but increasingly audits are concerned with questions of value for money. Since the 1982 Local Government Finance Act, the Audit Commission has been responsible for all local authority audits, although they are actually conducted either by the District Audit service or by auditors in private service. In 1985/86 councillors in Lambeth and Liverpool faced surcharge and disqualification for wilfully delaying the fixing of the annual rates. There are other principles of judicial control besides *ultra vires*. The main ones are *mandamus*, which requires an authority to carry out an obligatory duty; *prohibition*, which prevents an authority from proceeding further in an area where it might be exceeding its jurisdiction; and *certiorari*, where the activity proceeds but the authority may have its decision reversed at a later stage by the High Court. Finally, there are a variety of *statutory appeal* procedures by which the citizen can contest the decision of a local authority. These appeals are most commonly found in matters relating to planning decisions and schemes involving private properties.

There is one further kind of supervision that does not strictly fit into any of these three major categories. Although perhaps better described as an 'influence' rather than a 'control', the role of the local ombudsman should not be overlooked when considering the range of supervisory forces that act on local government. Their role is discussed in Chapter 8.

In large measure, the motivations for these central controls stem from the same centralising forces that were mentioned in the first chapter.

The desire for uniform provision in fields such as education and social services means that some degree of central supervision is inevitable. Similarly, central interference is a reflection of the need to recognise national interests. For example, highway construction and maintenance has national implications so that local schemes need to be compatible with national plans. Not least, there is the fact the local councils are a major part of the UK economy. Governments of all persuasions accept responsibility for managing the economy and it is only to be expected therefore that intervention in the financial affairs of local government is one of the prices to be paid. It is significant that questions of expenditure have been at the heart of central–local relations since 1979. In broad terms, the motivation of central government in regulating local government is its perception and pursuit of national as opposed to local interests. Even with the best will in the world, the pursuit of national interest by central government and that of local interest by local government will invariably lead to frequent clashes.

Central controls have been evident throughout the modern history of local government. In the field of health provision, for example, the nineteenth century Local Government Board provided advice for local authorities in a range of matters. Indeed, in some fields – notably health, police and education – a system of local inspection had been established well before the end of the nineteenth century. The extent of central supervision, however, has increased markedly since 1945 and, significantly, it has done so irrespective of the party in power. The first post-war Labour Government, for example, was anxious that its ambitions for social and economic reform should not be frustrated by unco-operative local authorities. As a consequence, it legislated in a number of local government fields, especially education, police, planning and social welfare. In order to ensure that ministers had sufficient powers to control the way in which local authorities provided these services, statutory instruments which allowed ministers to intervene were included in the clauses of the parent Acts. It has been suggested that by the middle of the twentieth century government departments had developed three different traditions of local control – *laissez-faire*, regulatory and promotional.[26] The *laissez-faire* approach allowed local authorities to please themselves about local provision and was perhaps most evident in the fields of health and housing. The regulatory approach was possibly best illustrated by the attitude of the Home Office, which saw its role as the careful supervision of local authorities in order to ensure that nationally determined regulations were implemented locally. The promotional approach, encouraging but not requiring local authorities to do certain things, was illustrated in the field of education. However, in the intervening period education has become more controversial politically. In the late 1960s, the Labour Government was intent upon introducing a system of comprehensive education nationally (DES Circular 10/65). The opposition of some Conservative-controlled authorities led to considerable conflicts between central and local government. Since 1979, the Conservative Government has had its own share of disputes with local authorities about education matters. The DES has taken a close interest in educational provision, especially regarding expenditure, curricula and training schemes. It has been proposed that there should be a national core curriculum and by European standards, Britain is unusual in not having a common school curriculum. Under the 1944 Education Act, only religious education is stipulated as a compulsory school subject. In the light of recent events in the sector, the relationship between the DES and local education authorities might be described now as a 'regulatory' rather than a 'promotional' model.

The relationship between central and local government has become more controversial since 1972. The 1972 and 1973 Acts did, in fact, remove some controls: they reduced the number of statutory officials and committees; the power of the district auditor was limited; and they increased the level and provision of the clause allowing limited spending in the interests of the community. However, the policies of both Labour and Conservative governments since then have resulted in a tightening of central control over local government. In the late 1970s, for example, Labour reintroduced a policy of comprehensive education and began to attempt to control the overall level of spending by local authorities. When the Conservatives came into office in 1979 they pledged to rationalise controls over local government and there has been some relaxation of controls and a reduction in the number of Whitehall circulars sent to local councils. Nevertheless, while under the 1980 Local Government, Planning and Land Act controls were eased in certain areas, others were put in their place. Particularly contentious were the new capital expenditure controls procedure and the new form of block grant which was subsequently reinforced by the device of 'rate-capping'. Even some Conservative-controlled authorities contested these measures. The sale of council houses has been another disputed policy.

Local government has never been free of central control and supervision, although the strength of these controls has varied between periods and between service sectors. Although it is fashionable to ascribe the present level of control to the Conservative Government's desire to control local expenditure, no one party can take all the blame for the current degree of central intervention. Perhaps the real difference between the parties is in their motivation for intervention: in the case of the Conservatives this has been primarily a consequence of their commitment to reduce public expenditure; in the case of Labour, intervention in local affairs is a consequence of their commitment to socialist policies which, by their very nature, usually presume the construction of nation-wide schemes. The motivations vary, but the effect is much the same. How far these controls limit the freedom of local authorities is open to debate. Some people contend that the effect has been to subordinate local government entirely to the will of central government and, in so doing, to diminish public interest in local politics. The integrated planning of local services is made more difficult by the fact that individual local authority services are subject to pressure from central government departments – central policies may well conflict with local schemes. As is usually the case, the reality is probably less clear-cut. For one thing, it should be recognised that there has never been a 'golden age' of local government when it was free from all central government interference. Controls have certainly become stronger, especially in matters of finance, but local authorities remain politically independent. There is still considerable scope for local authorities to respond to their own perceptions of local need and stamp their own ideas on the community.[27]

THE INTERDEPENDENCE OF LOCAL SERVICES

In meeting the needs of local areas and people, local authorities are not independent actors, but must work closely with a range of other bodies and agencies. Few organisations are able to achieve their objectives without the co-operation of external agencies. This is especially true of a local authority and, in this case, principal external actors will include central government as well as, in some instances, other local authorities either in adjacent areas or at other levels (county/district/parish). Moreover, local authorities are not the only organisations concerned with the well-being of the community and with providing services for local residents. Rather, they are at the centre of a network of bodies, some statutory and others voluntary, all of which have some impact on the local community. A good deal of collaboration is, therefore, necessary if local needs are to be met effectively. There has to be constructive liaison, even integration – from policy-making levels to those of day-to-day service provision – if all these organisations are to work together effectively and harmoniously in the interests of those who consume services.

Relationships within and between local authorities

The first stage of co-operation should take place within the authority itself between its various departments – 'intra-authority co-operation' – and all local authority departments will have connections with adjacent departments. The education service, for example, has close ties with local authority social service departments in respect of deprived children. Equally, there are strong links between the work of housing and social service departments.[28] 'Social' factors, for instance, are taken account of in calculating housing allocation. The provision of sheltered and adapted housing for disabled people also brings the two departments into contact, as does the housing of children and one-parent families. The provision of housing schemes for the mentally handicapped mainly involves local authority housing stock. In reality, however, collaboration between departments is not always easy to achieve. One reason (discussed in the next chapter) is that local authority departments are organised more according to the requirements of professional staff than they are according to the needs of clients. There are, therefore, organisational obstacles to be overcome as well as, in many cases, differences in approach between different professional groups. The Barclay Report, *Social Workers: Their Roles and Tasks*, for example, observed that: 'Housing officers are concerned to apply objective standards of priorities for the allocation of houses . . . Typically a social worker's emphasis on the individual problems of the client may strike the housing officer as over-protective, while the social worker thinks the latter's attachment to objective factors, inflexible and bureaucratic'.[29]

Collaboration between authorities – inter-authority collaboration – is similarly necessary, but often equally difficult. Even the structure itself creates a potential for conflict because of the way in which functions are divided between county and district levels outside London and the Metropolitan areas – a potential which increases when control of the collaborating authorities is in the hands of different political parties. One of the reasons why the Redcliffe–Maud Commission favoured all-purpose unitary authorities was that they removed one potential source of conflict – disputes between county and subordinate levels. Proponents of all-purpose local councils have pointed to their distinctive virtues in this respect:[30]

1. All-purpose authorities are simple and *easy to understand*. They avoid fragmentation between different levels of local government and are easier for the public to understand. One authority provides all local services.

2. *Interrelated services* can be administered by a single authority. Housing issues, for example, are linked to land-use planning matters which, in turn, affect transport and traffic schemes. Under the present system, outside the 36 metropolitan districts, housing is a district responsibility and the others are county functions.

3. Allocating all services to a single unit allows *coherence of political policy*. Local councillors are able to consider the needs of the locality in their totality; they are not limited to considering some services, while others are the responsibility of councillors in another tier.

4. All the needs of the local area could be *articulated by a single authority* which, it is alleged, would strengthen the voice of individual local authorities against central government.

The advantages and disadvantages of single-tier and two-tier systems of local government are not merely of academic and historical interest. Abolition of the GLC and the metropolitan counties means, in effect, that the two-tier and single-tier structures now exist alongside each other, albeit in a slightly modified manner since the metropolitan districts are required to establish joint boards for the provision of police, fire and transport services.

Wherever there is a division of responsibility, there is a potential for dispute: relationships which are essentially *interdependent* – where two or more bodies need each other's co-operation for the achievement of a particular objective – can break down very easily. In fact, there are many sectors which necessitate one local authority being dependent upon the co-operation of another for the achievement of the former's objectives. It follows, therefore, that there are opportunities for things to go wrong. Among other things, successful inter-authority relationships require the following:

1. Agreement about overall objectives and priorities (for example, a district authority which is committed to low rates could find this objective frustrated by a county authority imposing a large rate precept to pay for a cheap transport policy).

2. Agreement about the time-span of objectives (it is easy for short-term to conflict with longer-term structure plans).

3. Compatible structures and internal working procedures (if, say, one authority has a high degree of internal delegation of power and another is more formalised and hierarchical in its internal power structure, then there could be some difficulty in deciding the appropriate level of contact between officers of the relevant authorities).

4. Clear allocations of responsibility between organisations (where

there is uncertainty about 'who does what' then there is opportunity
for disputes which may lead to interference by central government).

5. Agreement about the use made of local resources – i.e. land,
   manpower and finance (one authority may wish to use land for the
   purposes of industrial regeneration; another authority may wish to
   stress the recreational nature of land).

6. Willingness to respond to ideas from outside one's own authority
   (one of the characteristics of most organisations is a resistance to
   ideas from other bodies; much the same is true of individuals).

Clearly, a great deal of goodwill and co-operation is required if local
authorities are to work together effectively and in the common interests
of the locality. Not least of the problems is the fact that differences in
party political control may lead county and district authorities to adopt
opposing policies. This was seen when some of the Conservative-
controlled London boroughs that were concerned about the level of
rates campaigned against the subsidised transport policy of the Labour-
led GLC. Even if the same party is in power at both county and district
level, there is no guarantee of agreed objectives. However, in some areas
a number of councillors sit on both county and district authorities and
this can help reduce tensions. Also, many authorities have responded to
the suggestion in the Bains Report that there should be joint committees
comprising councillors from the county (or region in Scotland) and
constituent district councils 'to co-ordinate the interaction of all county
and district functions and policies for the locality'.[31] The report
approved the ideas of one commentator:

Objectives should not be set by one authority in isolation . . . what is sought is
joint planning, not just a joint plan. It must be recognised that there will be
different authorities with different objectives who will not always agree. The
outcome of joint planning may be greater awareness and understanding rather
than agreement. But that will be a step forward.[32]

Joint boards and committees

Sometimes collaboration between local authorities extends to the joint
provision of services.[33] Since the abolition of the metropolitan county
councils, for example, police, fire and civil defence, and public transport services have been administered by joint boards comprising
councillors drawn from constituent districts (and also, in the case of the
police boards, local magistrates) according to rules which specify the
allocation of seats both to districts and to party groups. Although these
are the only major joint boards created following the abolition of the
metropolitan counties, similar arrangements are permitted, and even

encouraged, in respect of other services. A joint committee to oversee trading standards was required by statute and districts have been encouraged to collaborate in respect of granting aid to voluntary groups in the fields of arts, recreation and community services. Similarly, if the district authorities in the former metropolitan areas failed to agree satisfactory arrangements for the disposal of waste, the minister has been given residual powers to create a further joint board to operate this service.

Not surprisingly, the transfer of powers from the metropolitan counties to the districts has resulted in various patterns of joint action. Three approaches were possible: a 'county-orientated' approach with a county-wide central service unit located in a single place and administered by a joint board; an 'intermediate' approach with a county-wide unit located within one of the district authorities but responsible to a joint committee of all districts; and a 'devolved' approach where staff were dispersed and there was only a minimal retention of county-wide units with only weak co-ordinating joint committees and effective control being handed to a single lead district.[34] As might be expected, many of the county authorities wished to pass on a legacy of county-wide action – this was official Labour Party policy – and to leave *in situ* as many remnants of previous organisations as possible, whereas the Conservative Government showed a preference for the intermediate approach, partly because this seemed the most likely to maximise the financial savings from abolition. The ability of the former metropolitan counties to achieve their objective depended in part upon how far a sense of identity had been achieved within their county during the twelve years of existence, as well as the effectiveness of political links between the county and its constituent districts and between the districts themselves. Both of these links tended to be stronger if the parties in control were the same in all cases. In the event, the area which seems to have achieved most collaboration at the level of the former county is West Yorkshire and, by contrast, West Midlands, Tyne and Wear and South Yorkshire have least joint machinery. The latter three areas, for example, have all devolved arrangements for waste disposal. Greater Manchester and Merseyside – both of which have created joint authorities for waste disposal – fall somewhere between the two extremes.[35]

Although the three major joint boards have been meeting since December 1985, most of the joint arrangements are relatively new and it is, therefore, only possible to make a preliminary assessment about how these bodies will operate. Even at this early stage, however, it is notable that party politics is having an important effect on their style of operation and party loyalties rather than attachment to districts seems to guide the decision-making process. Similar practices have been discerned in other joint undertakings, as John Stewart has observed:

. . . past experience would suggest that the members of a joint board become isolated from the authority nominating them. Often they do not report back to the local authority, and if they did who would there be to advise the council on policy on that joint board whose experience is comparable with the officers of that joint board?[36]

One reflection of this is that there has developed a tendency to hold party group meetings before joint board sessions and for voting subsequently to take place on party lines. The significance of party politics within the joint boards has been exacerbated in the case of the police joint board where appointed magistrates hold one-third of the seats. This has sometimes resulted in them holding the balance of power between party groups and there have been particularly difficult relationships between the police forces and the joint boards in Merseyside and in Greater Manchester. One final feature of these joint authorities that is perhaps worth mentioning is the nature of their memberships. A crude measure by which the importance attached to the joint boards may be assessed is the seniority of those who are nominated to serve on the authorities. Much seems to depend upon the perceived status of the board in question. Thus, whereas the police and public transport boards have attracted leading district councillors as members, there seems to be much less enthusiasm for serving on the fire and civil defence joint boards.

LOCAL AUTHORITIES AND STATUTORY AND VOLUNTARY BODIES

So far, the discussion has focused on intra- and inter-authority relationships, but much the same requirements for co-operation apply to relationships between local authorities and statutory bodies which administer related functions. There are many such bodies and there are especially close relationships between local government and the public utilities (gas, water and electricity), the health authorities, other transport undertakings (British Rail), the Post Office, the Countryside Commission, national parks, tourist authorities, development agencies, etc. In addition there are the relationships with new town corporations and UDCs discussed in Chapter 4. Frequently, local authorities indirectly elect councillors to be members of these authorities and there is often considerable cross-membership between the local authority and associated statutory bodies. The Committee on the Management of Local Government discovered that over two-thirds of councillors

belonged to some kind of statutory body in addition to their membership of the local council.[37] The links between local government and
these bodies operate at various levels – from the policy-making level at
the top to the day-to-day co-operation between those employed by the
respective organisations. Local authority education departments, for
instance, work very closely, via their youth employment services, with
the Manpower Services Commission and with a number of voluntary
youth associations in respect of their youth and community services.

A particularly close relationship exists between local authorities and
related bodies in the National Health Service. Until 1974, the NHS was
based upon a tripartite structure with local authorities furnishing one
part of health service provision. Public health has been an important
local authority function in Britain. Following the National Health
Service Reorganisation Act 1973, hospital management committees, the
family practitioner services and local authority health services were
unified in new regional and area health authorities. However, the links
with local authority services – especially social service and environmental health departments – were not overlooked and there are close
relationships between these bodies. At the policy-making level, this is
manifested by district health authorities being required to allocate a
specified number of places to elected representatives from constituent
local authorities. This is also true of the community health councils
which monitor health service provision in the locality. Such links are
facilitated by conterminous geographical boundaries in many instances.
There are also close day-to-day working relationships as may be seen in
many aspects of local authority environmental health provision. In
1987, for example, one local authority brought together its environmental health and education departments to work with the area health
authority to produce a film on AIDS for showing in local schools.
Environmental health departments – sometimes referred to as public
health departments – have many causes to work closely with the regional
and district health authorities in the control of infectious diseases.
District community physicians, who used to be known as local medical
officers of health, illustrate the link between the health authorities and
local environmental health departments. Cases of communicable
diseases must be notified to the district community physician who,
having decided upon an appropriate course of action, will rely upon the
environmental health department to carry out the necessary duties. The
work of the public health laboratory is another link between these two
sectors.

The other area of local authority work which relates closely to the
health services is social services. Both have many common interests,

especially concerning specific groups in society: the elderly, the mentally handicapped and those newly released from hospital. For all three groups there has to be a careful balancing of services that are available in the community through local authorities and those provided in hospital by the health authority. The elderly may call upon a range of people and services drawn from both sectors – doctors, district nurses and health visitors from the NHS, and social workers, home helps and sheltered housing from the local authority. For the provisions to work effectively, there has to be good liaison and co-operation. At the policy-making level, co-ordination is sought through joint planning machinery comprising a joint consultative committee (JCC) for members and a joint care planning team (JCPT) for officers. There is even finance available from the DHSS specifically to foster joint schemes between the health and social service sectors. In 1985/86 the figure allocated was £105 million. The importance of collaboration has become even greater since 1981 when the DHSS published a consultative document *Care in the Community*, which stressed the desire to provide more long-term care in the community rather than in hospitals. The effect of this has been to transfer more responsibility for care to local authorities. Effective liaison is, of course, just as important at the 'sharp end' of health and social service provision through good working relationships between fellow professionals as it is at the policy-making level.[38]

The ten regional water authorities also have a close relationship with local government. As with health services, local government has always been involved in the provision of water services, although following the Water Act 1973, the major responsibility for water supply and sewerage facilities moved to the regional water boards. Until 1983, local councillors comprised a majority of the membership of the water authorities. However, since then members have been appointed by the Secretary of State. With the prospect of privatisation, the relationship could change yet again, but it is inevitable that local authorities will always be involved in some aspects of water supply and sewerage undertakings. Environmental health departments, for example, are charged with the responsibility of ensuring that the quality of water supplied is satisfactory. This involves them in a close working relationship with the water boards and, indeed, some local authorities undertake certain sewerage and water services on an agency basis on behalf of the water authorities.

In addition to the many statutory bodies, there is an even greater array of voluntary agencies working alongside local government. Although these bodies have no statutory powers, they are a vital component of the local political landscape. While they are primarily dependent upon the energies of volunteers, some are very large and have full-time professional staffs. Voluntary bodies include agencies like the NSPCC, the Marriage Guidance Council and the National Association for Mental Health (MIND), organisations concerned with welfare and help for the elderly, meals on wheels service, civic trusts, tenants' associations, church bodies, professional and trade bodies, sporting clubs, youth associations, environmental groups, and so on. In a study of three London boroughs, it was discovered that there were no fewer than 2,700 voluntary groups – 1,500 of which were in 'periodic contact with councillors and departments'.[39] The Maud Report found that, on average, local councillors belonged to six or seven such bodies. Part of the role of local voluntary agencies is to act as a pressure group in local politics, voicing the views of a particular section of the community, a function that is discussed in Chapter 8. However, equally important is their contribution to the provision of local services. Their efforts in this respect complement those of local authorities. The voluntary sector is especially important in the field of social services, both as a provider of voluntary help and as a monitor of local need. In the London survey, voluntary bodies in the social service field 'ranged from organisations which acted as agents for the local council (e.g. Family Planning Association) to small and very localised luncheon clubs for the elderly. Voluntary organisations assisted departments in several ways – providing services for the council, pioneering services and supplementing council-provided services.'[40] According to one local authority official, 'We can only run our services with the goodwill of the local community'.[41] They focus especially on three client groups: children, the elderly and the handicapped. Local authorities in turn help voluntary agencies through financial aid, the provision of professional support, sometimes through secondment schemes, and cheap premises and accommodation. Many of the smaller voluntary organisations operate under the umbrella of a larger association, the local Council for Voluntary Social Services, which has daily working relationships with local authority social service departments. Indeed, they have almost become an extension of the department and make an essential contribution to the provision of local welfare services.

The social services area is the one in which voluntary associations have the closest relationship with the local authority. In other fields, voluntary bodies are probably more likely to act as spokesmen for consumers than as service providers. Nevertheless, there are few areas of local authority work where a close working relationship with the voluntary sector is not an important aspect of local government's relations with the community it serves.

Local authorities do not operate in isolation from other organisations:

central government, statutory bodies, agencies in the voluntary sector and other local councils all have an impact on the work of local government. It is a complex network of relationships, made even more complicated by the fact that it has not been designed as part of a coherent plan. It is often as confusing to those who work in local government as it is to those who consume services. The scene is further complicated by the links between local authorities and the private sector. Privatisation, putting services out to tender and collaborative schemes between private and public sectors for the regeneration of inner-city areas means that local councils find themselves working increasingly with private sector organisations. Good relationships are crucial if they are to work well. This chapter has focused on the external relationships of local authorities; the next turns to relationships within local councils.

Notes

1. D. N. Chester and F. M. G. Wilson, *The Organisation of British Central Government* (Allen and Unwin, 1968).
2. W. Thornhill, *Public Administration* (ICSA, 1985), p. 30.
3. A useful review of the major approaches can be found in J. Stanyer and B. Smith, *Administering Britain* (Fontana, 1976), pp. 95–105. For a fuller discussion see B. Smith, *Decentralisation: The Territorial Dimension of the State* (Allen and Unwin, 1985).
4. For example, C. B. Fawcett, *The Provinces of England* (Williams and Northgate, 1919) is still relevant to the issues of local government structure.
5. W. Hampton, 'Local Government and Community', *Political Quarterly* (1969), p. 155.
6. Several useful studies of community action are to be found in R. Darke and R. Walker, *Local Government and the Public* (Leonard Hill, 1977).
7. R. E. Dickinson, *City, Region and Regionalism* (Kegan Paul, 1947). Useful extracts from this and related readings appear in W. Thornhill, *The Case for Regional Reform* (Nelson, 1972), Ch. 3. A valuable discussion of some of the main geographical ideas is to be found in E. Jones, *Towns and Cities* (OUP, 1966), Chs. 5 and 6.
8. *Cmnd 4040–1*. See also D. Senior, 'The City Region as an Administrative Unit', *Political Quarterly* (1965).
9. B. Keith-Lucas and P. G. Richards, *A History of Local Government in the Twentieth Century* (Allen and Unwin, 1978) provides an excellent review of the major events and ideas.
10. *Ibid.* p. 200.
11. Local Government (County Boroughs and Adjustments) Act 1926.
12. Keith-Lucas and Richards, *op. cit.* p. 205.
13. *Committee on Local Authority and Allied Personal Social Services*, Cmnd 3703 (1968).
14. Keith-Lucas and Richards, *op. cit.* p. 229.
15. *Royal Commission on the Constitution*, Cmnd 5460 (October 1973), and *Memorandum of Dissent*, Cmnd 5460–1.
16. Keith-Lucas and Richards, *op. cit.* p. 36.
17. See, e.g. *Report of the Machinery of Government Committee of the Ministry of Reconstruction* (Haldane Report), Cd 9230 (1918); and *Reorganization of Central Government*, Cmnd 4276 (1970).
18. P. G. Richards, *Delegation in Local Government* (Allen and Unwin, 1956).
19. There is an equally extensive literature on regionalism. The more useful books include: Thornhill (1972), *op. cit.*; B. C. Smith, *Regionalism in England* (Acton Society Trust, 1965); C. B. Fawcett, *op. cit.*; 'Regionaliter', 'The Regional Commissioners', *Political Quarterly* (1940); P. Self, *Regionalism* (Fabian Society, 1948); J. P. Mackintosh, *Devolution of Power* (Pelican, 1968).

20. Fawcett, *op. cit.*
21. See notes 7 and 8 above.
22. A. E. Smailes, 'The Urban Hierarchy in England and Wales', *Geography* (1944) ; and R. P. Smith, 'The Changing Urban Hierarchy', *Regional Studies* (1968).
23. *Royal Commission on the Constitution 1969–73*, Report, Cmnd 5460; *Memorandum of Dissent*, Cmnd 5460–1.
24. V. Bogdanor, *Devolution* (OUP, 1979).
25. R. Rhodes, *Control and Power in Central–Local Relations* (Gower, 1981).
26. J. A. G. Griffith, *Central Departments and Local Control* (Allen and Unwin, 1966).
27. Rhodes, *op. cit.*; L. J. Sharpe and K. Newton, *Does Politics Matter? The Determinants of Public Policy* (OUP, 1984).
28. See B. Hudson, 'In Pursuit of Coordination: Housing and the Personal Social Services', *Local Government Studies*, March/April 1986.
29. *Ibid.* p. 59.
30. G. W. Jones, 'The Local Government Act 1972 and the Redcliffe–Maud Commission', *Political Quarterly* (1973).
31. *The New Local Authorities: Management and Structure* (Bains), Department of the Environment (HMSO, 1972), para. 8.6.
32. *Ibid.* para. 8.10.
33. N. Flynn and S. Leach, *Joint Boards and Joint Committees: An Evaluation* (INLOGOV, 1984).
34. S. Leach, 'The Transfer of Power from Metropolitan Counties to Districts: An Analysis', *Local Government Studies* (March 1987). The section which follows draws upon the findings of the research project outlined in this article.
35. *Ibid.* p. 42.
36. J. D. Stewart, 'The Conditions for Joint Action', *The London Journal* (Summer 1984), p. 62, quoted in Leach, *op. cit.*
37. *Committee on the Management of Local Government*, Report (HMSO, 1967), Vol. 2 'The Local Councillor', Table 6.5.
38. For a review of the various aspects of the relationships between local authority social services departments and the health sector, see P. Lloyd, *Services Administration by Local Authorities* (ICSA, 1985), pp. 166–70.
39. P. F. Cousins, 'Voluntary Organisations and Local Government in Three London Boroughs', *Public Administration* (1976), p. 79.
40. *Ibid.* p. 76.
41. *Ibid.* p. 76.

7

INTERNAL ORGANISATION AND DECISION-MAKING PROCESSES IN LOCAL GOVERNMENT

The main issues involved in the organisation of local authorities are essentially the same as those in any large organisation: they concern the division of labour inside the authority. How should the many functions of the local authority be divided into manageable tasks? How should these various tasks be brought together in order to ensure that there is unity of purpose in the overall work of the authority? The former question is about *differentiation* and the latter about *integration*. It is also relevant to examine how local authorities actually go about their work, in particular the role of officers and that of councillors in local government and the relationship between these two groups. In the past two decades, all of these issues have been the subject of much debate. Four major reports have been devoted to these matters – the Maud Committee on the Management of Local Government (1967), the Bains Report on Local Authority Management and Structure (1972), the Paterson Report on Organisation and Management Structures in Scotland (1973) – and most recently the Widdicombe Report on the Conduct of Local Authority Business (1986). Not least, all the new authorities that were established in 1974 and 1975 have had to make decisions about the organisation of their own particular authorities. It is possible to consider how local authorities are organised in the light of general principles of organisation and of the social and political context in which they operate.

ORGANISATION: RECENT MODELS

Certain aspects of local authority organisation are determined by statute and, to this extent, the freedom of local authorities to create their own internal organisation is circumscribed. The main aspects that are determined by law are the following:

1. The full council, comprising elected members of the authority, is designated the formal governing body of the local authority. Only this body, for example, can levy rates. The council is required to meet annually in order to elect a chairman and transact other business. Thereafter, the council usually meets monthly or quarterly, but the frequency is not specified by statute.

2. There are some statutory appointments: all relevant local authorities must appoint a chief constable, chief education officer, director of social services, chief fire officer and chief inspector of weights and measures (before 1974, there were additional statutory officers.) There is also a legal obligation to appoint parallel committees in most of these fields, which may be required to include co-opted members (e.g. the police and education committees must have a proportion of local magistrates or educationalists, respectively, as members).

3. There are certain regulations about the procedure and conduct of business (Part XI and Schedule 12, Local Government Act 1972). These regulations include the notice to be given about meetings, the publication of minutes, etc. Most procedures are set out in the council's own standing orders which may be based upon model standing orders issued by central government. These concern such matters as: order and conduct of business at meetings; presentation of agendas and minutes; declaration of interests by officers and members, etc.

Outside these matters, however, local authorities are free to determine their own management arrangements and styles of decision-making and, to some extent, these will reflect particular local traditions. In the years immediately after the new authorities were created, however, there were many similarities in the way that local authorities organised their management structures. Now that local authorities have become better established, the particular needs of the locality have been recognised, and local political parties have had the opportunity to stamp their own ideas on the authority, management structures have become more distinctive. Indeed, one of the more significant issues about internal organisation is whether it is possible to design a single management structure that is suitable for all local authorities or whether each council needs to design its own unique structure in order to reflect the particular local circumstances.

The main features of a local authority organisation are committees and departments, which reflect the division of labour between elected members and officers, respectively. Sometimes other terms are used –

'directorates', for instance, is sometimes used to describe a large division on the officers' side – but the essence remains the same. Committees may, in turn, be divided into subcommittees and still further into panels. Given the random manner in which local authority functions have been amassed over the years, the usual pattern was for local authorities to establish committees and departments in parallel for each major separate function as and when needs arose. Much the same thing has happened in central government whenever a new 'need' has been perceived; the Department of Energy and the Northern Ireland Office are two recent examples of this tendency. The division of labour inside a local authority can be either vertical or horizontal. The former applies where a specific service sector forms the basis of the division (e.g. police, education, environmental health, housing, etc.) and the latter where the division is based on an activity that embraces the whole of the local authority (e.g. staffing, finance, land use). Horizontal divisions tend to be based on resource matters and vertical divisions on service provisions and, in a broad sense, horizontal departments and committees help present an overall view of the local authority, while vertically based departments and committees have the effect of fragmenting the authority. A common pattern for local authority organisation in the mid-1960s was the existence of a range of departments (usually on the basis of vertical divisions) with a parallel committee structure (Fig. 7.1).

This simple structure has some obvious virtues: it is fairly clear – each department has a committee both to scrutinise its work and represent its interests on the full council; new committees and departments can be added as new powers are given to local authorities or, conversely, existing structures can be dismantled as functions disappear. However, there are also weaknesses, in particular the fragmentation of local authority services. Differentiation is easily achieved by this simple framework; what is more difficult to achieve is the integration of the work of these various units into some kind of overall purpose and objective for the local authority. It is important not to lose sight of the fact that, ultimately, the purpose of local government is to respond to community needs, which are not generally separated into conveniently discrete aspects. A popular perception of how bureaucratic structures work (and local authority organisation is an example of a bureaucratic structure) is that of being 'passed around from department to department'. No doubt there is sound logic from the point of view of the organisation that provides services about the way in which tasks are divided and allocated, but this logic may not be apparent to the consumer of these services. To take an extreme example, a single-parent mother who is homeless and destitute, and whose child plays truant

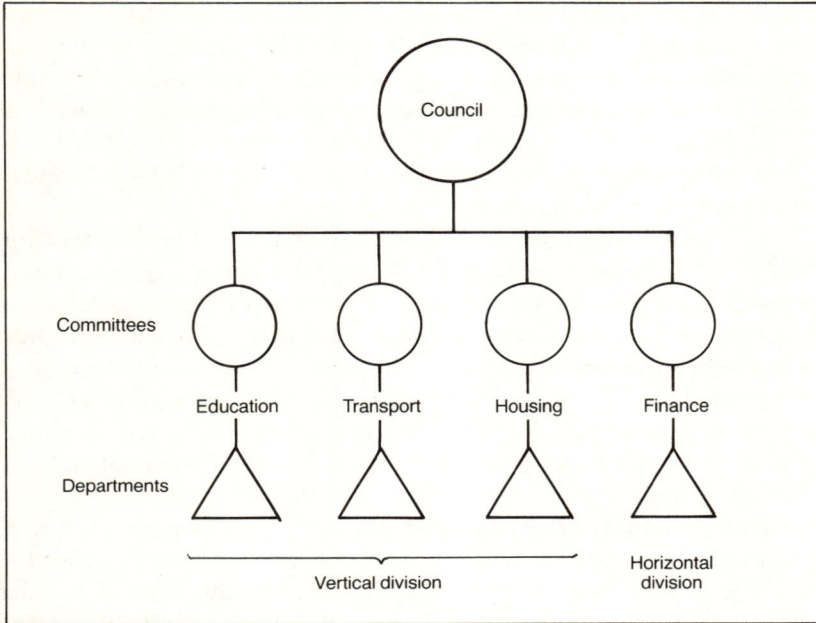

Fig. 7.1 Simple local authority structure

from school and instead goes shoplifting, is potentially likely to call upon four local services: housing, social welfare, education and police. The local authority will have to respond in all four areas and involve four separate departments, but from her perception, of course, all the problems are related. She may well find it difficult to comprehend the internal divisions of the local authority. The problems are compounded if, as well may be the case, some 'needs' relate to the district authority and others fall to the county tier or even to another body altogether such as the local health authority. It is very easy for a large organisation to lose sight of the needs of clients in responding to their own requirement to construct structures that are functionally satisfactory.

Fragmentation was regarded as the main problem of local government organisation in the mid-1960s. As the Maud Committee on the Management of Local Government observed, 'The separateness of committees contributes to the separateness of departments and the professionalism of the department staff feeds on this separateness'.[1] The latter point refers to the fact that in local government, as contrasted with the civil service, the careers of most officers are restricted to one particular department. Promotion is usually within, rather than between, service sectors. Another criticism made by the Maud Report was the time taken in committee work to the detriment of other aspects of the councillors' and officers' roles. Their survey discovered that it was not uncommon for authorities to have more than 30 committees and even more subcommittees. Another consequence of this practice was the massive amount of paperwork that was generated as a result.

According to the Maud Report, the two major problems of internal organisation were the following:

1. The fragmentation of the local authority's work. This was true for both officers and members, the former through excessive 'departmentalism' and the latter because of the excessive number of committees in most authorities. (Some had approximately 30 committees and even more subcommittees. Forty-two per cent of all councillors belonged to six or more committees.) The net results of this, according to Maud, were that too much time was spent on trivial matters and too little effort was made in planning the overall needs of the local area.
2. The failure to delegate non-controversial matters to paid officers.

Since the focus of the Maud Report's criticisms had been the effects of the committee system, it is appropriate to say something about the advantages and disadvantages of the committee system in local government. The main purposes of the committee system are as follows:

1. To divide the work of the authority in a way that allows councillors to be involved in both broad policy (via the full council) and the detailed planning of particular sectors. Some councillors are motivated to seek election to a local authority because of their special interest in a particular service sector.
2. To keep control over officers.
3. To allow councillors to make contributions to particular schemes.
4. To allow subjects to be considered in detail and related issues to be considered alongside each other.
5. To allow councillors to develop specialisms.
6. To allow discussions to take place in a less formal and possibly less partisan atmosphere.
7. To allow the co-option of outsiders either because of their expertise or because of their value in representing an external group or organisation. All committees, except finance ones, can co-opt and some are required to do so.

However, as Maud found, the proliferation of committees could have detrimental consequences:

1. It 'disintegrates' the work of the council and can lead to excessive concentration on minutiae and detail.
2. It can lead to delay in reaching decisions.

3. It allows insufficient delegation to officers.
4. It encourages councillors to spend their time more as 'committee members' than as 'constituency representatives' liaising with their electors.

The Maud Report proposed radical solutions to the problems of local authority management. In particular, the Report favoured a much more clear-cut relationship between councillors and officers in local government, where the councillors would be responsible for deciding broad policy matters, but would leave the details and the implementation of schemes to officers. The recommendations were also intended to promote better 'integration' of work on both member and officer sides of the authority. In the case of the former, it was argued that this could be achieved by the creation of a 'management board' – a kind of local authority cabinet – comprising between five and nine councillors who would be responsible for the development of major policies and for monitoring their implementation (Fig. 7.2). Integration on the officers' side would be achieved through the appointment of a chief officer in each local authority who would act as the general manager of the authority and co-ordinate the work of the various departmental chief officers. Finally, committees would no longer have executive responsibilities but would become deliberative bodies, with their number reduced drastically to approximately six per authority.

Maud's recommendations would have meant considerable changes in existing local authority management and while many local authorities took the opportunity to review their committee structure, few displayed much enthusiasm for the idea of a management board or for that of removing the executive role of committees. One implication of both these suggestions was that it would have meant having two classes of councillor – to use a parliamentary analogy – 'front-benchers' and 'back-benchers'. Not surprisingly, this was not acceptable to the majority of councillors who wished to retain their executive roles inside the local authority.

The reorganisation of local government following the 1972 and 1973 Acts opened the way for a more successful review of local government management. New authorities meant a rare opportunity to start an organisation structure from scratch and two working parties – the Bains and Paterson Groups – were established to look at optimum management structures in respect of the new English and Welsh, and Scottish local authorities, respectively. Both Groups were dominated by local government officers and their approaches were similar in outlook and in substance. Neither report was radical, and both were influenced by the idea of 'corporate management' which had become fashionable by that

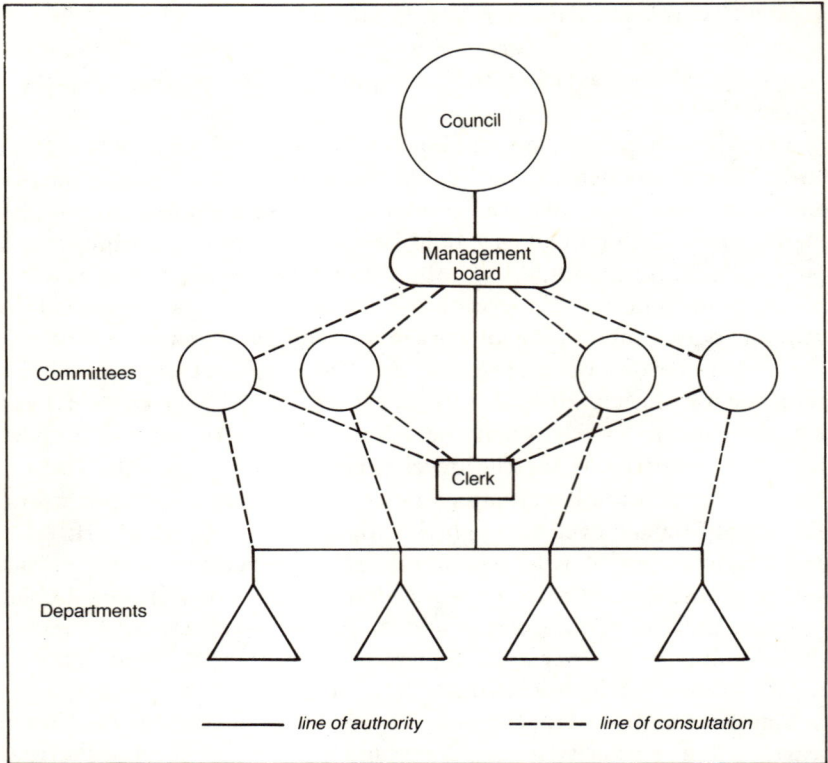

Fig. 7.2 Local authority organisation: 'The Maud Model'

time. Both Bains and Paterson stressed the need for unity of approach and this philosophy was reflected in their recommendations. Unlike the Maud Report, which had attempted to distinguish a clear division between the respective roles of officer and councillor, these reports stressed the 'duality' of local government – it was a partnership between member and officer and, although each had their own major area of responsibility, neither should regard any aspect of local authority work as their exclusive preserve.

A central concern of the Bains and Paterson Reports was the need to improve integration and co-ordination across the range of the authority's activities and all of their recommendations looked towards this central objective. In part, this was to be achieved by greater emphasis on horizontal departments and committees – groups which spanned the authority, rather than divided it up. It was also to be sought by widening the focus of both committees and departments by grouping related

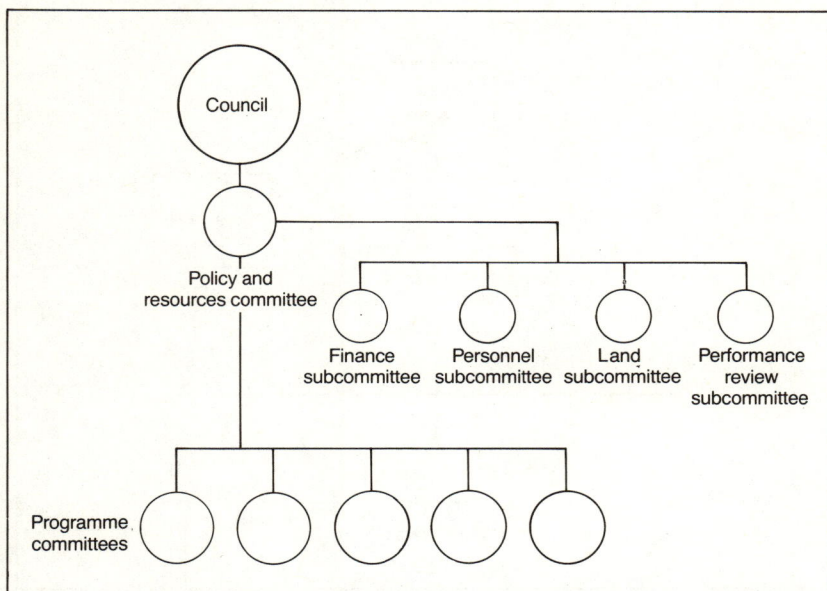

Fig. 7.3 'The Bains Model': organisation of members

activities together and creating larger committees and departments, 'programme areas' and 'directorates' respectively. However, the main way in which it was intended that integration could be achieved was through the establishment of a 'central co-ordinating team' on both member and officer sides.

The organisation of the local authority on the members' side would centre upon the establishment of a new policy committee, the Policy and Resources Committee. Its role was:

To assist the formulation and carrying out of the overall plan for the community . . . [it] would aid the authority in setting objectives and priorities, co-ordinating and controlling the implementation of these objectives and monitoring and reviewing performance.[2]

The Policy and Resources Committee was to have four subcommittees, three covering the main resource areas (finance, personnel and land) and another monitoring performance and the achievement of objectives (Fig. 7.3). It was proposed that membership of the Policy and Resources Committee should not be limited to the ruling party in councils where there was a majority party – indicative, perhaps, of the fact that the Bains Group itself did not contain political representatives.

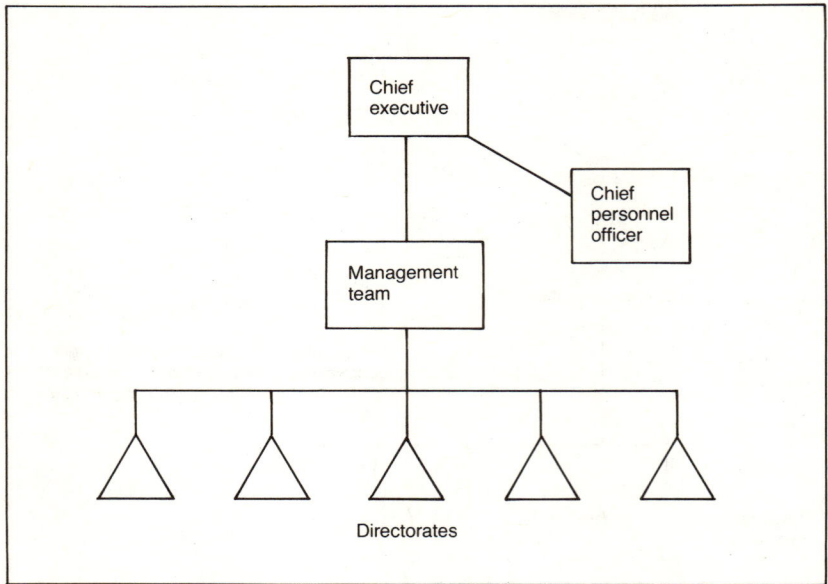

Fig. 7.4 'The Bains Model': organisation of officers

The proposed management structure at officer level was similar and the Policy and Resources Committee had its officer equivalent, the management team, comprising a number of departmental chief officers. This group is not to be confused with the management board – a body of councillors – recommended by Maud. Another device intended to facilitate co-ordination of the authority on the officer side was the appointment of a chief executive who would be the formal head of the paid officers. Unlike the old position of clerk of the council, there was no requirement that this person should possess legal qualifications and, indeed, when the new authorities were created a few of the more imaginative ones looked outside local government altogether in order to fill this post. Chief executives are the authorities' general managers (similar posts have recently been introduced into the health service) and their purpose is to provide leadership and co-ordination on the officer side of the council (Fig. 7.4).

The prospects for the Bains and Paterson Reports were much better than they had been for the Maud Report five years previously. This time the proposals were based upon existing good practice in some local authorities, corporate management enjoyed widespread favour and, not least, they were making recommendations for new authorities rather than trying to persuade existing ones to change their management structures. As a result, nearly all the new local authorities used the Bains or Paterson Reports as a model when designing their management structures.[3] Corporate management had become the vogue concept and innovative local authorities had already moved towards a more integrated approach by the early 1970s; their successor authorities continued this approach and not only adopted the Bains structure, but also had the motivation to make it work. Others adopted the new form, but did not possess attitudes that were consistent with this new approach. Corporate management is about attitudes and procedures as well as structures and to be effective, therefore, it needs to permeate structures and not just be an objective at chief officer level. In the decade since the new authorities were created, corporate structures have been modified and even sometimes dismantled in favour of the previous organisation. A decade after reorganisation, management practices in the new local authorities were subjected to a detailed examination by the Widdicombe Inquiry into the Conduct of Local Authority Business. The Widdicombe Report – along with its four volumes of research and no less than eighty-eight major recommendations covering areas ranging from the roles and relationships of councillors and officers to the practice of discretionary spending – represents a major and authoritative investigation into the internal organisation and decision-making processes of local authorities.[4] In particular, in contrast to the Maud and Bains Reports, Widdicombe does not ignore the impact of party politics upon conduct of local authority business. Indeed, a starting point for the Report is the assertion that the traditional requirement for officers to serve the entire council is suited neither to the realities of 'party politics nor modern management needs'. Research conducted on behalf of the Widdicombe Committee revealed that over 60 per cent of councillors believed that their first duty was to implement their party manifesto and among Labour councillors the proportion taking this view reached nearly 90 per cent. Party politics, and the decision-making machinery that goes with it, is now a fact of life in all but a very few local authorities and the Widdicombe Report attempts to come to terms with this in respect of the internal organisation of local councils and, especially, the implications it has for relationships between members and officers.

COUNCILLORS AND OFFICERS: SHARED OR DIVIDED POWER?

Any examination of local authority organisation must have a clear understanding about the respective roles of the elected member and the paid officer. In discussing this relationship we are, of course, concentrating upon a particular group of local government staff – officers, rather than the other categories of employees. (Altogether there are in the region of 2.5 million staff employed by local authorities, the biggest single group of which are teachers (600,000)). The traditional view of this relationship is that of master and servant: the officer is the paid servant of the council and carries out the collective decisions of the elected members; members make policy and officers administer their decisions. This is implicit in the liberal democratic basis of our political institutions. However, as with politics at the national level, the practical divisions between these two groups are much less clear and, for example, the distinction between 'policy' and 'administration' is not so precise as might be imagined at first sight.

Two decades ago, the Maud Report observed that:

> It is the members who should take and be responsible for the key decisions on objectives, and on the means and plans to obtain them. It is they who must periodically review the position as part of their function of directing and controlling. It is the officers who should provide the necessary staff work and advice which will enable the members to identify the problems, set the objectives and select the means and plans to attain them. It is the officers who should direct and co-ordinate the necessary action, and see that material is presented to enable members to review progress and check performance.[5]

The Bains Report went further in recognising that the distinction between 'policy' and 'administration' and, therefore, between councillors and officers, was blurred. In explaining their view of the relationship, they referred to the analogy of a 'sliding scale' which had been given by a witness in evidence to the Group:

> As one moves through that management scale, the balance between the two elements changes from member control with officer advice at the 'objective' end to officer control with member advice at the 'implementation' end.[6]

The analogy can be expanded and depicted as a diagram (Fig. 7.5).

For the purposes of illustration, the decision-making/scheme-implementation process is divided into three sections, although in reality these stages will fuse into a continuous process. At stage 1, key decisions are taken about objectives, priorities and, therefore, where resources will be allocated. These decisions are the result of some input, which may come from a range of sources – some will be political sources such as election manifestos or party programmes whilst others may come from the officers and departments themselves. The need for a highway scheme, for example, is just as likely to emerge from the advice of an officer as it is to come from a party political source. At stage 1, the main responsibility belongs to the councillor, although even at this juncture the officer is not entirely excluded. Once a decision has been

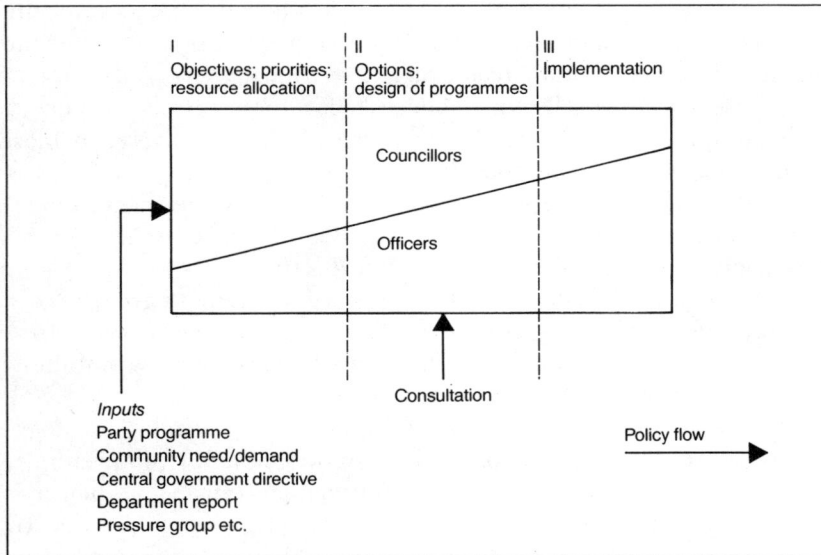

Fig. 7.5 Councillor/officer relationships: The Bains Analogy

taken, it is necessary to design programmes and look at alternative means of realising the chosen objective. At stage II, therefore, options might be presented alongside the 'costs' (financial and otherwise) of the various alternatives. This means the greater involvement of officers by this point in the decision-making process. Also, at around this stage, some form of public consultation might take place, either formally or informally. In certain matters, especially regarding planning matters, proposals have to be published and opportunities given for the public to air their views. In other matters the public might become aware of decisions which are in the pipeline in a less formal way, but will still make representations to the local authority. Finally, as the decision reaches its completion and implementation, the involvement of officials becomes greater, but even at this late stage, councillors might still make a contribution, if only to monitor the progress of the scheme. As we can see, therefore, at every stage both officers and councillors are involved.

This analogy of a 'sliding scale' is based upon the variable of *time* – as we move further along the time-scale of a decision, officers become more involved and councillors become less involved. There is a further variable: *the nature of the issue*. The more controversial or politically sensitive a scheme is, the more likely it is that councillors will take a close interest in all its various stages right until its implementation. In our diagram, therefore, the sloping line will be lower (i.e. giving the councillors a larger share of the activity) when deciding politically important matters and higher (i.e. giving officers a larger share of the activity) in respect of more technical and routine matters. A decision to reorganise schools or sell council houses falls into the former category; a decision about priorities for highway maintenance is likely, in most circumstances, to fall into the latter category.

In fact, there are other variables in the relationship between councillors and officers if we move beyond the analogy depicted in the diagram. These include some aspects of the political setting:

1. *Political control.* It is frequently suggested that Labour groups take a closer interest in departmental activities than their Conservative counterparts. This might result in part from their more ambitious perceptions about the role of local government.

2. *Perceptions and ideologies.* There might be a prevailing ideology, irrespective of the party composition of the council. If, for example, there is a general concern with 'management efficiency' then it is likely that there will be a high degree of delegation to officers. If, however, the prevailing ideology is 'accountability' then it might be expected that councillors will be much more involved in the day-to-day running of the authority.

3. *Size of majority.* In fact, this could work in two contrasting ways. A party with a large majority in a local authority may feel free to set the pace in that authority and keep officials under tight reins. Conversely, in an authority where party politics are not well-developed, or where there is a 'hung' council, officers frequently assume enhanced responsibilities.[7]

4. *Timing of elections.* An impending election is likely to encourage councillors to keep close control over the affairs of the authority.

5. *Personalities.* Finally, the simple factor of personalities should not be overlooked. Any relationship will be affected by individual personalities and this is just as true of those between members and officers. A determined councillor and a timid officer will have a different relationship from that where the personalities are reversed.

For the Widdicombe Committee, it was the role played by political parties that had led to the greatest impact on the relationship between councillors and officers in local government. As the Report observed:

Politics is now the main determining factor in the decisions of local authorities . . . It is however not recognised in the statutory arrangements . . . [which are] . . . corporate rather than adversarial in nature. The successful bridging between the formal statutory arrangements and the informal arrangements has relied much on improvisation . . . and the good will and good sense of councillors.

Local government institutions are in many respects poorly attuned to the modern political environment.[8]

Although the committee considered that abuses had only occurred in a few authorities, many more suffered from 'instability and uncertainty' in councillor-officer relationships. At the heart of the problem was the fact that whatever the statutory arrangements might suggest, the reality was that decisions were usually formulated inside party groups and that frequently officers had difficulties serving dual masters – the full council and, where one existed, the majority party group on the council. Widdicombe concluded that a redefinition of relationships was necessary. In broad terms, the Report suggested that 'councillors should leave day-to-day implementation of council policies, including staff management, as far as possible to officers, and officers should demonstrate that they are sensitive to the political aspirations underlying these policies'.[9] The Committee was especially concerned to discourage the intervention of councillors in routine matters and to limit their control of staff recruitment and management. The various roles played by senior officers are categorised under three headings: professional *managers* of specific departments, *advisers* guiding the work of the council and its committees, and *arbitrators* ensuring that council business is conducted fairly and with propriety. In all three capacities, they are called upon to walk a narrow tightrope neglecting neither the interests of the whole council and minority groups, nor the legitimate concerns of majority political parties. The Report considers that, as a consequence, officers are often placed in a highly ambiguous position.

The Report briefly considers alternative management approaches, in particular: the management board/ministerial model with a decision-making body akin to the cabinet in central government, and a separate directly elected executive. Both these approaches were rejected. Instead the Committee favoured a sharpening of the division of roles between officers and councillors combined with a strengthening of the role of chief executives as heads of the officer side of the authority. A particularly important recommendation concerns the machinery for the formulation and deciding of council policies. A distinction is made between legal 'decision-taking' and 'policy formulation' – the former was decreed to be the exclusive preserve of councillors which should take place in as open a manner as possible in committees that accurately reflect the overall political balance of the council, while policy formulation, it was thought, could operate quite properly through deliberative, as opposed to decision-taking, committees. The Widdicombe Committee realised that if they gave no place to party group deliberations inside the local authority, then such meetings would simply move outside the formal structure. By incorporating a place for party deliberations, they hoped to be able to regulate the process by which such discussions took place.

The wide-ranging recommendations which are intended to give substance to these ideas cover various areas of local authority management. The more important ones are the following:

1. All decision-taking committees should comprise councillors only.
2. Such committees should reflect the overall political composition of the council, the chief executive to be responsible for ensuring the application of this rule.
3. Deliberative meetings of party groups to formulate policy may be held in private but procedures about attendance and standing orders should be tightened up.
4. Powers may be delegated to chairmen of committees to cover urgent matters, the chief executive to agree the issue in question.
5. All local authorities should be required to appoint a chief executive (an independent assessor should sit on the appointments committee and the chief executive should only be dismissed with the agreement of two-thirds of the members of the council), to be responsible for the propriety of all council business including the composition of committees, the rights of councillors to inspect official documents, the registration of councillors' interests and the delegation of power to chairmen of committees.
6. The chief executive should be responsible for the appointment, disciplining and dismissal of staff at or above the rank of principal officer.
7. Officers at or above the level of principal officer should be prohibited from seeking elected office in other local authorities.
8. Officers may be attached to advise party groups or their leaders in limited numbers and with appropriate safeguards.
9. The attendance allowance for councillors should be replaced with a flat rate allowance supplemented in some instances by a special responsibility allowance.
10. A statutory upper limit of 26 days per year should be allowed to public service employees for council duties.

In view of the range and extent of the recommendations of the Widdicombe Committee, it is not surprising that the report attracted considerable comment and caused a great deal of controversy. This was especially the case with regard to the recommendations concerning the extension of the powers of chief executives (particularly since some authorities had dispensed with this position) and the ban on political activity by senior officers. Many councillors were understandably concerned that the recommendations would result in a diminution of their role and it is therefore inevitable that a good deal of further discussion will take place before it is known to what extent Widdicombe's ideas will be put into practice. Perhaps the most important contribution of the Report is that it marks the first real attempt to come to terms with the impact of party politics upon the internal management and decision-making processes inside local government and, rather than ignoring the place of party deliberations about policy, attempts to respond to and formalise the contribution made by political parties.

FACTORS AFFECTING LOCAL AUTHORITY ORGANISATION

Like the relationship between members and officers, the overall management structure of local authorities is inevitably affected by particular local circumstances. It would be unrealistic to expect that a single model structure could serve the organisational requirements of all authorities since, as we have seen, the needs and problems of local areas and communities vary widely. If these needs and problems are to be met effectively, then it is essential that the management structure of the local authority should be tailored to accommodate them. A local authority with particular inner-city problems, for example, will wish to ensure that its organisational structure facilitates rather than inhibits an effective response by the authority to the multifaceted needs of the inner-city area. This may be expressed by the creation of an inter-departmental 'task force' involving, among others, representatives of police, social services, housing and education departments. Another example of tailoring structure to meet local need is to be found in the creation of economic development departments in some local authorities. Although not an obligatory function of local government, many local councils, especially those in areas where there has been a decline of basic industries like steel and coal, see economic regeneration as one of their responsibilities and have created departments specifically to pursue this objective. An illustration of this initiative is the Department of Employment and Economic Development in Sheffield, a city which has been badly affected by the decline of manufacturing industry in the past few years. In 1971, half of Sheffield's workforce of 281,000 was employed by manufacturing industry. In 1986, fewer than 58,000 of the 225,000 in work were employed in the manufacturing sector and if the rate of decline were to continue, all manufacturing jobs would be lost within another 25 years.[10] Other cities have faced similar problems and they too have appointed specific committees and departments to focus on economic and industrial matters. Indeed, these stuctures are to be found not only in the traditional industrial areas. In North Yorkshire, for example, which is not an area usually associated with manufacturing industry, the Policy and Resources Committee has a subcommittee concerned specifically with economic development. This is in addition to the other four subcommittees which are broadly as recommended by the 1972 Bains Report. It is perhaps a sign of how much the economic situation has changed since 1972 that the Bains Report made no mention at all of economic development activities in their discussion of local authority management organisations.

A further illustration of fashioning structures to fit particular needs can be seen in seaside towns where 'resort service' departments and committees reflect the significant contribution made to the economic life of the area by the tourist industry. This is equally true of several 'inland resorts' like Harrogate or York, and even in some areas which have not in the past been regarded as centres for tourism – places such as Bradford and Sheffield – the local authority has established tourist sections to pursue the economic opportunities of tourism and conference business.

There are many other examples of fitting internal structure to meet particular local need and one final circumstance ought to be mentioned – territorial range. Reorganisation in 1974 and 1975 both reduced the number of local authorities and increased their size. North Yorkshire, the largest county in territorial terms, has several times the land coverage (3,209 square miles) of its neighbour Cleveland (226 square miles). In Scotland, the Fife region comprises 500 square miles compared with 10,000 square miles in the Highlands. Larger authorities in this respect will require organisational arrangements that reflect the territorial span of their areas. One organisational response is the creation of area offices. Most authorities have some kind of area organisation, if only local rent offices for payment of council rents. In the larger county authorities, however, the need for an area structure extends much beyond this simple convenience. North Yorkshire's County Hall in Northallerton is approximately 70 miles from its most distant borders, and services such as highway maintenance would be impractical without an area structure. The Bains Report put forward three main reasons for area offices:

   (i)   to bring services to the place of need;
  (ii)   to provide a point of ready public access to the [county] organisation;
 (iii)   to properly deploy resources of staff, plant and equipment and materials.[11]

Some of the larger local authorities have general area management structures; others have area organisation for those services where territorial range is particularly significant.

A basic issue of management structure is how the range of local authority activities can be divided for the purpose of organising departments and committees. This is similar to the issue of delimiting local authority areas and there are some interesting parallels to be drawn. One approach is to look at general principles that can be used to separate one service sector from another. At least two principles of organisation were raised by Aristotle who, 2,000 years ago, considered whether it was better to give magistrates responsibilities on the basis of the subject matter or the class of persons concerned. These two principles are still relevant and, together with two further principles (area and work process), they form the basic approach to the issue of differentiation in organisations:

1. *Function*. Organisations can be divided on the basis of identifying discrete functions or responsibilities. It is usually assumed that 'functions' are easy to identify: education, social services, housing and highways appear distinct and easily distinguished services. However, it should be remembered that 'functions' have developed by a gradual process of change (note, for example, the changing definition and responsibility for public health during the last century) and each of these 'functions' involves a wide range of specific duties and separate pieces of legislation. What is defined as a function can change over time as illustrated, for instance, by the introduction of economic development departments. Is 'public protection' a single function or an umbrella term covering police, fire, consumer protection, etc.? Is economic development now a 'function'?

2. *Clientele*. This would mean that an organisation would be divided on the basis of the various client groups served, e.g. children, women, ethnic groups, deprived, elderly, etc. There are obvious limits to the widespread application of this principle. It would hardly be practical, for example, to have separate social service or education provision for each of the client groups listed. It tends instead to be used as a secondary principle, i.e. when a new duty is undertaken by a local authority, that responsibility is tacked on to an existing department which has closest involvement with the group concerned. A good example of the clientele principle used in this way was the schools health service, which used to be an aspect of the work of the local education authority since the latter had contact with all children under the age of 16. Ever since the health authorities took over this responsibility in 1974, the provision of health care for children results in doctors, dentists, health visitors, school nurses and others visiting schools and therefore requires considerable collaboration between the education and health authorities. The principle is

used when, for instance, a local authority focuses on the needs of a specific group such as the deprived or an ethnic minority (see Chapter 3).

3. *Area*. Like clientele, area tends to be used as a secondary principle. The range problem of the larger county authorities referred to above demonstrates how organisation by area as a second-level approach helps them cope with the needs of distant parts of the county. Again, this can be illustrated by reference to the education service. Most LEAs outside the metropolitan districts have area or divisional offices. The duties of these offices vary between authorities but are concerned with such matters as day-to-day management, links with teachers, parents and students, governing bodies, school catchment areas.

4. *Work process*. This is where a common service – legal, architecture, building, printing, personnel, public relations – is provided across the local authority. There are obvious economies of scale to be achieved if one legal department or one architecture department serves the authority as a whole and with these professional services there is little dispute about their value. Other matters, however, may be more contentious. Should each department, for example, be responsible for its own recruitment and have its own personnel section or should there be a central personnel unit responsible for recruitment throughout the authority? Should teachers, for example, be recruited by the personnel department or the education department's own personnel division?

Local authority organisations reveal all four principles in operation. Not surprisingly, 'function or major purpose served' is the most widely applied principle and is the usual basis of vertical differentiation in the management structures of local authorities. The important point is that these 'functions' are not static, but change in response to evolving ideas and circumstances. If it were intended to devise a rational organisation for local authorities, then it would be necessary to review the totality of the authority's responsibilities and then, perhaps using the principles outlined, to determine the size and scope of departments accordingly. Moreover, it would involve a continuous process of organisational review since both the duties imposed on the local authority and the demands placed upon it are themselves continually evolving.

The Bains Group gave little attention to these matters in putting forward its proposals for both committee and departmental structures. Although it favoured wider groupings, partly to improve co-ordination and partly to reduce inefficiency, the Report gave little theoretical basis for the departments and committees recommended. In the case of the

COMMITTEE	RESPONSIBILITIES
*Education**	Education Libraries Museums Art galleries
Social services	Social services
Planning and Transportation	Planning Highways and transport planning Traffic Parking Road safety Lighting Aerodromes Public transport
Amenities and Countryside	Country parks Footpaths Caravan sites Gypsy sites Recreation and tourism Smallholdings Land drainage Refuse disposal Entertainment
Public protection	Consumer protection Emergency services Health education Registration and licensing
National Parks (if appropriate)	National parks
*Police**	Police

*Statutory committees

In addition, a Policy and Resources Committee with four subcommittees on finance, land, personnel and performance review.

Fig. 7.6 Committee structure in non-metropolitan counties: Recommendations of Bains Group

non-metropolitan county, the Bains Report proposed the committee areas shown in Fig. 7.6.

This model structure can be compared with that of North Yorkshire County Council (Fig. 7.7). Setting apart the Joint Committee with the component district authorities (which was also recommended in the Report), the structure is clearly derived from the Bains approach. However, there are some significant modifications including, for example, recognition of the importance of economic development by the creation of a special subcommittee of the Policy and Resources Commit-

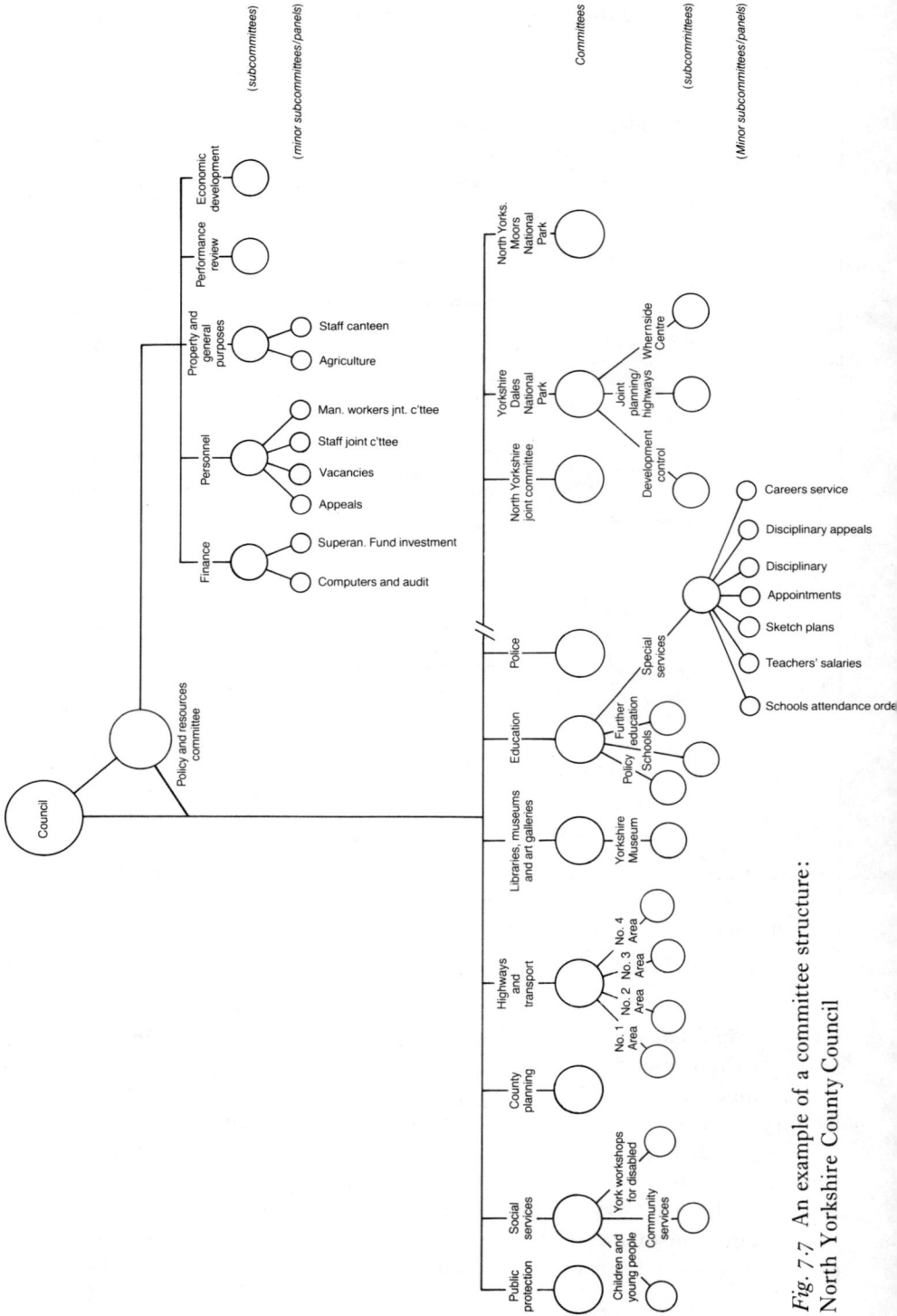

Fig. 7.7 An example of a committee structure:
North Yorkshire County Council

tee. At main committee level, the significant differences are the splitting of highways and transport from planning and of libraries, museums and art galleries from education. The chart also shows how in some fields – notably education – there are several further subdivisions within the service sector. North Yorkshire County Council is not atypical in its committee structure and in 1974 most other local authorities took the Bains model, adapted it to meet their particular circumstances and political ideas and have subsequently modified it as needs and ideas have changed.

Circumstances as well as principles affect organisation and it is possible to speculate about the kinds of external factors that will lead to differences in the way local authorities structure their internal management. Greenwood *et al.* have suggested that six factors might be expected to have some effect on the internal structure of local authorities.[12] These factors or 'contingent variables' are the following:

1. *Size*. This can be defined by size of the population served, the territorial span of the authority or the number of elected councillors. As noted earlier, a larger geographical unit will almost certainly require more 'area organisation'. Equally, the larger authority will probably have more specialist staff – legal, personnel, architects, etc. – with their own departments.

2. *Environment*. The salient factors here might be population density and the 'wealth' of the area. An authority with a problem of urban decay, or one with a particularly deprived community might be expected to focus on this problem through the creation of departments or committees which tackle specific aspects of community needs. A wealthier locality has less need and therefore might require fewer committees.

3. *Type of authority*. Some local authorities – counties and metropolitan boroughs/districts – have more service committees and departments as well as a wider range of responsibilities and might be expected to have a greater need for central co-ordinating bodies on both officer and councillor sides.

4. *Interdependence*. As noted in the previous chapter, local authorities are involved in a large number of interdependent relationships – with other authorities, statutory bodies and the voluntary sector. It might be anticipated that the greater the number of dependent relationships, the more likely it is that an authority will need central co-ordinating departments and committees in order to unify all these external links.

5. *Political control*. This could also be expected to affect internal organisation. Labour-controlled authorities are often seen as giving

greater emphasis to the 'corporate approach' (stressing the overall impact of the authority's activities on the local community), while Conservative-led authorities are considered more 'federalist' in inclination (regarding the various activities and duties as essentially separate). If this distinction is valid, then Labour authorities would tend to be more centralised internally and Conservative authorities more decentralised in their management structure.

6. *Ideology*. This is a related concept and is based on the hypothesis that the prevailing ideology in the local authority, if one can be detected, will affect organisation. Thus, for example, a local authority which stresses 'participation and accountability' might tend to be more differentiated in order to allow greater community and citizen involvement, with larger numbers of committees, public relations units, etc. In contrast, in an authority where the key phrase is 'efficiency' there are likely to be fewer vertical committees and greater emphasis on resource management committees and departments.

These contingent variables were tested against the management structures of local authorities immediately after their creation in 1974. In particular, their impact was assessed on the extent of differentiation (i.e. the number of committees and departments and the number of specialist departments) and on the extent of integration (co-ordinating committees, central departments, chief executives, management teams) inside local authorities. The research revealed that, in the aftermath of reorganisation, although the Bains Report's recommendations were widely implemented – rather more so in the counties and the metropolitan districts than in the shire districts – they were adapted to fit local ideas and circumstances. Perhaps the most widely accepted recommendation was that concerning the creation of a central Policy and Resources Committee. The impact of some of the variables outlined above on the organisation of local authorities proved to be significant. Size (in all its aspects), the range of duties, ideology and population density all had generalised effects on how a local authority designed its internal management: the larger local authorities with the more extensive range of duties, not surprisingly, required more *differentiation* and, subsequently, more *integrative* devices. Other factors such as geographical area and wealth appeared to have more specific effects on how particular aspects of the local authority's organisation was designed.

The importance of using contingent variables to explain differences in local authority management structure is that it emphasises how this aspect of local government is also affected by the nature of the community that it serves. In earlier chapters, we stressed how communities vary in terms of their needs and resources and how local authorities have to match their response to these distinctive circumstances. In this context, the local authority response is most obviously manifested in terms of its policies and services. However, the effect of the community setting is also felt in organisational terms, and the ability of the authority to meet the community's needs will be significantly affected by the 'goodness of fit' between the management structure of the local authority and the community setting.

AREA ORGANISATION

There is one particular form of local authority organisation that is especially appropriate to the needs of local communities: area-based services. As the 1969 Royal Commission discovered, it is impractical to create major units of local government that correspond to the public's own perception of community. There is a mismatch between the size of areas required for operational purposes and those to which people identify and feel a sense of belonging. Although some form of community administration can be achieved through a 'third tier' of the local government structure (community and parish councils), the popular idea of communities makes them too small to be useful for the purposes of most local government services and, therefore, for the construction of principal local authorities. Communities are, however, meaningful to the electorate and have needs which are often unique to that location and which involve several local authority sectors. It follows, therefore, that if there is a concern to involve the local community and to respond to its particular needs, this can best be achieved by decentralisation of internal administration and procedures within local authorities.[13]

Area organisation is where the authority focuses its services on a locality smaller than the local authority itself. It can refer to a single service but more usually involves linking several service sectors together at the level of a specified area. It can also be adopted in respect of one or two particular problem areas – inner-city areas are frequently targeted – or can be a widespread approach applied to the local authority as a whole. Area organisation illustrates the use of 'area' as a secondary principle of division of work. The philosophy behind area organisation – the term 'area management' is sometimes used – was expressed in the Seebohm Report on Local Authority and Allied Personal Social Services (1968)[14] and the Skeffington Report *People and Planning* (1969). The Seebohm Report recommended that social services should be run via area teams, each comprising approximately 12 social workers and serving populations of around 100,000 people, the latter figure to be reduced as more staff became available. Community involvement was also a feature of the report: 'Implicit in the idea of a community-oriented family service is a belief in the importance of the maximum participation of individuals and groups in the community in the planning, organisation and provision of the social services . . .'[15] Similar sentiments in respect of planning procedures were echoed in the Skeffington Report the following year: 'Local planning authorities should consider convening meetings in their area for the purpose of setting up community forums . . . to discuss collectively planning and other issues of importance to the area . . . Community development officers should be appointed to secure the involvement of those people who do not join organisations.'[16]

In fact, some area-based initiatives preceded both reports.[17] In 1967/ 68, *Educational Priority Areas* were recognised and accorded special building programmes. Also in the field of urban deprivation were *Urban Programme Priority Areas* (1968), with a particular emphasis on problems of overcrowding, unemployment and minorities, and *Community Development Projects* (1969). Twelve Community Development Projects were sponsored by the Home Office to look into new ways of responding to the needs of people in areas of high social deprivation. One such project in Oldham established area committees to bring together councillors and residents to discuss matters of mutual concern.[18]

Although area organisation has been primarily deployed as a means of concentrating on inner-city deprivation or in the social services sector, some authorities have recognised its wider potential. Stockport and Newcastle, for example, have experimented with more generalised area-management schemes.[19] In Newcastle, teams comprising county and district councillors in the appropriate wards and officers from the housing, planning, social services and education departments liaised with the local community and were allocated annual budgets of up to £50,000 for local projects. In Stockport, a system of eight area committees was established, each comprising district and county councillors 'to assess planning and environmental matters concerning the area and to identify expenditure priorities during the council's budget-making process'.[20]

Area organisation at both officer and councillor level is a means of adapting local authority structure to focus on the needs of neighbourhoods and communities. In practice, not many local authorities have introduced formal area organisations. However, even those that have not find themselves in a dialogue with community and neighbourhood-based groups since one of the features of local government in the last 15 years or so has been the growth of community politics. This has developed alongside demands for greater opportunities for public participation in local affairs. More recently, much attention has been given to the concept of 'public service orientation' as a means of narrowing the gap between local councils which provide services and those people who consume the services. The concept of public service orientation stresses that local authorities should respond to community need in terms that are essentially in the interest of the client rather than those of the local authority. According to John Stewart and Michael Clarke, it should be recognised that services are provided *for* and not just *to* the public. They challenge those senior managers who:

- judge the quality of service by organisational or professional standards,
- devote little time to learning about the customer away from the central office in which they work,
- provide no training for staff on quality of customer service,
- do not involve customers in decisions on the services provided or projects undertaken,
- have not considered whether reception arrangements help the customer.[21]

In practice, however, local services are frequently the result of judgements and decisions made by politicians and professional officers with relatively little reference to the clients' own preferences. If the public service orientated approach is to work then it requires local authority structures and processes which are *comprehensible* and, therefore, *accessible* to the consumers as well as the professionals. One way that this might be achieved is through the further decentralisation of service administration to area or neighbourhood teams which provide integration between related service sectors and easier access for members of the community. Structural change has to be accompanied by changes in *attitude* and *perception* – this is equally true of service providers and consumers, not least those groups who are usually most excluded. It requires a shared approach at all levels and by all participants. The relationship between the local authority and the service user is the subject of the next chapter.

LOCAL AUTHORITY ASSOCIATIONS AND RELATED BODIES

Throughout the development of local government strong professional relationships have existed between local authorities and also between particular professional groups within the local authority services. By 1906, for example, the *Local Government Directory* listed no fewer than 140 associations and societies representing local authorities and their staffs.[22] The most important bodies were the associations representing the four main types of local authority – the Association of Municipal Corporations, the County Councils Association, the Urban District Councils Association and the Rural District Councils Association – all of which had been established by the end of the nineteenth century. Each of these four associations developed in different ways during the twentieth century and relationships between them were not always harmonious, partly as a result of differences in the political composition of these national bodies. The AMC was subject to particularly notable shifts in political direction. More recently, the AMC and CCA clashed over their views regarding the reform of local governments structure in the earlier 1970s.

Since reorganisation the common interests of local authorities have been promoted through organisations representing the new local authority structure. In England and Wales, there are now three local authority associations: the Association of County Councils (ACC), the Association of Metropolitan Authorities (AMA) representing the metropolitan districts, and the Association of District Councils (ADC) representing the interests of districts authorities in the non-metropolitan areas. There is also a National Association of Local Councils to bring together parish and community councils. Scottish local authorities are represented by just one association, the Convention of Scottish Local Authorities (COSLA). As might be expected there are differences in political control of these bodies and that while the AMA is generally dominated by Labour representatives the converse is true with regard to the ACC. Some have argued that separating the interests of county and district authorities in this way, especially given the likely differences in political control, means that the collective voice of local government against central government is weakened.

One of the more important achievements of these associations has been the formation of a number of joint bodies which advise on technical and support services for local government. Some significant examples of these bodies are: the Local Authorities Management Services Advisory Committee (LAMSAC), established in 1967 to co-ordinate research and training activities in the fields of management services, the Local Authorities Conditions of Service Advisory Board (LACSAB) established in 1948, which advises on pay and conditions of employment, as well as other bodies concerned with such matters as joint purchasing schemes. Mention should also be made of the work of the Local Government Training Board (LGTB) established in 1967 with the remit of promoting training of local government officers. This latter activity has also been much encouraged by the work of the Institute of

Local Government Studies (INLOGOV) at the University of Birmingham, as well as by the National and Local Government Officers' Association (NALGO) (which has its own education department for this specific purpose) and the many professional bodies represented by local government services.

Notes

1. *Committee on the Management of Local Government* (HMSO, 1967).
2. *The New Local Authorities: Management and Structure* (HMSO, 1972), p. xv.
3. See R. Greenwood *et al.*, *The Organisation of Local Authorities in England and Wales* (INLOGOV, L.5, 1975).
4. *Committee on the Conduct of Local Authority Business*, Cmnd 9797, 1986. Research volumes: (1) The Political Organisation of Local Authorities, Cmnd 9798, (2) The Local Government Councillor, Cmnd 9799, (3) The Local Government Elector, Cmnd 9800, (4) Aspects of Local Democracy, Cmnd 9801.
5. Maud, *op. cit.* para. 145.
6. Bains, *op. cit.* para. 3.15.
7. See R. Wendt, 'Decision-making in Central and Local Government in the Absence of Political Majority', *Public Administration* (1986); and C. Mellors, 'Political Coalitions in Britain: The Local Context' in L. Robins (ed.), *Updating British Politics* (Politics Association, 1984).
8. Cmnd 9797, paras. 4.17–4.21.
9. *Ibid*, para. 4.39.
10. In January 1987 the city's Department of Employment and Economic Development with the council's Central Policy Unit produced a strategy for increasing employment by 25,000 jobs in two years: *Sheffield: Working it Out*.
11. Bains, *op. cit.* para. 5.79.
12. The section which follows draws upon R. Greenwood, C. R. Hinings and S. Ransom, 'Contingency Theory and the Organisation of Local Authorities', *Public Administration* (1975).
13. See, for example, W. Hampton, 'Local Government and Community', *Political Quarterly* (1969).
14. Cmnd 3703, esp. Ch. XVI.
15. *Ibid.*
16. *People and Planning*, Ministry of Housing and Local Government (HMSO, 1969), para. 253.
17. This section draws upon J. Gyford, 'Diversity, Sectionalism and Local Democracy', *The Conduct of Local Authority Business*, Vol. IV, Cmnd 9801, pp. 111–15.
18. L. Corina, 'Area Councillors: An Experiment in Consultation', *Public Administration* (1977).
19. K. J. Harrap *et al.*, *The Implementation and Development of Area Management* (INLOGOV, 1978).
20. Gyford, *op. cit.* p. 113.
21. J. Stewart and M. Clarke, 'The Public Service Orientation: Issues and Dilemmas', *Public Administration*, Summer 1987.
22. B. Keith-Lucas and P. G. Richards, *A History of Local Government in the Twentieth Century* (Allen and Unwin, 1978), p. 180.

8

COMMUNITY INVOLVEMENT IN LOCAL GOVERNMENT

A central theme of this book has been the need for information. If a local authority is to respond to the needs of its area, then it must be well informed about the condition of its people and their environment. This need for information, however, extends beyond data about population size and structure or other aspects of the social and physical setting of local government discussed in earlier chapters. There is in addition a vital need for information-sharing which means effective communication between the local authority and its people. We can justify the cost and complexity of our system of elected local government only if the links between people and local authorities are valued by both sides. Otherwise, a system of decentralised administrative bodies might serve us just as well. One writer expresses the idea succinctly '. . . local democracy . . . involves having a well-informed public, well-informed elected representatives and, indeed, well-informed local authorities'.[1]

FORMAL LINKS BETWEEN THE CITIZEN AND THE COUNCIL

Popular interest in local government

There are many ways in which we might attempt to gauge the interest of the community in local government and perhaps the simplest is to measure turnout and involvement in local elections. In 1967, the Maud Committee observed that 'the degree to which local authority elections are contested and the proportion of the electorate which votes are measures of the public's interest.'[2] At that time, both measures indicated that public interest was not especially high. Turnout in local elections was and remains much lower than in general elections and much lower than in other countries. The percentage of uncontested seats in the mid-1960s – approximately 9 per cent in county boroughs, 20 per cent in non-county boroughs and UDCs, and around 70 per cent in RDCs – seemed to confirm the low level of public interest in local political affairs. Overall, 40 per cent of councillors had secured election without an actual contest. It might be expected that this last figure would be reduced after 1974, since reorganisation drastically cut the number of councillors from 42,000 to 26,000. This did in fact occur. For example, in the English county elections of May 1985 less than 2 per cent of seats were uncontested. Researchers for the Widdicombe Committee were 'told on several occasions that in the 1985 elections all county council seats had been contested for the first time within memory'.[3] In metropolitan boroughs and districts the proportion of uncontested seats is now less than 1 per cent. It is possible to speculate on what other factors besides the reduced number of councillors have caused the increasing competition for council membership. There are three possible causes: the increased involvement of political parties in local elections; the formation of the Social Democratic party which, in alliance with the Liberals, is anxious to secure a local electoral base for its bid for national success; and, perhaps, the greater political controversy surrounding local government in recent years.

However, the second measure of popular interest – turnout – has not changed. In 1964, for instance, the average turnout in county council elections was 41 per cent (the average turnout in local elections in West Germany and Sweden was 70 and 80 per cent respectively). In 1985, the average turnout in the English counties was still 41 per cent. There are, of course, differences in the levels of turnout, particularly between rural and urban areas, between different types of authority and between 'safe' and 'marginal' seats. As with national elections, marginal contests generally attract higher turnouts. The stability of the local population is another possible influence on the level of the poll. After taking all these factors into account, however, the stark fact remains that if turnout is used as a measure of public interest in local government, the indications are that the degree of involvement is not great. Significantly, this measure of public interest has not changed since local government was reorganised in the mid-1970s.

Other tests of the citizen's involvement in local politics and the knowledge about local government produce interesting results. On the whole, the Maud Committee was depressed by its findings 20 years ago. The level of people's knowledge about local government was limited – one in five of the electorate was unable to name a single service provided by local government, even though 98 per cent of them consumed some

Table 8.1 Electors' knowledge of local government (percentages)

		Well or quite well informed	Poorly informed or uninformed
Age	18–34	47	53
	35–54	56	44
	55–64	60	40
	64+	46	54
Sex	Male	62	38
	Female	43	57
Class	AB	66	34
	C1	56	44
	C2	43	57
	DE	40	60
Education*	16 or under	48	52
	over 16	66	34
Party Supporter	Con.	57	43
	Lab.	49	51
	Alliance	61	39

* Age at completing full-time education.

Source: Conduct of Local Authority Business (Cmnd 9800) 'The Local Government Elector' based on Tables 2.1, 2.2, 2.3, 2.4.

form of local authority service. Moreover, local councillors and officers made little effort to improve this level of knowledge. As might be expected, not all sections of the electorate were equally knowledgeable – on average, men were better informed than women, the middle-aged better than the young or old, and those in higher social groups and with better education more than those in lower socio-economic groups. In 1986, the Widdicombe Committee felt less concerned about the level of public awareness. Its survey suggests that 52 per cent of electors could be considered quite well or well informed.[4] Again, there were differences between the various sectors of the population (Table 8.1).

The question arises as to whether low turnouts indicate apathy or satisfaction with the way that local councils are run. Both the Maud and the Widdicombe Committees attempted to answer this question. In 1967 'just over a quarter . . . thought their local (borough or district) council was run very well and just under a quarter thought their county councils very well run'.[5] However, the proportion of electors who were 'very satisfied' with specific services was much higher: welfare clinics (83 per cent), public libraries (80 per cent), refuse collection (67 per cent), schools (65 per cent) and council housing (48 per cent).[6] Widdicombe also looked at electors' satisfaction with local services, although some account should be taken of the difficulty of comparing two different surveys. On the general question about 'how well' the council is run, approximately 70 per cent considered their authority to be run 'very' or 'fairly' well.[7] There was no significant variation either by type of elector or type of local authority. The Widdicombe survey does not separate 'very' from 'fairly' well and, if we combine the two equivalent categories in the earlier Maud survey, then the level of general satisfaction jumps from 25 per cent to over 75 per cent – higher than that found by Widdicombe. Turning to specific services, the level of satisfaction declines slightly from the findings 20 years earlier: schools (54 per cent), council housing (39 per cent), street cleaning (67 per cent), home helps for the elderly (37 per cent), refuse collection (87 per cent), dealing with planning applications (32 per cent), fire service (77 per cent).[8] This time there are significant variations, both between services (as was also the case with Maud's survey), and between different groups in the electorate. Newcomers to an area, for example, tended to be less satisfied than those who had lived in the area for more than five years. Non-ratepayers were less satisfied on the whole than those who paid rates in full or were partly rebated. However, the 'most striking finding is . . . the relatively low levels of satisfaction expressed by those respondents living in London and in other metropolitan areas in respect of the principal local services, schools and housing'.[9]

Variations in the levels of satisfaction with specific services and between this specific assessment and satisfaction with the way in which the council is run more generally raise another important distinction. Links between electors and the council may be divided into two broad categories: those concerned with the *formulation* of policy (i.e. at the pre-decision stage) and those concerned with the *implementation* of policy (i.e. those taking place after a decision has been made). The two matters are, of course, interlinked since if policy is formed badly and without proper prior consideration of public needs and desires, then unsatisfactory implementation will result with all the attendant public opposition. Indeed, the Skeffington philosophy about involving people in planning decisions can be criticised on the grounds that its recommendations involved people too late in the planning process. The proposals were mainly about 'how schemes should be implemented' rather than 'what schemes should be undertaken'. Consultation about how schemes should be implemented is rather different from involvement at the initial planning stage. Nevertheless, it remains the case that for most of the community, at least the overwhelming majority who are not especially involved in formal or informal political activity, their contacts with the authority are about the 'implementation' rather than the 'formulation' of local authority policies. This is one reason why most links between the citizen and the council operate through officials rather than elected members.

Local officials and the community

Successive surveys have demonstrated that the most frequent contacts between the local authority and the electorate are via the local authority department or official.[10] There is good sense in this since most matters relate to specific issues or grievances, many of which can be rectified without the intervention of a local councillor or, indeed, if this fails to produce satisfaction, with resort to alternative routes either formal (via courts, ombudsman, ministers, etc.) or informal (via political parties, pressure groups, the local media, etc.). In 1967, Maud found that 27 per cent of the electorate had had some contact 'with the local town hall or council office' during the preceding 12 months. This compared with 17 per cent of the electorate who had *ever* contacted a councillor. Most contacts with the council were 'by personal visit' which is a major reason why local authority premises need to be within easy travelling distance of all parts of the authority's area.

Widdicombe looked at the level of satisfaction of those citizens who had been in contact with local authority officials. Not surprisingly, those who simply 'contacted' the officials for one reason or another were significantly more satisfied than those who had been in touch to 'complain' about some aspect of the authority's work. Of the former, 68 per cent were reasonably satisfied, compared with 26 per cent of the latter. Both figures, however, were lower than those where the contact had been with an elected member of the authority. The Widdicombe survey discovered that electors are roughly twice as likely to complain via officers as they are via local councillors.[11] When asked who they would most likely contact when faced with a 'really wrong' decision by the authority, electors seemed just as likely to approach their MP as their councillor.[12] Indeed, slightly more thought that MPs would be the more effective in obtaining redress. Again, there are differences between social groups. On the whole, the better educated and higher social class groups are more likely to use several routes simultaneously to pressurise the council.

It is instructive to look at the subject matter of complaints to the local authority. In general, the Widdicombe survey found that half the issues that were likely to stimulate complaints were 'public' matters which could affect a community or area, rather than services which are essentially consumed personally. Council housing was the only 'personal' provision that rated highly in the list of likely complaints. The subjects were: council housing/rents (21 per cent), rates (3 per cent), planning (10 per cent), education (4 per cent), street cleaning/refuse (15 per cent), roads/traffic/parking (23 per cent). It should be stressed that these results refer to 'likely subjects of complaint' and are not a breakdown of *actual* complaints. The latter is something that the Maud Committee did consider. In respect of the services provided by county councils, the main subjects of enquiry/complaint were: education (31 per cent), welfare services (16 per cent) and building and planning (15 per cent). At the then borough/district level, the major subjects of enquiry/complaint were: council housing (35 per cent), building (16 per cent), street cleaning and refuse (16 per cent). Again, a word of warning about interpretation is necessary, since there is a considerable difference between an *enquiry* and a *complaint* and the figures cannot be compared with those in the Widdicombe survey.

There is one other source that can be used to reveal the major subjects of concern – the annual reports of the Local Commissioners for Administration (the local ombudsmen). Again the figures have to be treated with some caution because these indicate the subject matter of complaints submitted via local councillors where it is believed that 'maladministration' (literally a bad decision-making process) has occurred in the authority. Also, some matters are excluded from the local ombudsman's purview, notably personnel matters, contractual matters, management of education, issues where there is another channel or mechanism of complaint and, significantly in this context, matters which affect all or most citizens in a particular area. The last restriction, of course, excludes those 'public' matters which were the most likely subjects of complaint in the Widdicombe survey. The most common subject matter of complaints referred to the ombudsman are: planning, housing, education, land and highways.[13]

Councillors: the representative link

The key link between local authorities and their publics is the local councillor. Every local authority is governed by an elected council which, in the case of the principal local authorities in Britain, comprises between 28 and 120 members. Like MPs, councillors are elected to represent particular constituencies – local government wards – which are periodically reviewed by the Local Government Boundary Commissions. Each councillor serves an average population of 1,800 citizens and is elected for a fixed four-year period. This constituency size is larger than that in other West European countries. Metropolitan districts and boroughs are elected by 'thirds' (i.e. one third retires each year with no

election every fourth year), and counties and all Scottish authorities are
re-elected every fourth year by an all-out election. Non-metropolitan
districts have a choice between the two systems, with most operating the
'all-out' pattern. Elections are held the first Thursday in May.

Like any other representative, it is possible to assess how 'representative' local councillors are in a variety of ways. The word representative
can be used to denote three distinctive meanings – someone who is freely
elected; someone who is typical of the electorate; and someone who acts
as a delegate on behalf of a given group or community.[14]

In most senses, councillors are freely elected although critics might
argue that the British electoral system distorts the true feelings of voters.
A more specific concern about local elections is the extent to which they
are used (by both voters and political parties) as a reflection upon
national party performance. Where common party labels are used, it is
inevitable that electors will equate local party with national party and,
therefore, with issues and performances in national politics. It is almost
axiomatic that in a mid-term, when national governments tend to be
unpopular, there will be an adverse reaction to that party in the local
elections. Each May, *The Economist* and the *Local Government
Chronicle* produce analyses of voting behaviour at local level and it is
invariable that comment is made about how closely local electoral
behaviour mirrors feeling at national level. In effect, therefore, the local
electorate is, in part at least, using the local election as an opportunity to
make a judgement upon national parties rather than on the performance
of their councillors locally. There are 'local swings' and 'local issues'
which seem to go against the tide of national political feeling, but the
impact of national feelings is considerable. Certainly, national parties
themselves use the May local elections, like by-elections, as nation-wide
barometers of political feeling in the country. They are the best opinion
polls available to the party leaders at Westminster.

The second aspect of 'representative' requires an examination of the
kind of people who become councillors. The belief that our elected
representatives should reflect society as a whole in their social characteristics is based upon the belief that an effective relationship requires
councillors to be able to identify with their electors and, perhaps even
more importantly, with their experiences and values. It is not sufficient
to be 'with' the people, or 'for' the people, there is also an importance
attached to being 'of' the people. It assumes, in a neo-Benthamite
manner, that if elected members share the backgrounds of their electors
then in pursuing their own values and ideas, they will also pursue the
values and ideas of those who elected them. This close social relationship between councillors and electors is perhaps doubly important at

local level since, unlike at national level, councillors are required to be 'locals' and, as they are not paid a full-time salary, they are expected to retain as best they can a normal place in the local community. However, in assessing the backgrounds of people who become local councillors, it has to be remembered that only certain things can be measured. It is a simple task to record attributes such as age, sex, educational and occupational background; it is more difficult to measure experience, outlook, motivation and integrity.

No representative assembly is a microcosm of society. This is true of local councils, although councillors are, in fact, slightly more typical of their electors than are Members of Parliament. There are three major sources of data on the background of councillors – the Maud Committee, the Widdicombe Committee and the Robinson Report on the *Remuneration of Councillors* (1977). Although the findings vary slightly, the major patterns of councillors' backgrounds are similar in all three reports (Table 8.2). Councillors tend to be older, better educated and in higher occupational groups than their electors. Women are slightly better represented now than 20 years ago, although they are still the most underrepresented group of people when compared with the electorate as a whole. As in national politics, the proportion of manual workers elected has receded since 1964, though not to the same extent.[15]

There are two main reasons why councillors are not typical of their electors – motivation and opportunity. Most people are not motivated to become politically active to the extent of seeking representative office. Those that are tend to be socially atypical. They may, for example, belong to families where there is a tradition of political involvement or be attracted to politics as a result of being in contact with those who are involved through their social life or work. Much has been written about the circumstances that have attracted or deterred people entering politics.[16] Inclination has to be matched by opportunity and any potential councillor, therefore, has to balance the satisfaction of public life, however that may be defined, with the costs to his/her career and social life.[17] Some careers are more easily combined with political activity than others.

The third test of representation is perhaps the most important. How far do councillors fulfil their roles as delegates? In practice, councillors are called upon to undertake several duties – as case-worker, as watchdog and as a local spokesperson. A lack of time, let alone resources, prevents councillors performing all of these roles equally. Instead, they tend to specialise in particular aspects of council work depending upon their own circumstances and ambitions. In 1967, according to the Maud survey, the average councillor devoted 13 hours per week to council

Table 8.2 Some characteristics of local councillors (percentages)

		Maud (1964)	Robinson (1976)	Widdicombe (1985) (%)	Population (1985)
Sex	Male	88	83	81	(49)
	Female	12	17	19	(51)
Age groups	21–34	4	9	7	(29)
	35–44	15	17	19	(17)
	45–54	26	24	25	(14)
	55–64	31	30	27	(15)
	65+	23	21	22	(25)
Education*	Degree or equiv.	7		22	(5)
	Other HE qualification	14		9	(8)
	'A' Levels	3		8	(6)
	ONC/Diplomas ⎱	13		5	—
	'O' Levels ⎰			25	(17)
	Other			8	(14)
	None	44		23	(48)
Occupation*	Professional	9		9	(3)
	Employer/manager ⎱	48		32	(11)
	Intermediate ⎰			18	(9)
	Non-manual	13		10	(18)
	Skilled manual	17		16	(23)
	Semi-skilled manual	7		4	(18)
	Unskilled	3		1	(6)
House tenure	Owner-occupier	66	76	85	(57)
	Council house	16	16	10	(32)
	Other	18	8	4	(11)
Length of council service	0–3 years	26	28	25	
	4–9	31	35	40	
	10+	43	36	35	

* Not all figures in these categories are strictly comparable and some discretion has been used in allocation of figures to groups in respect of the earlier survey. Also, non-respondents are excluded, so figures may not total 100.

Source: Committee and Management on Local Government, Vol. 2 (1967) Remuneration of Councillors Vol. 2 (1977), Conduct of Local Authority Business, Vol 2 (1986).

business – a third of a normal working week and much of it during 'unsocial' hours. In 1977, the Robinson survey put this figure much higher at an average of nearly 20 hours per week. The Widdicombe survey in 1985 suggested a slightly lower figure of 18 hours, but still much increased since the mid-1960s. The extended workload has not spanned the range of councillors' duties, but has instead been mainly as a result of increased commitments in council and committee meetings (Fig. 8.1). It will be remembered that, even in 1967, Maud had been concerned at the amount of time taken in committee and council meetings.

To some extent, the pattern of council work reflects the nature of

Public consultation meetings (2)

Meeting other organisations (8)

Council party group meetings (5)

Dealing with electors/pressure groups (13)

Other (10)

Meeting other organisations (5)

Dealing with electors/pressure groups (8)

Preparation/travel to meetings (18)

Preparation/travel to meetings (25)

Council/committee meetings (11)

Council/committee meetings (21)

1964   1985

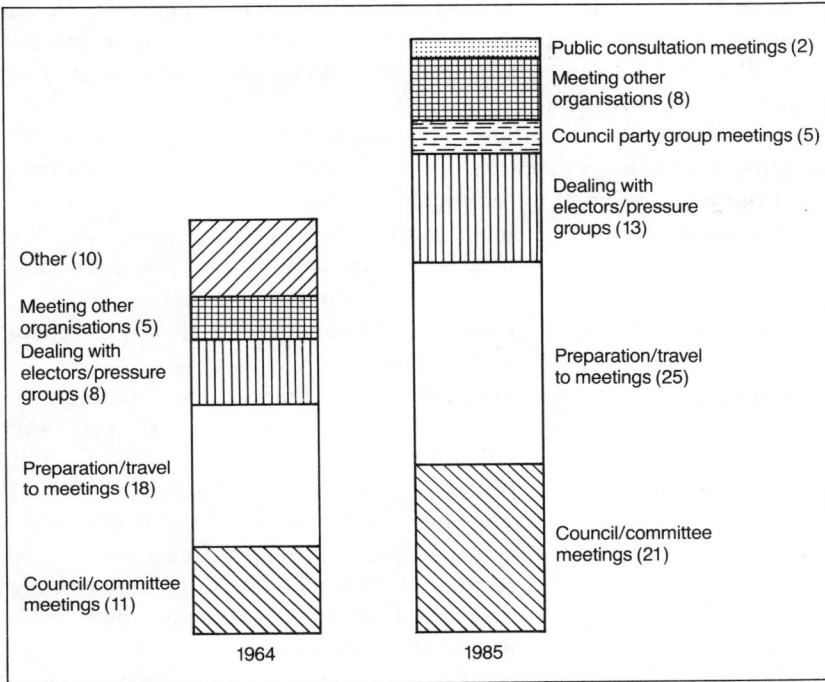

Fig. 8.1 Time spent by councillors on council business in 1964 and 1985 (hours per month)
Source: *Management of Local Government* (1967): *Conduct of Local Authority Business* (1986)

councillors' remuneration. Until 1974/75, councillors could claim a loss of earnings allowance, but since then attendance allowances have been payable in respect of all council and committee meetings and other 'approved duties'. The definition of the latter term varies between authorities and in some includes 'surgeries' for local electors. Nearly all local authorities pay additional allowances to the council chairman and, since the Local Government Planning and Land Act 1980, special responsibility allowances have been payable to leading members of the authority. Although a few local electors occasionally criticise the allowances claimed, in many cases they probably do not compensate for loss of income incurred through council work. However, they probably encourage councillors to spend more time in their 'policy-making' role than in their 'constituency' role. The issue of paying local councillors a salary has been raised on a number of occasions, most notably in 1977 following the Robinson Report. This recommended a payment scale for all councillors comprising a small basic payment together with an expenses element, a lost earnings supplement and a special responsibility allowance for some councillors such as committee chairmen. The suggestion, however, was not taken up.

Studies of local councillors have suggested different schemes for labelling councillors' various roles. One such scheme,[18] for example, identifies five aspects of the councillor's work:

1. Representative — looking after the interests of the ward, the local authority as a whole or a particular group within the community.

2. Ombudsman — helping constituents with their grievances and problems.

3. Manager — overseeing the administrative organisation of the authority; ensuring fair play and efficiency.

4. Policy-maker — setting objectives and allocating resources. This may be further subdivided into those councillors who specialise in a given service sector and those who are concerned with the overall policies of the authority: the specialist and the generalist.

5. Politician — resolving conflicts and influencing others.

To make matters still more complex, it has been suggested that the 'representative' role itself may relate to five different groups of constituents:[19]

1. Representing a geographical area — from a ward to the whole authority.

2. Representing a group in the community — council tenants, ethnic minorities, women, etc.

3. Representing an organised group — welfare, church, etc.

4. Representing another local authority — where the councillor holds dual membership of authorities or, indeed, the role performed when the councillor represents a local authority on another statutory body.

5. Representing the individual citizen (this links with the ombudsman role).

Moreover, we need to add to all of this the particular circumstances of councillors: whether they are committee chairmen/vice-chairmen ('front-benchers') or not ('back-benchers'); the party they belong to; the time they have been on the council; and, not insignificantly, the scope of their ambitions. As in other countries, local government is an important training ground for Members of Parliament — about half of Labour MPs and a third of Conservative MPs previously served in local government —

and the more ambitious may well perform a different role in local government than those who see their purpose to act mainly on behalf of a small community or group and who do not aspire to national office.

We can see some of the effects of these factors in a study of councillors in Birmingham.[20] Committee chairmen, for example, were only half as likely to hold frequent 'surgeries' as non-chairmen; Labour politicians were twice as likely to hold regular 'surgeries' as Conservatives and got higher attendances. Those who had served more than 11 years on the council spent more than eight hours per month with other organisations compared with just over three hours for newer members. In general, newer members, Labour members and those who did not occupy leading positions on the council had more frequent contacts with individual electors, whereas council leaders who were mainly those with longer council service tended to consult more with organisations than with individuals. Labour councillors were more likely to be involved in party group meetings than their Conservative counterparts. It has also been suggested that occupational background can play a part in determining how the councillor divides scarce time between various demands: '. . . higher socio-economic groups prefer policy work while manual workers . . . prefer to deal with individual problems. New members and junior councillors also tend to emphasise ward responsibilities rather than preference for work on authority-wide policies'.[21]

One classification which has gained wide currency distinguishes three dispositions among councillors – delegates, trustees and politicos. *Delegates* act on behalf of their electors and in accord with their wishes. *Trustees*, by contrast, make decisions on the basis of their own personal judgement, conscience and their position of responsibility. *Politicos* balance judgement and public opinion, assessing each issue according to its sensitivity and political consequences. The suggestion is that, as political careers develop, the councillor moves from delegate through politico to trustee. Trustees tend to have fewer contacts with electors or their ward party organisation. They are much more likely to consider themselves policy-makers than ombudsmen for their constituents' grievances.

The various aspects of the councillor's role are matched by the different types and orientations of councillors themselves. Their orientation may vary according to their geographical perception (ward or whole authority); according to the scope of their policy interests (single service or broad policy); according to their perception of accountability (delegate, politico or trustee) and, finally, according to the extent of their commitment to a party political line. How councillors perform their roles and how they apportion their time will depend upon all of these factors. These questions in turn will determine how the links operate between the electorate and themselves.

Local ombudsmen: an additional link

For many electors, the only reason for contacting the local authority is to complain about the way in which a particular service is being provided. On the whole, however, local councillors do not spend a large part of their time helping citizens resolve particular grievances. Indeed, as we have seen, electors are just as likely to contact their Members of Parliament, and 'council problems' – housing, planning, education and social welfare – form a large proportion of the MP's postbag and figure large when they hold constituency surgeries.[22] Some MPs hold surgeries alongside local councillors in order to 'redirect' their constituents. The Local Commissioners for Administration (LCA) – the local ombudsmen – that were introduced under the 1974 Local Government Act and the 1975 Local Government (Scotland) Act are intended to complement the 'constituency' role of local councillors.[23]

Concern about the adequacy of the local authority complaints procedure had been evident for many years and was the subject of the Whyatt Report *The Citizen and his Administration*, a *Justice* report, in 1961. In view of the number of citizens approaching them about council matters, many MPs were persuaded of the need for strengthening the complaints procedure in local government. Pressure grew stronger after the Parliamentary Commissioner for Administration was established in 1967. During his first year, the PCA received 61 complaints concerning local administration which, being outside his jurisdiction, were rejected.

The 1974 and 1975 Acts provided a system for the investigation of complaints by the public where 'injustice is sustained in consequence of maladministration'. Three ombudsmen were appointed in England plus one each for Scotland and Wales. As with the Act establishing the PCA, 'maladministration' was left undefined, as was 'injustice', but the same kind of errors that concerned the PCA were intended to be the matters considered by the local ombudsmen. These errors are usually referred to in the terms that Richard Crossman used when establishing the PCA: neglect, delay, incompetence, failure to obey rules, bias. They concern the *way* in which a decision is made, rather than the *result* of a decision. This in itself creates some difficulties, since most aggrieved citizens will be concerned with what they consider to be a 'bad' decision; their concern is not that the decision was arrived at in an inappropriate manner. However, they must show this to have been the case if they are to challenge the decision. It is not possible to question a 'bad' decision if it has been arrived at properly. As noted above, certain areas are excluded: those matters where there is recourse to a tribunal or court and matters which affect all or most of the population. There is also a time limit of 12 months within which, in normal circumstances, a complaint must be lodged.

Like the PCA, local ombudsmen are seen as an adjunct to the elected politicians and complaints must go via councillors. However, over half of the 2,000 or so complaints received annually by the English Commissioners are still sent directly to the LCA. Direct access was, however, available if the citizen could show that the councillor had refused to refer the complaint and, since 1984, the LCA has been able to pass on complaints made directly to the Commission. Two-thirds of the cases investigated since 1974 have revealed injustice and maladministration.

The actual powers of the LCA are limited. Once an investigation has been completed, a report is sent to the citizen, the councillor and the local authority and where injustice and maladministration are found proven, the local authority is invited to inform the LCA what action it proposes to take regarding the matter. It may, of course, be too late to redress the grievance so far as the citizen is concerned. In the event of no action being taken, the LCA can issue a second report. The Commission has no power of enforcement and must, in the last resort, rely upon moral pressure to persuade the local authority to act. However, only in a few cases (less than one in ten) has the Commission been dissatisfied with the response of local councils. The Local Government, Planning and Land Act 1980 extended the Commission's right to see relevant documents in pursuit of an investigation.

The value attached to the local ombudsman varies. Some councillors remain sceptical and even concerned that their role is usurped. This is despite the fact that many of them do not devote much of their time to their own 'ombudsman' function. Officers can find investigations time-consuming and costly. However, simply by being there, the LCA perhaps makes administrators conscious of the need to adhere to proper decision-making procedures. Ultimately, the most important test is public reaction and the simple fact is that most electors are not aware of the existence of the LCA and would not, therefore, think about calling upon the Commission's help in pursuit of a grievance. The Widdicombe survey revealed that the ombudsman would be only the fifth choice of people when considering how they would challenge a bad decision by the council – councillors, MPs, officials and the local newspaper/radio were all more likely to be used and only the district auditor ranked below the LCA. When asked who they thought would be the most effective in remedying the problem, the ombudsman was again ranked fifth. Nevertheless, the Local Commissioners are an important and supplementary means of linking people and local authorities.

So far, we have considered the formal links between local government and the community – officers, councillors, local ombudsmen and, in previous chapters, the courts and ministers. Informal links – political parties, pressure groups and the local media – can be just as significant.

INFORMAL LINKS

Political parties and local government

Political parties are not new to local government although there has been a steady growth in their involvement in recent years and nearly all councils are now run on party lines. The use of national party labels in local elections is commonplace and party groups are often controlling influences on how local authority business is conducted. In the major cities, traditions of party political control have developed that closely resemble those at Westminster. The extent to which party political divisions surface in actual decision-making processes varies between authorities and also between issues. Even where party labels are present, much of the business of the local council can be conducted in a non-partisan atmosphere. Moreover, the different structures of government in local and national politics mean that the impact of political parties at Westminster is not entirely replicated in local town and county halls. The committee system and the fact that officers are servants of the council and not of the major party are important characteristics of the local setting. Nevertheless, the considerable growth in overt party involvement in recent years cannot be denied. In 1972, shortly before reorganisation, 59 per cent of county councils were run on party lines; now the proportion is 92 per cent.[24] The equivalent figure for non-county boroughs in 1972 was 63 per cent. This compares with the 92 per cent of non-metropolitan districts that are now run on party lines. Other figures confirm the rise of the party in town and county halls. In England and Wales, for example, 47 per cent of principal local authorities were controlled by Independents or non-party councillors in the last election prior to reorganisation. By 1985, the proportion had fallen to 14 per cent. In 1975, 4,802 councillors did not belong to any of the three major political parties. Ten years later the figure was 1,389 – a fall from 20.1 per cent to 5.9 per cent of all councillors. Even allowing for changes in nomenclature – many Independents in county halls were Conservatives in all but name – the change is dramatic.

Even in the nineteenth century, political parties were an important feature of the local government landscape. In 1835, for example, the Royal Commission on Municipal Corporations observed that local elections were 'often a trial of strength between political parties'.[25] By the third quarter of the century, parties were an established aspect of municipal politics in many cities.[26] At a time when political parties were developing their national organisations, an important reason for their growth at local level was the desire to keep the party organisation well oiled between general elections. Much the same need exists today. The steady growth in party involvement continued – more rapidly in London and the major cities than in rural areas – with the rise of the Labour party acting as a stimulus to anti-socialist groups in some areas. By the early 1970s, therefore, Independents and non-party candidates were really only features of local government outside the towns and cities. Reorganisation effectively speeded up the politicisation of local government but did not start a process that goes back to the nineteenth century.

Perhaps more important than the incidence of party labels at local elections is what happens after the election. Parties have a considerable impact on the management of local authority affairs and in this area, changes are more recent. An early turning point was the introduction by the Labour party of model standing orders for party groups in local government. These had the effect of focusing power on the party group and led to more disciplined behaviour on the council and its committees. Despite these orders, however, even by the 1960s it was not possible to detect a single pattern of party management in Labour-led local authorities.[27] Variations still exist, but the evidence suggests that during the last decade party control has strengthened. Two-thirds of Labour groups in local government now meet at a frequency of 2–4 weeks; Conservative groups meet less frequently, with two-thirds meeting monthly or less often.[28]

One way of assessing party control is to consider how disciplined party groups are when voting on the council. Cohesion among party groups, expressed in terms of consistent voting, is a prime requirement of party management in the local authority. This is something that the Widdicombe Report considered. In its survey, approximately 54 per cent of all groups in counties and metropolitan districts always voted together in the full council.[29] Disciplined voting was less apparent in shire districts and London boroughs and was also much lower in committees, where a less partisan atmosphere seemed to prevail. There was also considerable difference between the parties. Across the various types of authority, 59 per cent of Labour groups always voted together compared with only 23 per cent of Conservative groups. The equivalent figures in respect of committee votes were 15 per cent and 5 per cent respectively.

Party domination is also seen in the distribution of committee chairmanships and places. Irrespective of the type of authority, and with minimal differences between the parties, it is almost universal that the party (or coalition of parties) which has a majority on the council will take all the committee and subcommittee chairmanships and vice-chairmanships.[30] In strict constitutional terms, it is improper to refer to an 'administration' in local government. In *de facto* terms, however, majority parties can be described as such in all but name. Having captured all the committee chairmanships, majority parties consolidate their power base by assuming a majority of committee places. According to Widdicombe, the majority party/parties take the majority of seats on all committees in 87 per cent of local authorities.[31] This figure would probably be even higher were it not for the number of 'hung' county councils where no one party has a majority, and the Alliance has been successful in obtaining a proportionate distribution of committee places as the price for its support of one of the other parties. A final manifestation of party politicisation is to be found in the growing phenomenon of the 'full-time' councillor – someone who spends more or less the whole of their working week on council matters. The Widdicombe survey indicated that over half of local authorities had at least 'one or two' such members.[32]

The desirability or otherwise of political party involvement in local government has long been debated. In so far as their involvement is so firmly established the debate is, of course, now largely academic. In favour of parties it is generally argued that public interest and, therefore, participation in local government is stimulated as a result of party involvement. Parties also give a clearer sense of purpose to the running of local services by offering the local electorate the opportunity to vote for a programme of policies which are intended to be structured, comprehensive and coherent. In local authorities without disciplined party control, there can often be conflicts and inconsistency between the various sectors of local authority provision. Politics is about choice and party manifestos mean that at least the electorate knows what to expect. Party control also gives leadership to local government officers who might otherwise dominate the conduct of local authority business.

Critics of parties in local government argue that their presence deters some people from standing for election who might otherwise do so. They point also to the effect of national parties on local electoral behaviour. However, just as the principal virtues of parties in local government are to be found inside the authority, so too are their major vices. Partisanship and ideological conflicts tend to colour all areas of council business, even to the detriment of the real interests of the local community. The temptation to score party political points can become irresistible, not least in those authorities where the council is in conflict with central authorities. At a time when party politics have become polarised at national level, some would suggest that parallel developments have occurred in certain local council chambers. Indeed, it was a concern about these developments that led to the establishment of the Widdicombe inquiry into the conduct of local authority business. The inquiry sought the views of the electorate about the party politicisation of local government; 52 per cent considered the non-party system better, compared with 32 per cent who favoured the party system.[33] This preference for Independents was across age, sex and class groups, although it was particularly strong in social groups A and B and among those who were better 'informed' about local government.[34] Only one group of electors revealed a distinct preference for the party system – Labour voters. Among Conservative voters, the preference for a non-party system was nearly 2:1 in favour.

Since it is impossible to turn back the clock, even if the electorate so wished, the important thing is not to debate the advantages and disadvantages of political parties in local government, but rather to understand their effect on local authority business. One effect has been an increased workload for councillors. Meetings have tended to be longer and councillors more involved in the details of policy implementation as well as its formulation. This has led to changes in the relationship between members and officers as the former have become more involved in the details of administration. This even extends in some cases to their relationships with junior officers. Naturally, practices and norms vary between authorities and, in the same way as internal structures depend on local circumstances, so too do the patterns of party management. The range of duties, the nature of the local economy, the political traditions of the authority and the composition of the council all have a vital impact on the party management of the council.[35]

There is need for a postscript about parties since an increasingly common feature in local government is the 'hung' council – local authorities without a majority party.[36] Approximately 17 per cent of British local councils are 'hung'. Among English and Welsh counties the proportion is much higher and following the May 1985 elections, 24 of the 47 counties were left without single-party majority control. Since these authorities operate the 'all-out' election system, this means that unless there is a succession of by-election changes, the balanced situation will remain until May 1989.

There are many consequences for the organisation and procedures of the 'hung' authority. Whatever arrangements are made to run the council – and they will depend upon such factors as the political traditions of the authority, the relationships between the party leaders, the ideological nature of the parties and the economic context – the situation will almost certainly slow down the decision-making process as well as move the location of decision-making. Councillors will need more time to construct deals between party groups, and officers will require time to liaise with the various leaders and to brief all involved. Meetings are invariably longer – in Avon the meeting that produced the annual budget in March 1986 lasted 30 hours. In hung authorities, the focus of decision-making shifts from committees to the full council, which is no longer just a 'rubber stamp' for decisions made elsewhere. Decisions can and do change as they proceed up from committees to the full council. It can also be difficult to ensure that various decisions fit together since voting patterns can fluctuate considerably between one meeting and another. Not surprisingly, much of the extra burden of work falls upon officers, who need to keep the authority running smoothly; in order to do so, they are frequently required to display considerable tact and political skill. They often have two particular problems – ensuring fair treatment for all groups and getting decisions out of reluctant councillors. One measure of the unpredictability can be illustrated by the fact that in some hung councils it is not unusual to elect a fresh chairman at the beginning of each committee meeting. For some local authorities, a balance of power has become a way of life and if the fortunes of the Liberal–SDP Alliance continue then it is something with which many other authorities will have to cope.

Pressure groups in local politics

Links between the community and the local authority are supplemented by other channels of communication and influence. One important link is that provided by pressure groups, which operate in much the same way in the local political arena as they do in national politics. Pressure groups are a way of reinforcing existing and formal channels by offering a means of articulating specific demands, in contrast to elections which are necessarily generalised in nature. The citizen has only one vote to cast at a local election and, therefore, has to register support for one candidate or one party on the basis of a broad range of policies. It is unlikely, however, that even the most committed supporter of a political party will be in full agreement with that party in all areas of policy. Pressure groups focus on specific issues and, unlike political parties, do not themselves seek office but rather attempt to influence decisions. They also strengthen the link with the electorate by being a channel of communication between elections. This is especially important in local authorities where elections are held at fixed four-year intervals.

Both the mode of operation and the determinants of effectiveness are similar for local and national pressure groups. Basically, there are two types of group: 'interest' and 'attitude'. The former comprises people with a common interest or attribute (usually defined in economic terms) where political activity may be only a by-product of group membership (AA, trade union, etc.), and membership levels are stable but wide in social terms. 'Attitude' groups are organisations of people with a common view or cause (RSPCA, CPRE, Campaign for the North) and which exist solely to pursue that cause. Theoretically, anyone can become a member of an attitude group; in practice, members tend to be middle-class and middle-aged.[37] Unlike interest groups, a major problem for the organisers of attitude groups is persuading members to renew their annual subscriptions. If a group is to persuade a local authority that it speaks for a significant body of opinion, it is important that it can command a large and stable membership. Like any other pressure groups, those operating primarily in the local political arena attempt to influence policy by focusing their activities where they are likely to have the greatest effect – the 'stiletto principle'. How precisely they go about voicing their demands will depend upon the following:

1. *The nature of the group*. Some groups may have expertise to offer the local authority (e.g. the county trusts are often consulted on many conservation issues by local councils), while others may face a difficult struggle in attempting to change existing attitudes.

2. *The political culture*, both external to the group and internal. The former determines the general acceptability of group involvement in local politics and the latter the kinds of action that memberships will support. There is good evidence that one of the factors affecting likely success is the method of communicating demands. A study of groups in Kensington and Chelsea observed that the more successful groups adopted 'proper' styles of action that did not embarrass senior officers and councillors, made 'reasonable' demands and were considered 'helpful' in being able to provide the council with useful information.[38]

3. *The 'real' source of decision-making*. Groups will focus on the spot where the decisions are made that they wish to influence. In some

cases this will mean elected members; in other cases it will mean approaching officers. Social services and environmental groups, for example, tend to have closer links with officers. Groups concerned with housing demands or rights for minorities may be more likely to focus attention on the elected politicians.

The likely effectiveness of groups will also depend upon a number of factors including, among others, the following:

1. The acceptability of the cause and its compatibility with existing local authority policies.
2. The size, organisation and funds of the group.
3. The extent of political and media support it can achieve.
4. The expertise of the group and its value to the local authority.

It is almost impossible to gauge accurately the number of pressure groups in the local government setting and some groups are active only occasionally. However, one study of Birmingham calculated that there were 4,000 voluntary groups, many of which did engage in pressure group activity.[39] The two areas in which local pressure groups are probably most active are social welfare and the environment. The number of local amenity societies, for example, has doubled every six or seven years since 1955.[40]

One advantage that local pressure groups have over their national counterparts is that councillors tend to be more accessible than MPs. Councillors live locally and therefore are relatively easy for pressure groups to lobby. However, this in itself is unlikely to guarantee success and the evidence of several studies is that their achievements are closely related to the character of the group, the nature of the demand and the means of articulating this demand. Groups such as those working in partnership with local authority social services departments or those civic groups working closely with planning departments stand much better chances of success than organisations placing extensive demands on the authority but offering little in return.

Participation and community action

Although Mill referred to the desirability of public involvement in local affairs over a century ago, the idea of direct citizen participation has gained fresh vigour over the last two decades. Its impact has been felt most deeply in the area of planning which, since the 1968 Town and Country Planning Act, has been one field in which local authorities are statutorily required to involve the public in a process of consultation. However, since the Skeffington Report and subsequent town planning legislation, the ethos of citizen involvement has spread to other areas and, in some local authorities, has been actively fostered by sympathetic council leaders.

Participation in local politics can take two main forms: direct public involvement in the administration of a particular local service or organisation (e.g. parents as school governors), or a process of consultation between the council and the local people in respect of a given service. The latter is the more usual meaning attached to participation in local government. Consultative processes are not always easy to achieve – even after reorganisation the world of local government remains complex and inaccessible in the eyes of many electors. The professionalism and expertise of officers is not always readily compatible with the lay opinions of those who consume local services. Even the 'language' of professionals can make it difficult for the public to understand what is really being proposed and it thus deters effective public involvement. Not least, any consultative process is time-consuming. All in all, the professional local government officer might find consultation to be something of a distraction. As one town planner observed: 'Trained planners with the public interest in mind are best left to get on with the job'.[41] There is also the crucial question of whether participation is regarded as an event or a process. If the former is the case, then all that is being sought by the local authority is a public ratification of proposals which have reached a more or less finalised state. The crucial 'gestation' period when policies are devised and shaped has passed by the time the public is invited to give its views and at best, therefore, all it might be expected to contribute are some suggestions about change at the margin of the scheme. The more ambitious understanding of participation is that it is a process – a continuing relationship between the authority and the public. As such it is 'an integral part of ongoing processes of policy formulation, decision-making, implementation and monitoring within various local government services or within local government generally'.[42] In practice, participation tends to be an 'event' rather than a 'process', with specific time periods set aside for public consultation exercises.

Most experience of public participation relates to the field of planning since this was the first area to require public consultation, and the obligations to do so remain the greatest. Since 1968, however, consultation has become a limited requirement in some additional areas. The 1980 Housing Act, for example, obliges local authorities to inform tenants about certain aspects of housing management. However, it does not lay down the mechanisms and procedures for making this information available and local authorities have adopted a variety of means of meeting the requirements of the Act, including, for example, the formation of consultative committees, co-option of tenants on to housing committees, opinion surveys and *ad hoc* public meetings.[43] Other new consultative procedures include: those with respect to the local business community (the 1984 Rates Act compels local authorities to consult non-domestic ratepayers about the rates), ethnic minorities (there has been a convention of liaising with local community relations councils but the consultative links between authorities and ethnic organisations have considerably expanded since the inner-city 'riots' of 1981) and, in some areas, women's groups.[44] Still more recently, parent consultation and involvement in the control of schools and their curricula have become an important feature of the Conservative Government's education policies.

Community politics derive from the idea of citizen participation in local affairs, although there is an important difference between various aspects of community politics. *Community action* is essentially radical and seeks change in existing practices through self-help groups, while *community development* is concerned with collaborative links between the council and local groups.[45] Community politics can relate to either geographical or social concepts of the community, although they tend to be more concerned with the former. An early landmark in community development was the report of the Seebohm Committee (see page 146), and since the late 1960s community politics have become an increasingly important characteristic of local political life. Both the Liberal and Labour parties have been closely concerned with the phenomenon of community politics. For the former, vigorous encouragement of participatory democracy is a key electoral strategy as well as a philosophical conviction. The 1970 Liberal Assembly endorsed a resolution on community politics which referred to the role of local Liberals as being 'to help people in communities to organise, to take and use power, to use our political skills to redress grievances and to represent people at all levels of the political structure'.[46] Labour's approach to community politics has been more concerned with the forging of a 'coalition of interests at local level between groups that have not previously been influential in local politics: environmental, tenants', women's and ethnic minority groups'.[47]

The most direct forms of contact between community action groups and the public are through public meetings. In one Sheffield study, for example, tenants' associations used bingo sessions as a means of collecting complaints and welfare problems.[48] Especially important are community broadsheets as a means of disseminating information and forging links between members. Significantly, the Sheffield survey suggested that the territories for community action groups were as often defined in accordance with externally imposed administrative boundaries (i.e. those appearing in planning studies) as they were 'natural areas' defined by the group themselves.

Local authorities have often encouraged the formation of community groups and helped foster community identities by their own organisational arrangements. This has been especially the case in Liberal- and Labour-controlled local authorities.[49] Following their taking control of Richmond in 1983, for example, the Liberal group initiated schemes of area consultation through area management committees and public consultative meetings. In Labour-controlled Walsall, 32 neighbourhood offices were opened in the early 1980s. Labour authorities in London and in several northern cities have pursued similar objectives. In Sheffield, for instance, there is a series of area housing committees with tenant representatives, and experimental neighbourhood forums containing 'councillors, council officers and representatives from tenants', residents', youth, parent and church groups'.[50] Few local authorities have been as bold as this in their desire to involve community groups in helping decide the shape and content of local authority policies and not all party groups or, indeed, officers welcome the move towards community politics. Nevertheless, community action groups are now a feature, to a greater or lesser degree, of local government's relationship with the public. Even in rural areas, where dispersed settlement patterns militate against the formation of large groups, some forms of community action can be discerned.

The local media, local government and public access

The most obvious way in which people learn about local politics is through the local and regional press. Eighty per cent of the adult population reads some kind of local newspaper. In 1967, the Maud Committee observed that generally the only information 'the public get about the local authority's work is through the local press and even that does not appear to make a very striking impression'. It is of some concern, therefore, that the evidence suggests that the space devoted to local government matters has declined from its peak in the late nineteenth century.[51] In part this is due to the loss of many provincial newspapers – although there has been a tenfold increase in free local newspapers during the last decade – and also to the editorial difficulty of finding space for the 'less newsworthy and entertaining' aspects of local government. Problems are also caused by the fact that newspaper circulation areas do not necessarily coincide with local authority

boundaries. Some newspapers lack specialist local government correspondents and assign the duty of covering local council meetings to
relatively junior reporters. The problems are exacerbated when local
authorities themselves appear to be less than enthusiastic about opening
their doors to the press. Even though the provisions for press and public
access have been widened since the Public Bodies (Admissions to
Meetings) Act 1960, not all local authorities have demonstrated a spirit
of openness to coincide with the intentions of the relevant legislation.
The provincial press tends to be of two types: newspapers belonging to a
national group and which often include syndicated material, therefore
reducing the space available for special 'local' material, and independent
newspapers which are often weekly circulations. Both kinds have been
accused of 'trivialisation' and 'personalisation' of local politics. There is
little space devoted to and, newspapers would argue, little interest in,
substantial detail about local political matters.

Other forms of the media have a potential involvement in local
politics. In addition to the regional commercial television companies
and the regional network of BBC television, there are now over 100 local
radio stations in Britain. The latter have considerable potential significance for the coverage of local government affairs and were seen by some
as a means of rectifying the 'communication gap' which many felt
existed by the late 1960s. Indeed, the white papers that heralded the
new local radio stations 'charged them with the task of "fostering a
greater public awareness of local affairs and involvement in the community" '.[52] In practice, these expectations have not been fully met.
Relatively few local radio stations have full-time local government
correspondents and a similarly small proportion devote regular slots to
local government topics – and the ones that do are mainly BBC rather
than ILR stations.[53] Even coverage of local elections is spasmodic. As
with newspapers, one problem is the lack of conterminous boundaries
between broadcast areas and local government units. At the very least
this leaves the radio station with difficult choices about which, if any,
local authority should receive some media coverage. One IBA survey
concluded that, like press coverage, most local radio stations displayed a
'dutiful rather than enthusiastic' attitude[54] towards their own coverage
of local government. Implicitly or explicitly, most broadcasters retain
the belief that local politics are of little interest to the public in general
and, therefore, not something that should figure prominently in their
programme scheduling. The same attitude prevails in the local press
although it has become a chicken-and-egg situation. Does the public's
limited appetite for media coverage of local government affairs reflect a
lack of interest or is it a result of the scant attention that the media

currently give to local affairs? Local media in other countries are often more generous in their coverage of local politics.

Relations between the press and the local authority raise the issue of access to the local authority and its meetings. Before 1960, these matters were regulated by the Local Authorities (Admission of the Press to Meetings) Act 1908, which gave the press the right to be present at full meetings of the council. This right, however, did not extend to committees and a council had only to resolve to exclude the press 'in the public interest' in order to preclude its attendance. By going into committee, the council could achieve the same effect – a technique used regularly by many local authorities.

A Private Members Bill introduced by Margaret Thatcher led to the Public Bodies (Admission to Meetings) Act 1960, which extended to the public the right to attend council meetings, the education committee and committees comprising the full membership of the council. However, both public and press could be excluded by the resolution of councillors, again in the 'public interest' because of the 'confidential nature of the business' being discussed or 'for other special purposes'. Unlike the 1908 Act, the press could not be excluded by the simple device of going into committee; the precise reasons for excluding it had to be disclosed. The 1972 and 1973 Local Government Acts extended the provisions of the 1960 Act to allow access to committees, but not subcommittees.

The legislation still gave the more secretive local authorities sufficient scope to limit press and public access to their proceedings either by extensive use of the exclusion provisions or by transacting much business in subcommittees. The Department of the Environment expressed its concern about this practice in a circular in 1975,[55] which pointed out that the 1960, 1972 and 1973 Acts established minimum rights of access and that local authorities could go beyond these standards and, at the very least, respect the spirit of the legislation. A more powerful criticism was levelled by the Community Rights Project (CRP) which, in January 1984, reviewed the way in which 61 local authorities met their duties under the 1960 Act and subsequent legislation.[56] None of the authorities surveyed met all their obligations and some failed to meet their statutory requirements in eight out of ten matters.

Not all local authorities were equally reticent about allowing press and public access to council and committee proceedings. In 1978, for example, the London borough of Hillingdon opened all committees and subcommittees to the public except in specific circumstances.[57] The CRP put forward a draft bill that was intended to extend access to subcommittees and to make local authorities be more explicit in justifying those occasions when the public was to be excluded. Like the Act in 1960, the measure was taken up as a Private Members Bill and became the Local Government (Access to Information) Act 1985. It supersedes the 1960 Act. Although not entirely what the CRP had intended, the measure does in fact extend access rights to subcommittees and oblige local authorities to be specific about the reasons for excluding the press at some meetings. By the time that the measure took effect, however, fewer than 20 local authorities had voluntarily met all the provisions of the Act. Besides increasing access, the 1985 Act also requires that authorities make available minutes of meetings, agendas and reports and, perhaps most radical of all, relevant background papers. Originally the Bill had been intended to include all documents discussed in public by the authority – not just council documents – but this clause was lost during the Bill's passage through Parliament.

The effectiveness of the measure will, like its predecessors, depend ultimately on how far local authorities wish to follow the spirit as well as the letter of the law. One local authority changed its standing orders immediately the Bill was presented in order to implement its provisions. It has followed this up by applying similar open access provision to JCC meetings with the local health authority and, since 1986, to all meetings of school governors. Other local authorities will, no doubt, be less forthcoming. Like other aspects of local government organisation and procedure, much will depend on particular local values and traditions.

CONCLUSION

There will always be a need for the local delivery of services. There are, however, means other than local government through which local services may be provided . . . . Local government is government *by* local communities rather than *of* local communities.[58]

Like many other institutions, local government in Britain has undergone significant changes in recent years and further change seems inevitable. Both its structure and internal organisation have been overhauled and there has been a marked shift in the relationship between central and local government. Major reform of the financing of local government has to take place if local autonomy is to be maintained to any real extent. By any test, local government has undergone, and continues to face, a period of uncertainty and challenge.

Besides these structural and organisational reforms, there have been important developments in the political, economic and social environment in which local authorities operate. One such development is the increasing politicisation of local government, which has affected not only the conduct of local elections but has also had such an impact on the decision-making procedures in local councils and upon relationships between elected members and professional officers. No less important are the new demands that result from social and economic change. Local authorities are being required to meet new needs in various fields: the growing number of elderly people, for example, results in ever greater need for community care, which not only increases the load on local authorities but also brings them into even closer contact with the health authorities and the large number of voluntary sector bodies that also provide support for this section of the community. Changing economic circumstances resulting in the decline of some industries and increases in unemployment have also brought new challenges. Local authorities have often been at the forefront of employment initiatives and in this area too, they have collaborated closely with other agencies, both local and national.[59] Unemployment has had a secondary effect upon local service provision – the need to cater for the recreational needs of those out of work. There are many other ways in which social and economic trends have added to community needs, for example responding to the number of deprived families, coping with the problems of renewing out-of-date housing stock, and dealing with increasing crime rates.

Local authorities are unable to meet any of these needs without the involvement of other bodies, public, private and voluntary. They are not independent or self-sufficient actors in the local community and sometimes their primary role may be to mobilise and co-ordinate the actions of other bodies. The needs and problems of local communities are interdependent. Effective reaction by those who deliver services to the local community requires a similar degree of integration: '. . . corporate working not just within the local authority but by a network of public and voluntary agencies, corporate working not just at county or district headquarters but at the level of the social worker, the school, the police station, the general practitioner and the housing estate'.[60] One of the most important things to appreciate about the relationship between the local council and the local community, is that collaboration is an essential characteristic of an effective link. This is true both inside the authority and between the authority and adjacent organisations.

The role that local government will play in delivering local services to the community in the future will depend to a large degree upon how two opposing forces are resolved. In ideal terms, local government should be *local*, and we have already seen how decentralising pressures have led to the establishment of area and neighbourhood levels of operation. Meeting the needs of the community is most effective if these needs are met at a level which is understood by, and accessible to, the community itself. At the same time, however, local authorities have faced strong centralising pressures, most clearly seen in the financial control of local government by central government. The immediate future of local government will therefore depend on the balance that is achieved between these two forces – localism and centralism.

Local government after the 1987 general election

Following its re-election in June 1987, the Conservative Government indicated that it intended to legislate in a number of fields which would affect local government. In their first two terms of office, the Conservative Government had introduced over 40 major pieces of local government legislation and these new proposals will, if enacted, have a considerable impact upon the status and workings of local government. The proposals concern: inner cities (notably the expansion of the urban development programme and the possible introduction of new mini-UDCs); the introduction of the Community Charge in England and Wales (possibly over a phased period), putting more local authority services out to private competitive tender; implementation of some of the Widdicombe proposals; housing (notably allowing estates and tenants to opt out of local authority control); and, not least, the field of education (notably, the introduction of a national curriculum for schools within two years, the creation of city technology colleges, the removal of polytechnics from local authority control, financial delegation to schools and allowing schools to opt out of local authority control). The pace of the reform can be gauged by the fact that within five weeks of the Queen's Speech announcing the education changes, five consultative documents had been published – *Collective Worship in Schools*, *Admission of Pupils to Maintained Schools*, *Financial Delegation to Schools*, *Grant-Maintained Schools* and *The National Curriculum 5–16*.

The decision to extend the practice of compulsory competitive tendering to a wider range of services than those covered by the Local Government, Planning and Land Act 1980 is consistent with the more commercial approach to the provision of services favoured by the Government. In practice, a few local authorities already put services out to private tender and a recent survey revealed that approximately ten per cent of local councils – mainly Conservative-controlled councils – adopt this approach on a voluntary basis.[61] The services put out to tender include: cleansing, routine property maintenance, leisure management and catering. However, the scale of these services is relatively minor and represents a cost of only £120 million out of a total budget for these authorities of £34 billion. Contacts between local authorities and the private sector will also be extended by the proposals for the revitalisation of inner cities, since a partnership approach between public and private sectors is regarded as the most effective means of tackling the problems of these areas. Some local authorities already have well-established collaborative links with commercial organisations in this connection.

Whatever the motivation for introducing these measures – limiting the expenditure of local authorities or extending choice in the delivery of local services – their implications will be considerable. They will mean that local government will lose direct control over certain services and will be required still further to collaborate with other bodies in the locality – statutory and voluntary, public and private. In some ways they mark a return to the *ad hoc* principle, as opposed to the *multi-purpose* principle, as the preferred means of delivering services to the local population. There is also a potential paradox in that the proposed reforms which, whilst extending choice and strengthening account-ability in some ways, would also reduce the powers of local government and increase its subordination to central government. It will, therefore, become even more important that local authorities, possibly in col-laboration with others, remain conscious of the needs and desires of the local community *to* whom and *for* whom they provide services.

Notes

1. P. Kershaw, 'Democracy and the Management of Local Authorities' in R. Darke and R. Walker (eds.), *Local Government and the Public* (Leonard Hill, 1977).
2. *Committee on the Management of Local Government* (Maud), Vol. 3, 'The Local Government Elector' (HMSO, 1967).
3. *The Conduct of Local Authority Business* (Widdicombe), Vol. 1, 'The Political Organisa-tion of Local Authorities', p. 42.
4. Widdicombe, *op. cit.* Table 4.
5. Maud, *op. cit.* p. 62.
6. *Ibid.* Table 92.
7. Widdicombe, *op. cit.* Table 3.1.
8. *Ibid.* Table 3.6.
9. *Ibid.* p. 46.
10. See, for example, J. Bonner, 'Public Interest in Local Government', *Public Administra-tion* (1974); *Committee on the Management of Local Government*, Vol. 3, Ch. 2; *The Conduct of Local Authority Business*, Vol. 3.
11. Widdicombe, *op. cit.* Table 4.6.
12. *Ibid.* Table 4.7.
13. Report of the Commission for Local Administration.
14. A. H. Birch, *Representation* (Macmillan, 1971).
15. C. Mellors, *The British MP* (Gower, 1978), Ch. 5.

16. See, for example, R. V. Clements, *Local Notables and the City Council* (Macmillan, 1969).
17. Some useful observations on the personal satisfactions and frustrations of council work can be found in *Management of Local Government*, Vol. 2, Ch. IV.
18. T. Byrne, *Local Government in Britain* (Penguin, 1986), pp. 128–29.
19. G. W. Jones, 'The Functions and Organisation of Councillors', *Public Administration* (1973).
20. K. Newton, 'Links Between Leaders and Citizens in a Local Political System', *Policy and Politics* (1973). See also K. Newton, *Second City Politics* (OUP, 1976).
21. Darke and Walker, *op. cit.* p. 53.
22. A. Barker and M. Rush, *The Member of Parliament and his Information* (Allen and Unwin, 1970); L. Cohen, 'Local Government Complaints', *Public Administration* (1973).
23. C. M. Chinkin and R. Bailey, 'The Local Ombudsman', *Public Administration* (1976).
24. Byrne, *op. cit.* p. 109.
25. *First Report of the Royal Commission on Municipal Corporations* (1835), p. 35.
26. K. Young, 'Party Politics in Local Government: An Historical Perspective' in Research Vol. IV, 'Aspects of Local Democracy', *The Conduct of Local Authority Business*, Cmnd 9801.
27. J. G. Bulpitt, *Party Politics in English Local Government* (Longmans, 1967).
28. *The Conduct of Local Authority Business*, Vol. I, Cmnd 9798, Table 2.2.
29. *Ibid.* Table 2.3.
30. *Ibid.* Table A13–A15.
31. *Ibid.* Table 2.8.
32. *Ibid.* Table 3.4.
33. *The Conduct of Local Authority Business*, Vol. III, Cmnd 9800, Table 6.5.
34. *Ibid.* Table 6.7.
35. *Ibid.* pp. 204–6.
36. C. Mellors, 'Coalition Strategies: The Case of British Local Government' in V. Bogdanor, *Coalition Government in Western Europe* (Heinemann, 1983) and 'Political Coalitions in Britain: The Local Context' in L. Robins, *Updating British Politics* (1984).
37. See P. Lowe and J. Goyder, *Environmental Groups in Politics* (Allen and Unwin, 1983), pp. 10–11.
38. J. Dearlove, *The Politics of Policy in Local Government* (CUP, 1973).
39. K. Newton (1976), *op. cit.*
40. Lowe and Goyder, *op. cit.* pp. 88–89.
41. Quoted in Darke and Walker, *op. cit.* p. 95.
42. *Ibid.* p. 98.
43. Gyford, *op. cit.* p. 122. See also A. Richardson, 'Tenant Participation in Council House Management' in Darke and Walker, *op. cit.*
44. Gyford, *op. cit.* pp. 122–27.
45. D. Hill, *Democratic Theory and Local Government* (Allen and Unwin, 1973), p. 154.
46. Quoted in Gyford, *op. cit.* p. 115. See also A. Greaves, 'The Future of Community Politics', *New Outlook* (1980) and M. Clay, *Liberals and Community* (ALC, 1985).
47. Gyford, *op. cit.* p. 116.
48. S. Lowe, 'Community Groups and Local Politics' in Darke and Walker, *op. cit.*
49. The section which follows draws upon Gyford, *op. cit.* pp. 118–21.
50. *Ibid.* p. 119.
51. I. Jackson, *The Provincial Press and the Community* (Manchester University Press, 1971).
52. A. Wright, 'Local Broadcasting and the Local Community', *Public Administration* (1982).
53. *Ibid.* pp. 311–13.
54. *Ibid.* p. 317.
55. DoE Circular 47/75, *Publicity for the Work of Local Authorities*.
56. R. Bailey, 'Secrecy in the Town Hall' in D. Wilson (ed.), *The Secrets File* (Heinemann, 1984).
57. *Ibid.* p. 67.

58. *Report of the Committee of Inquiry into the Conduct of Local Authority Business*, Cmnd 9797 (1986) paras. 3.34–5.
59. See, for example, K. Dyson (ed.), *Local Authorities and New Technologies*, (Croom Helm, 1987); T. Bovaird, 'An Evaluation of Local Authority Economic Initiatives', *Local Government Studies*, 1981.
60. K. Davey, *Local Government Chronicle* (17 October 1986) p. 1185. In 1986 INLOGOV completed a major study, 'The Review of the Future Role and Organisation of Local Government', which it had undertaken at the request of the major local authority associations. Their twelve major discussion papers, five introductory papers and over fifty working papers provide a wealth of material on the options facing local government.
61. *Local Government Chronicle*, (3 July 1987).

SELECT BIBLIOGRAPHY

The following represents a selection of further reading. It is not intended as an exhaustive list and the interested reader will find many additional references in the works which are cited. Since the circumstances of local government are changing so rapidly, the reader who wishes to keep up-to-date with events is also referred to the several journals in this field, most of which have annual indexes. The main ones include: *Local Government Studies*, *Local Government Policy-making*, *Local Government Administrator*, *Policy and Politics*, *Public Administration*, *Local Government Chronicle*, *Municipal Review*, *Municipal and Public Services Journal*, *Local Government Review*, *County Councils Gazette*, *District Councils Review*. In addition, there are a number of valuable annual publications containing useful information such as the *Municipal Year Book* (Municipal Publications).

LEGISLATION AND OFFICIAL PUBLICATIONS

Legislation

Education Act, 1944
Education Act, 1980, 1981
Housing Act, 1980
Housing Finance Act, 1972
Local Authority Social Services Act, 1970
Municipal Corporations Act, 1835, 1882, 1883
Local Government Act, 1888
Local Government Act, 1894
Local Government Act, 1958
Local Government Act, 1972
Local Government Act, 1974
Local Government Act, 1985
Local Government Act, 1986
Local Government (Access to Information) Act, 1985
Local Government, Planning and Land Act, 1980

Local Government (Scotland) Act, 1973
National Health Service Reorganisation Act, 1973
New Towns Act, 1946, 1965
Community Land Act, 1975
Rates Act, 1984
Transport Act, 1985
Water Act, 1973, 1983
Historic Buildings and Ancient Monuments Act, 1953
Ancient Monuments and Archaeological Areas Act, 1979
National Heritage Act, 1983
Town and Country Planning Act, 1947, 1968, 1971
National Parks & Access to Countryside Act, 1949
Countryside Act, 1968
Civic Amenities Act, 1967
Control of Pollution Act, 1974
Inner Urban Areas Act, 1978
Wildlife & Countryside Act, 1981
Local Government Act, 1971

Royal Commissions and other inquiries

Royal Commission on the Constitution, 1969–1973 (2 vols.) (Kilbrandon) Cmnd 5460–1 1973
Royal Commission on Local Government in England, 1966–1969 (Redcliffe–Maud) Cmnd 4040 1969
Royal Commission on Local Government in Scotland, 1966–1969 (Wheatley) Cmnd 4150 1969
Royal Commission on Local Government in Greater London, 1957–1960 (Herbert) Cmnd 1164 1960
Royal Commission on Standards of Conduct in Public Life (Salmon) Cmnd 6524 1976
Committee on the Staffing of Local Government (Mallaby) 1967
Committee on Management of Local Government (5 vols.) (Maud) 1967
Committee on Local Authority and Allied Personal Social Services (Seebohm) Cmnd 3703 1968
Committee on Public Participation in Planning (Skeffington) 1969
The New Local Authorities: Management & Structure (Bains) 1972
The New Scottish Local Authorities; Organisation and Management Structures (Niven/Paterson) 1973
The Remuneration of Local Councillors (Robinson) Cmnd 7010 1977
Committee on the Conduct of Local Authority Business (Widdicombe) Cmnd 9797 1986

Other

Organic Change in Local Government, Cmnd 7457 1979
Streamlining the Cities, Cmnd 9063 1983
Paying for Local Government, Cmnd 9714 1986

The Conduct of Local Authority Business: Research Vols.
    1. The Political Organisation of Local Authorities, Cmnd 9798
    2. The Local Government Councillor, Cmnd 9799
    3. The Local Government Elector, Cmnd 9800
    4. Aspects of Local Democracy, Cmnd 9801

THE PURPOSE OF LOCAL GOVERNMENT

D. Hill, *Democratic Theory and Local Government* (Allen and Unwin, 1974).
W. Eric Jackson, *Local Government in England and Wales* (Pelican, 1969).
G. W. Jones and J. Stewart, *The Case for Local Government* (Allen and Unwin, 1985).
W. J. M. Mackenzie, *Theories of Local Government* (LSE, 1961).
J. S. Mill, *On Representative Government* (1861).
I. Bowen Rees, *Government by Community* (Charles Knight & Co. Ltd., London, 1971).
L. J. Sharpe, 'Theories and Values of Local Government', *Political Studies* (1970).
J. Stanyer, *Understanding Local Government* (Fontana, 1976).
J. Stewart, *The Conditions for Local Choice* (Allen and Unwin, 1983).
C. H. Wilson (ed.), *Essays on Local Government* (Blackwell, 1948).

HISTORY AND REFORM

A. Alexander, *Local Government in Britain since Reorganisation* (Allen and Unwin, 1982).
H. Elcock, *Local Government* (Methuen, 1982).
B. Keith-Lucas and P. G. Richards, *A History of Local Government in the Twentieth Century* (Allen and Unwin, 1977).
J. Redlich and F. W. Hirst, *The History of Local Government* (Macmillan, 1970).
P. G. Richards, *Reformed Local Government System* (4th Ed., Allen and Unwin, 1980).
K. B. Smellie, *A History of Local Government* (Allen and Unwin, 1968).
W. Thornhill (ed.), *The Growth and Reform of English Local Government* (Weidenfeld and Nicholson, 1971).
B. Wood, *The Process of Local Government Reform 1966–74* (Allen and Unwin, 1976).

AREAS AND STRUCTURE

J. Brand, *Local Government Reform in England* (Croom Helm, 1974).
S. Bristow *et al.*, *Redundant Counties?* (Hesketh, 1983).
J. Craig, 'Which Local Authorities Were Alike in 1981?' *Population Trends 36* (Summer 1984) p. 25.
J. Dearlove, *The Reorganisation of British Local Government* (CUP, 1979).
N. Flynn *et al.*, *Abolition or Reform?* (Allen and Unwin, 1985).
T. W. Freeman, *Geography & Regional Administration* (Hutchinson U.L., 1968).

G. W. Jones, *The Local Government Act 1972 and the Redcliffe–Maud Commission* (Political Quarterly, 1973).

B. Massam, *Location and Space in Social Administration* (Edward Arnold, 1975).

I. B. Rees, *Government by Community* (C. Knight, 1971).

P. G. Richards, *The Local Government Act 1972: Problems of Implementation* (Allen and Unwin, 1975).

B. C. Smith, *Decentralisation: The Territorial Dimension of the State* (Allen and Unwin, 1985).

W. Thornhill, *The Case for Regional Reform* (Nelson, 1972).

J. Webber & J. Craig, 'Socio-Economic Classifications of Local Authority Areas', *Studies in Medical & Population Subjects No. 35*, (OPCS, HMSO, London).

B. Wood, *The Process of Local Government Reform 1966–1974* (Allen and Unwin, 1976).

POPULATION AND LAND

L. Allison, *Environmental Planning, a Political and Philosophical Analysis* (Allen and Unwin, 1975).

A. Cox, *Adversary Politics & Land* (CUP, 1984).

J. W. House, *The U.K. Space* (Weidenfeld & Nicholson, 1982).

P. Lowe & J. Goyder, *Environmental Groups in Politics* (Allen and Unwin, 1983).

FINANCE

D. E. Ashford (ed.), *Financing Urban Government in the Welfare State* (Croom Helm, 1980).

H. Aughton, *Local Government Finance for District Councillors: A Brief Guide* (Rose, 1973).

R. J. Bennett, *The Geography of Public Finance* (Methuen, 1983).

F. R. Flexman, *Local Charges as a Source of Local Government Finance* (Inst. of Municipal Treasurers and Accountants, 1968).

N. P. Hepworth, *The Finance of Local Government*, (7th Ed. Allen and Unwin, 1984).

Clive Holtham, *Value for Money* (University of Birmingham, 1981).

A. Midwinter, *The Politics of Local Spending* (Mainstream, 1984).

K. Newton & T. J. Karran, *The Politics of Local Expenditure* (Macmillan, 1985).

T. Rhodes & S. Bailey, 'Equity, Statistics and the Distribution of the Rate Support Grant', *Policy and Politics* Vol. 7 (1979).

FUNCTIONS OF LOCAL AUTHORITIES

Report ed. C. Bazlinton, *Inquiry into British Housing* (National Federation of Housing Associations, 1985).

J. B. Cullingworth, *Housing & Local Government in England and Wales* (Allen and Unwin, 1966).

J. B. Cullingworth, *Town and Country Planning in Britain* (Allen and Unwin, 1976).

J. B. Cullingworth, *Essays on Housing Policy* (Allen and Unwin, 1985).

B. Davies, *Social Needs & Resources in Local Services* (Joseph, 1968).

P. Dickins, S. Duncan, M. Goodwin & Fred Gray, *Housing, States & Localities* (Methuen, 1985).

D. Donnison & C. Ungerson, *Housing Policy* (Penguin, 1982).

N. Falk and J. Lee, *Planning the Social Services* (Saxon House, 1978).

H. Glennerster *et al.*, *Planning for Priority Groups* (Martin Robertson, 1983).

M. Goldsmith, *Politics, Planning and the City* (Hutchinson, 1980).

J. Higgins, *Government & Urban Poverty* (Blackwell, 1983).

M. Kogan, *Educational Policy-making* (Allen and Unwin, 1975).

S. Leach & J. Stewart, *Approaches in Public Policy* (Allen and Unwin, 1982).

P. Lloyd, *Services Administration by Local Authorities* (ICSA, 1985).

D. Regan, *Local Government and Education* (Allen and Unwin, 1977).

P. G. Richards, *Delegation in Local Government* (Allen and Unwin, 1956).

CENTRAL AND LOCAL RELATIONSHIPS

D. Butler & A. H. Halsey (eds.), *Policy & Politics* (Macmillan, 1970).

J. A. G. Griffiths, *Central Departments and Local Authorities* (Allen and Unwin, 1966).

J. Gyford and M. James, *National Parties and Local Politics* (Allen and Unwin, 1983).

G. Jones (ed.), *New Approaches to the Study of Central–Local Relationships* (Gower, 1980).

R. Rhodes, *Control and Power in Central–Local Government Relations* (Gower, 1981).

B. Smith, *Regionalism in England* (Acton Society Trust, 1964–65).

INTERNAL ORGANISATION AND MANAGEMENT

L. G. Bayley, *Local Government – Is it Manageable?* (Pergamon, 1979).

N. Boaden, *Urban Policymaking* (CUP, 1971).

J. K. Friend and W. Jessop, *Local Government and Strategic Choice* (Tavistock, 1969).

R. Greenwood *et al.*, *The Organisation of Local Authorities in England and Wales* (INLOGOV, 1975).

R. Greenwood *et al.*, *Patterns of Management in Local Government* (Martin Robertson, 1980).

R. Hambledon, *Policy Planning and Local Government* (Hutchinson, 1978).

K. J. Harrop, *The Implementation and Development of Area Management* (INLOGOV, 1978).

R. J. Haynes, *Organization Theory and Local Government* (Allen and Unwin, 1980).

G. W. Jones, 'The Functions and Organisation of Councillors' *Public Administration*, (1973).

R. S. B. Knowles, *Modern Management in Local Government* (Butterworth, 1971).

R. MacAllister & D. Hunter, *Local Government, Death or Devolution?* (Outer Circle Policy Unit, July 1980).

K. P. Poole, *The Local Government Service* (Allen and Unwin, 1978).

J. D. Stewart, *The New Management of Local Government* (Allen and Unwin, 1986).

J. D. Stewart, *The Responsive Local Authority* (Charles Knight, 1974).

PARTY POLITICS AND ELECTIONS

A. Alexander, *Borough Government and Politics* (Allen and Unwin, 1985).

J. G. Bulpitt, *Party Politics in English Local Government* (Longman, 1967).

J. Dearlove, *The Politics of Policy in Local Government* (CUP, 1973).

W. P. Grant, *Independent Local Politics in England and Wales* (Saxon House, 1978).

J. Gyford, *Local Politics in Britain* (Croom Helm, 1976).

W. Hampton, *Democracy and Community* (OUP, 1970).

G. W. Jones, *Borough Politics* (Macmillan, 1969).

K. Newton, *Second City Politics* (OUP, 1976).

L. J. Sharpe, *Voting in Cities* (Macmillan, 1967).

LOCAL GOVERNMENT AND THE ELECTORATE

R. Benewick and T. Smith, *Direct Action and Democratic Politics* (Allen and Unwin, 1972).

N. Boaden *et al.*, *Public Participation in Local Services* (Longman, 1982).

R. Darke and R. Walker, *Local Government and the Public* (Leonard Hill, 1977).

D. Hill, *Participating in Local Affairs* (Penguin, 1970).

Justice, *The Citizen and His Council* (Stevens, 1969).

INDEX